MEDIUM RARE

THE TRUE LIFE STORY OF SPIRITUALIST MEDIUM RONNIE BUCKINGHAM

10.4.17

To Nicky / Amy
With Love + Best Wishes
Ronnie Buckingham
x

Ronnie Buckingham
with Ruth Baker

ISBN: 978-0-9956793-0-6

Ronnie Buckingham & Ruth Baker

Braintree, Essex, United Kingdom

Book cover photography by Amelia Bullett Photography

Published by: Ronnie Buckingham Publishing

Dedication

I dedicate this book to:

My late father, Ronald Gordon Snr.,
The late Lee Armstrong, for the humour and kindness he showed me,
The late and wonderful Anne Walmsley, for her help on my spiritual path and the fun times.

Ronnie Buckingham

Acknowledgements

There are so many people to whom I owe much gratitude for their impact in my life:

My special thanks to my darling wife, Nicky, who has made me complete.

A big thank you to Margaret and Bill Dawson, for all of their support, the Buergi family for their help when I needed it most, Carol and the late Bob Martin, for being there for me, Nicky's family for putting up with me and Andy Reid for thirty five years of friendship.

A massive thank you to my 'dragon lady,' Lyn Younger, who moulded and guided me to become the medium I am today.

I am grateful to my brother Lee, for always having my back, to Ruth Baker, for putting my life into words, the late Gordon Van Sertima, for showing me how to train and stay fit.

I am sincerely grateful to all of those who have frequented my shows, promoted and stood by me, and the countless, wonderful people, who have allowed me to read for them and have shared their joys and sorrows, for they truly have been the most incredible teachers.

My heartfelt thanks to all of those dear friends who have allowed me to write of their experiences in this book.

Finally, to my daughters, Marie, Vicky and Sarah, thank you for being in my life, I am so proud of you.

With much love to you all,
Ronnie Buckingham

Contents

FOREWORD

Two dates that will be etched in my mind for the rest of my life:
17th August 1989, the birth of my second son.
15th December 2001, his death.

I remember it was a dry, sunny afternoon, towards the end of April in 2001, that my ex-wife called me at work to say that our twelve year old son Ross had to go to hospital for a blood transfusion. Apparently earlier that day she had taken him to see the doctor (this was about the fourth time). He was feeling unwell and seemed unable to shift a cold and cough he'd been suffering from for some months.

This time, his own doctor was the duty doctor on call in the surgery that morning. Immediately, upon seeing Ross, he took some blood and expedited the results, due to my son's anaemic appearance. I arrived at the hospital and was told to go to a particular ward on the third floor. It didn't even register that it was an oncology ward.

Ross was a very sporty lad and a football crazy, keen Spurs fan, but recently he had been suffering from a lack of energy. We thought it was down to his cold and cough. When I arrived, he was sitting on a hospital bed having his temperature and blood pressure taken. A doctor approached having realised that both his mum and dad were now present and asked if we could go into a side room for a chat. Still unaware what was going on, we both walked in and took a seat. The doctor then said that his blood results showed he was suffering from Acute Lymphoblastic Leukaemia (ALL). I remember Ross's mum breaking down in tears, followed shortly after by myself having now realised what we had just been told. Ross was unable to receive the specialist treatment he required at that hospital and would be transferred to the Royal London Hospital in Whitechapel, East London, which was purportedly the best at the treatment of ALL.

Wiping away the tears, now came the job of telling Ross. What should we say? How would we tell him he had cancer? At twelve years old, Ross was reasonably wise to the world and would be aware of how serious cancer is, so we decided to play it down. We told him that he had a problem with his blood that only a hospital in London could fix and he was going to go to that hospital straight away. Ross's mum took him up to London as we had arrived in two separate cars.

The following day, numerous invasive tests were carried out on him under general anaesthetic, one of which was to retrieve spinal fluid from his spine, in order that they could see how far progressed the ALL was. Unfortunately for Ross, the ALL had spread to his bone marrow, which meant that a more radical treatment would be required to try and cure him.

When we were told of his condition earlier, the hospital consultant had said that ALL was the most common form of Leukaemia and as such had a greater success rate at around 70%. With a 70% success rate in our minds, Ross definitely would fall within it we assumed, this unfortunately turned out not to be the case. We were told at that stage that curing Ross would be a long, uphill battle and not a pleasant one for all concerned, especially Ross.

This played out to be true, his mum, myself and, on occasions, his mum's partner, lived and breathed at the Royal London Hospital. We used to do shifts of three to four days each a week, twenty four hours a day. It was difficult enough for us let alone Ross.

Each few weeks we were taken down the corridor to a family room and each time they broke bad news to us that he wasn't responding to the chemotherapy. Therefore there was only one course of action left open to them which, if successful, would involve a stem cell transplant, something fairly new at the time, but it was his only chance of survival.

Every time we had the family room meeting, we would have to wipe away the tears before seeing Ross. Every time we tried to put a positive spin on it, generally talking about how positive the next stage of treatment was likely to be.

Following blood tests on Ross's mum, elder brother and myself, the doctors concluded that I was the best match at 68%, so I would be the donor. In order to generate the quantity of white blood cells required, I'd have to have a course of injections that would accelerate their production over a three week period. I was told that all the bones in my body would ache, which was the unfortunate side effect, but once the cells had been harvested the effects would disappear within a few days.

After a very intense period of strong chemotherapy and radiation treatment, Ross was ready for the transplant. This took place on the 7th November 2001. The transplant itself was successful, unfortunately several weeks later, due to his suppressed immune system, Ross caught an infection called Adenovirus, which affected his respiratory system. Just a few days later, at noon on the 15th December 2001, our beloved son Ross died in our arms.

Devastated we left the ITU and went our separate ways, his mum with her partner, myself with my wife. I remember the day being so strange, almost as if I were in a trance, trying to comprehend what had just happened, with the realisation that I would never see my son again. The daily hospital routine I had been used to for the past seven months had now ended.

Bereavement counselling was only given to the address where Ross lived, so at that time because he lived with his mum, that's where the counselling was offered. I remember feeling very alone at that time. I had three other kids, Ross's natural elder brother and his half-brother and sister, but I couldn't get out of my mind the sense of failure that engulfed me. I was supposed to save Ross, he was relying on me and I had let him down.

I ran a number of successful businesses employing over sixty people, but couldn't get myself motivated enough to get back into work properly, which didn't go unnoticed. One day, I received an internal email from one of my concerned employees, telling me that she felt, understood and could see my sense of loss. She also said that in the previous year she had lost her father but had been to see a spiritualist medium called Ronnie Buckingham, who had been able to pass on messages from her father, which had helped ease some of the pain she was experiencing. She gave me his telephone number and hoped that I didn't feel she was intruding.

The very thought of turning to a clairvoyant didn't go down well for me, I was hugely skeptical and for a few weeks ignored the email but thanked her for her thoughts of kindness. Yet the email continued to play on my mind. What had I to lose by going? If I didn't tell anyone then no one would be the wiser. I thought if people close to me knew that I was thinking of going, it would be frowned upon and I would feel even worse than I already did. I plucked up the courage to call Ronnie and left a message on his answerphone, giving minimal information. I didn't want him knowing my surname or where I lived, just in case he could search out information about me and what had happened. Ronnie called me back on my mobile phone and was very happy to offer me an appointment, which at that time was several months ahead. He didn't ask me any questions, which I remember being surprised about, he just gave me an address and postcode.

I used to have Ross and his elder brother Mark to stay alternate weekends, often having to rely on my parents to pick them up on a Friday evening due to work or traffic problems. It was nice for all the kids to spend alternate weekends together but it always seemed that I was late collecting them. This played on my mind when the day arrived for me to drive to see Ronnie. I was running late again talking to myself whilst en-route, saying to myself that I couldn't even get to this appointment on time but also hypothesizing that it would be a waste of time anyhow, so why worry?

As it happens the traffic was kind to me and I arrived five minutes early. I even had time to drive past the end of Ronnie's road to see where he lived. I didn't want him to judge me by my car or appearance, so I parked the car around the corner, out of sight. Still unsure as to whether I should go through with it or not, I found myself reluctantly ringing the doorbell.

A tall, well-presented and friendly man welcomed me in and offered me a cup of tea. I remember the first few minutes feeling totally wrong-footed. He wasn't at all what I expected, although what I was expecting I'm not totally sure, but it wasn't 'Mr Normal.' Surprisingly I felt at ease but nevertheless was determined not to let my guard down. 'Don't give him any clues about anything,' I kept saying to myself. We entered into a room that had a table and two chairs, the room was bright and airy, the table had some place mats and a box of tissues on it but no crystal ball. I'm not sure why I thought the crystal ball would be there.

Ronnie asked me to relax and to let him hold my hand so that he could get a connection, this I did with some reluctance. After what seemed like few minutes but was probably only fifteen seconds, tears started streaming down his face and a sense that a heavy weight had just landed on his shoulders as he slumped in his chair. I must confess that I found this all a bit strange and was waiting for Jeremy Beadle to jump out.

"Oh my God," he cried, "You've lost your son haven't you?"

I confirmed this was true but put this down to a lucky guess, after all he had a fifty per cent chance between a boy or a girl.

"What's his name then?" I asked.

"It's a short name," Ronnie replied, "With a very dominant 'S' in it, Scottish I believe."

Well that certainly made me sit up and pay a bit more attention.

"I can't hear clearly enough at the moment what your son is saying," Ronnie said, "So we'll come back to it later if that's okay."

I agreed, still intrigued by the seemingly accurate description of Ross's name.

"This was no accident, your son's passing," he continued. "It was an illness that travels around the body, immediately I know it's connected to the blood, so I'm assuming your son died of Leukaemia. Is that correct?"

I confirmed that it was, still a little apprehensive of what was being said to me.

"He's just told me his name really clearly," Ronnie told me. "It's Ross."

Immediately I reached for the tissues as tears welled up and then ran down my face. Oh my God, how can this be? Was Ross really here communicating with him? Now I was paying serious attention and was feeling some sense of relief. I had so many questions but couldn't get them out.

Ronnie then moved onto probably the most moving bit of all for me. After Ross had died his body was moved into the chapel of rest at the funeral home, where over a few days only close family were able to go and see him in his coffin if they wished. He was dressed in the new kit of his favourite football team, which was his Christmas present. His brothers and sister had placed a football annual in his coffin, together with a hand drawn picture from his younger brother Tom, who was four years old at the time, and his baby sister Madison, who was eighteen months old. On the picture was a message to Ross, 'We love you and will always miss you. Enjoy playing football with the angels. Love always, Tom and Madison.'

Ronnie stated that Ross was very moved by his funeral and had been there with us in spirit. Ronnie then went on to tell me that Ross was dressed in his favourite football teams kit and that it was the North London side

Spurs. He said that two other items were placed into his coffin with him, a book and a picture drawn by his younger brother and sister. He recited word for word what was written on the picture, even describing the picture as a football pitch with players, a goal and angels joining in. I was so moved at this point, there was no way that this information could have got to Ronnie. He knew nothing about me, no surname, just my first name and a mobile phone number.

I left a different man to the one that had arrived earlier, I knew that Ross was okay and when I felt the need to speak with him. I could go back and see Ronnie again. The remainder of the reading was just as good, he spoke about his elder brother, who had promised him on the day he died that he would make something of himself. Today, fifteen years on, he's a qualified interior architect with a degree.

My son - Ross Waters

I personally visit Ronnie every year and have done so since that first reading. I hear from Ross, and now my late father, about things that have happened in my life over the previous year and, to some extent, clues about things yet to happen. I've learned to cope with Ross's passing now, which I wouldn't have been able to do if I hadn't gone to see Ronnie. I will be eternally grateful to him in the knowledge that one day, I will be reunited with Ross on the other side of life, wherever that may be.

Graham Waters

INTRODUCTION

This morning, whilst I walked my dog, Bella, some thoughts popped into my mind that I'd like to share with you. You see, I believe experiences are what life is all about, this world, this life, is our schooling. It's where we gain knowledge through experiences both good and bad.

As you will read in this book, I've made many, many mistakes in my life. Some at a cost to others and many at a cost to me. I've pursued pointless love and yet shunned love shown to me, I've hurt and been hurt, known great happiness and health, great sadness and ill health, but everything needs to be seen as an experience and something to learn from.

I, like many of you, have repeated mistakes, repeated experiences, but in the end have learned from them. One of the main lessons has been the simple message that some things, as well as some people, are just not meant for us. It might be a career that you want to follow, or someone's heart you want to win but can't. Don't force it, learn from the experience and move on to what is, or who is, really meant for you.

If you want to be a singer but can't sing, or want to be a footballer but can't play well enough, or want to try and make someone love you who doesn't, then don't waste your time. Try something or someone else and in time it will all fall into place. Treat everything in life as an experience, learn from it, cherish it and move on from it and happiness and fulfillment can and will be yours.

Be proud of who you are now, don't regret what has happened in the past, it's all brought you here to this moment. Above all, take time to really listen to others, as their past experiences may be similar to yours and a problem shared is, as they say, a problem halved.

With love,
Ronnie Buckingham

Chapter 1
The Happening

Being a spiritualist medium is sometimes a funny old game. But then sometimes it isn't.

There were several of us sitting in the circle as usual on a Monday night, led by Lyn, the dragon lady, as she was fondly known. Usually, at the end of the sessions, we would go into the kitchen, some would go home but some would stay awhile. On this particular night, there was Lyn, a lady called Pat and myself, discussing what had happened during the evening. I sat opposite Lyn, who was animatedly chatting, whilst balancing a piece of cake and a cup of tea on her lap.

Without warning, my heart stopped beating. Everything slowed down as I plunged into a monochrome vastness. I could feel the colour being pulled from my cheeks as my life began slipping away. Lyn stared at me strangely as I lay my arms on the table, resting my head down. The thoughts in my head were grinding to a halt. Nothing made sense. Something had pulled the plug on my comprehension. My only thought was 'This is it, I'm going to die.'

Thunder echoed in my chest. Bang. Abruptly my heart gave a beat. 'Wait… wait…wait…,' My thoughts began to ricochet in slow motion off the walls of my mind. I could feel liquid oozing from every pore, as my body began to break out in a cold sweat. The shadow of fear turned towards me as I was thrust into complete blackness.

Bang. My heart gave another beat. Relief was swiftly followed by bewilderment, as my brain tried to grasp the implications of my declining heartbeat. I had no idea what to do. The ice cold hands of terror strangled rational thought from my brain.

"Lyn, Lyn, I've got to get home, there's something really wrong here." Rising panic escalated through my very core. "I've got to get to a hospital, I've got to get home."

"Come with me quick, back into the lounge," Lyn lead me back into the meditation room, the spirit room as we called it. Alarmed, Pat ran in behind us.

Lyn sat me down on the settee and continually told me to breathe deeply. In my puzzled state, I tried to focus on her face, clinging onto her voice. I was looking at Lyn, but to me she wasn't Lyn anymore. Lyn was still Lyn, yet to me for some reason, she wasn't Lyn. I couldn't see anything around her, she was all I could see. All the while I questioned 'Who is she? If not Lyn, then who?' Looking down it seemed as if my knees and legs had grown. My knees morphed into something so foreign. In the distance my mind yelled that they were much higher than they should have been. Nothing made sense.

"Lyn, my knees, my knees are so high, my knees shouldn't be that high," I cried, "You're not Lyn, what's going on? Please help me."

Lyn continued to stare intently at me as I began to sob. I sobbed and sobbed, like I've never cried in my life. My guts felt squeezed by the pressure in my body. Totally disorientated and unable to control myself, the tears poured down my cheeks. Lyn hugged me in an effort to calm me, then held me at arm's length.

"Ronnie, do you trust me?" her voice slapped my consciousness.

"Of course I trust you," I was perplexed by her question, "What's going on?"

"I want you to try and go into meditation," she told me. "Breathe deep, sit back, close your eyes, breathe deep," she instructed, "And please, really trust me."

Resisting the desire to simply curl up into the foetal position, I sat back, closed my eyes and dropped my head to my chest. I fought to control my breath. My heart beat so slowly, it felt as if I were barely alive. In a singular act of faith, I simply dropped into the silence. Even the air stilled as if it too held its breath. Nothingness enveloped me.

Then the strangest sense of movement crashed through me, as if I was being catapulted through an unavoidable collision . Opening my eyes, it seemed as if my knees had been left behind. I felt myself coming out of my body. At the same time, there was an odd sensation, as if someone was stuffing cotton wool into my mouth and up my nose. My mind struggled to comprehend the weird feeling of my face swelling.

"It's okay Ronnie," Lyn reassured me, "Please Ronnie, it's okay love. Just let yourself go, don't fight it."

Part of me wanted to resist but it was futile. Rapidly I became aware that my arms had come out to either side of me and they were shaking violently. I had no control. Was I having a fit? All the while, there was the feeling of cotton wool being poked into my face. My eyes felt like they were bulging out of my head. The sensations worsened. Attempting to keep a grip on a slither of normality, part of me became the observer of myself. One part of my mind endeavored to remain calm, whilst observing rising panic looming in the other part of my mind, as I tried to understand what was happening. What the fuck was going on?

A frightening straining in my throat threatened to choke me. It felt red raw, as if something was crawling up my throat, ready to erupt out of my mouth. My lips began to move and yet it didn't feel as if I was saying anything. More constriction in my throat gripped and I continued to have the feeling of being stuffed by a massive, unseen force.

Suddenly, I was back in the room with Lyn kneeling in front of me, holding my hands, tears streaming down her face. Pat stood beside her shaking, her face paled beyond all recognition.

"Lyn, what's happening?" I was totally confused, "What's going on?"

"You changed into my James," she sobbed, "My James just came through you."

God bless his soul, Lyn's son James. In a nanosecond, my brain snapped the pieces of the puzzle together. I'm six feet tall, James was six feet four inches tall. This, I realized, was the reason Lyn wasn't Lyn when I looked at her, because I had been looking through James's eyes. It wasn't Lyn, it was Mum. My knees had felt higher because his knees were literally higher than mine. The sense I had of sliding forward was to allow James's spirit to come in. The cotton wool feeling was because my face became his face, I'm quite sharp featured and his was a much fuller face than mine.

One afternoon, Lyn arrived home whilst James was out playing football. Almost immediately, she received a phone call to say he had passed out. She rushed out of the house and hurried over to the place where he was laid out. The moment she arrived, she knew he was dead. She did her best to resuscitate him until the ambulance could get to the scene, but knew in her heart he had gone. It was unclear what had caused his sudden collapse, it was thought perhaps drugs, but whatever the cause, it was too late. Suddenly and without warning, James had passed over.

It was devastating for her. A top rate medium and a wonderful teacher, but the event knocked even her faith. She asked questions of spirit. Why did her harmless, brilliant young lad have to go like that? Due to the slightly unusual circumstances of his passing, it was a few weeks before he was buried. Lyn went to visit him to see him in the coffin when he had been dead for about two weeks. The fingers on his hands had begun to turn black and that really affected her terribly, she couldn't get over it. Even mediums need proof sometimes.

Lyn held my hands, "Ronnie, I've held my son's hands a million times and these were his hands."

Not that my hands were black, nothing like that, just that she knew it was her son that had come through. I told her of the feeling in my throat and face and she repeated back what I had said to her.

"I'm sorry Mum, I'm so sorry," were the first words that came through me.

"You don't have to be sorry son," were her first words to James since his passing.

Lyn is a marvellous medium and I owe everything in my mediumship life to her. She saw the potential in me and in her own, very strict way, she helped and guided me to become the medium I am now.

That one event changed Lyn completely. It also changed the course of my life forever. Yet there had been no inkling in the earlier years of my life that I would become a spiritualist medium. There had been no belief in the afterlife, no interest in ghost stories, no conversing with angels, or suchlike. Far from it, as you're about to find out.

But before I tell you my story, I want to ask you, the reader of this book, a question. As you turn the pages of this book, keep in mind my question and ponder it. Because the answer may prove to be the revelation you seek. My question is simply this:

Is it possible for a leopard to change its spots?

Chapter 2
The Graveyard

Every family has its share of skeletons they say. Mine had a complete bloody graveyard. I was born in Hackney on 11th January 1954, minus a silver spoon, the oldest son to my father, Ronald Gordon, who I was named after. Home was 131 Wick Road, Hackney, which was shared with my parents, brother, grandparents and my uncle Sid.

The rattling of bones began with my mother, who was engaged to an Australian chap during the war years and conceived my brother Michael. She was, to all intents and purposes, going to move out to Australia to marry the father of her child and live there. In those days, conceiving a child out of wedlock was not the done thing at all.

My mother's father, Charlie Pollington, was a coal merchant, ex-boxer and professional referee. A very small yet violent man, he possessed a quick and vicious temper. My mother was one of several children, there were my aunts Renee, Lil, Bet and Nina, together with my uncles Patrick and Charlie. As a child my uncle Pat had a very serious illness, which I think was diphtheria. My grandfather was at his bedside for several weeks whilst he fought this terrible disease. Pat made a miraculous recovery and there was a huge celebration when he pulled through, as few children did in those days. Then tragedy struck during an air raid, which were common in London during the war years. My mother and the other children were in the bunker, which was hit by a bomb and Pat, who had survived diphtheria, was killed. It drove my grandfather beyond despair.

My mother went on to have my brother Michael, all the time waiting to join the man in her life in Australia. My grandfather was totally and utterly convinced that Michael was uncle Pat reincarnated and he absolutely doted on him. Elizabeth, my grandmother, was a lovely lady who sadly passed at a very young age with cancer. She knew that my mother intended to go to Australia with her lover, but dare not tell my grandfather because to him they would be taking Michael, who he considered was really Pat, away from him. A letter arrived for my mother containing boat tickets and the fares for her and Michael to go to Australia. Unfortunately, my grandfather opened the letter and went absolutely berserk. He knew that my grandmother was involved in this cover up, and that she wasn't going to tell him until my mother was safely on the boat and away. To say that he beat my grandmother almost to death is an understatement.

My mother came home from work and couldn't open the passage door. My grandmother lay in a crumpled, bloody heap on the floor. At that point, my grandfather came down the stairs and told my mother point blank that if she went through with it and took what he considered his reincarnated son away from him, then he would finish the job. There was no option but for my mother to turn her back on Michael's father, the love of her life. In order to protect my grandmother she stayed in England. As Michael grew older, the chap in Australia wrote to my mother and made it clear he was disgusted with her for letting him down. What could my mother say? Sadly her hands were bound.

A very talented lady, my mother was a gifted singer. Discovered by Carol Levis, who ran a very popular talent show, my mother and her sister Renee used to sing on the show regularly. This led to my mother singing with some of the big bands of the time and she could have gone far in the business. My parents were introduced to each other by one of my aunts. A very good looking man and younger than my mother by about six years, my father was totally smitten by her. He used to watch her sing and asked her out, luckily he was aware of Michael and accepted the situation. But that was where the fairytale ended for her. It turned out my father was a compulsive gambler.

My father's parents, Margaret and George, had several children, being my aunts Mil and Jean, together with my uncle George and my father.

Margaret's sister Amelia and her husband George Bates were unable to have children, so they basically took my father from my grandmother and were allowed to bring him up as their own. They completely spoilt and dominated him. They used to take him to the Hackney dog track and through this he became fanatical about greyhounds and betting, which shaped his life.

My father's parents absolutely hated my mother with a vengeance. To them she was a wanton woman and they defied my father to marry her. In fact my parents had to lie and say they were getting married on the Saturday. In reality they married on the Friday because they knew my father's family would be there in full force. Not so much his father but my aunt Jean, my grandmother and Mil, who had brought him up, were a force to be reckoned with. They turned up at the church on the Saturday to try to stop the marriage. Nicely side-stepping a showdown, my parents moved in with my grandfather Charlie. My brothers, Lee, Alan and Paul followed Michael and myself and we all jostled for room in the tightly packed space.

My brother Michael has always been my idol really. An incredibly smart and clever individual, he was one of the youngest people to pass 'the knowledge, which is an exam that taxi drivers in London have to pass in order to drive a black cab. Michael met the love of his life, his childhood sweetheart Jean, a lovely girl, and they married at a very young age. They have been together now for something like fifty-five years and they are still totally happy. I never considered Michael my half-brother, he was just my elder brother and is still the person I respect most in the world.

Money was always really tight when we were kids, mostly due to my father, who would get paid on the Friday and stop at the dog track. By the time he arrived home, his wages had virtually disappeared. The lack of money and space were problematic. My uncle Sid, who lived in one room upstairs, hated my brother Michael for whatever reason but daren't say anything to him because he was terrified of my grandfather Charlie. There we were in a three bedroom house with an outside toilet and no bathroom, occupying just the downstairs rooms.

As a child I detested school. I was always the scruffy kid as all my clothes came from the secondhand stalls. In those days, as my father worked in the print industry, he earned exceptionally good money, probably more in a week than a builder would earn in a month but as soon as he earned it, he spent it. He never had to suffer the ignominy of wearing rags because my aunt and uncle suited and booted him. They didn't give my mother a single penny but whatever my father wanted he could have.

There was one particular night, when my father came home with a greyhound in tow. Imagine in this little house, where we already had a mongrel called Peggy that I had rescued from somewhere, my father came in with another dog. It was at Christmas time and it had been snowing heavily. The story that my father told my mother was that the dog had fallen out the back of a van and that whoever was driving the van hadn't realised. He made out that he had rescued the dog and had taken it to the vets, who bandaged it up. My mother told him to take it to the RSPCA as we had enough to cope with. No wonder the dog growled at us kids. No matter, my dad wanted the dog and he kept it.

Even though times were hard, he went about building a kennel at the bottom of the garden for the greyhound. When he went out to the bookies, my mother undid the bandage and there wasn't anything wrong with the dog. An Irish stamp in its ear gave the game away, it was a racing dog. Clearly my father had bought the dog to race it or flap it, as they used to do around the flap tracks, which are for less 'official' races. I don't remember the dog being with us for a long time but it was the cause of many rows between my parents.

A bit of a wayward child, I wanted to be out of the house all the time. In the east end of London in the early 1960s, when I was around six or seven, there were still bomb sites everywhere, which became my playground. When I think back, I was a ragbag kid really, a bit of a naughty urchin as a lot of kids were. I preferred my own company but that was perhaps out of necessity, seeing as how I was the scruffy kid that most other kids didn't want to mix with. Yet I was always very daring and constantly into all sorts of mischief.

My father worked for the News of the World and other newspapers and used to bring them home. At that time, the News of the World was a massive broadsheet paper. Opposite the house in Wick Road were some old bombed houses surrounded by ash. One of my stunts was to take some sheets of the paper with me, fill them with the ash and screw them up to make an ash bomb. I would hide behind a wall of the flats opposite my house, where there was a bus stop. When the bus pulled up, I used to run out, throw my 'bombs' onto the bus and run back behind the wall.

Of course the paper would burst and the ash would fill the bus with dust and everyone would come out coughing and spluttering. Now I feel quite ashamed of that as it was a silly thing to do, but in those days smart phones didn't exist, so we had to make our own entertainment.

It all came to an abrupt end on my third attempt at a bombing raid. Luckily I had a thirty yard start and was wearing plimsolls, as this time the conductor jumped off the bus and gave chase. Blimey he was fast! My saving grace was that we used to have what was called the Bullring there. I had a fifty yard sprint to the Bullring, which had steps that went right around the edge but also a big concrete slide. Now this concrete slide was covered in some sort of varnish and kids could slide down it four abreast. With my plimsolls on I ran up the slide, just short of being caught by this man. Arriving at the top I looked back towards the conductor, whose attempts to catch me failed due to slipping back down because of his leather soled shoes, added to which the slide was too wide for him to grip the sides. It really did frighten the life out of me though and put an end to the ash bomb shenanigans.

There were a few incidents that, looking back, I can't believe I did. One was the time some new maisonettes were being built at the Well Street end of Wick Road. Piles of builders sand encircled the newly erected buildings and the kids would jump from the first floor balcony onto the sand. The really brave kids even jumped from the second floor balcony. I went one step further and actually climbed onto the roof, which was at least thirty five to forty feet high. Standing on the roof with the other kids egging me on, I tried to psych myself up to launch off the edge. I always wanted to make myself look bigger than the others to make up for my lack of material possessions.

An old chap opposite was watching us, he came out of his house yelling at the top of his lungs, "Get off that roof yer little bastard!"

Well, that gave me the impetus to jump, which I did. Landing in the sand, my chin came down to meet my knees and my teeth rattled in my head. I was so terrified of the old chap that I was up and away at such a speed it was a personal best.

Eventually, after my younger brothers were all born, my aunt and uncle decided that our family needed a place of our own. Now I have to go back into this story, because when I was born my aunt Jean and my grandmother Margaret's family wouldn't acknowledge Michael at all but were absolutely taken with me. You have to remember these were people who hated my mother with a vengeance yet they adored me. All that side of the family were publicans and they had pubs out in Essex, such as The Cock at Rayne, also one in Stambourne. My granddad on that side of the family had been ill and subsequently retired and lived in a cottage in Tiptree, Essex, where he died at a relatively young age. My grandmother and my aunts Jean and Mil would come down during the six weeks summer holiday and the Christmas holiday and they would literally drag me off. I never complained because they spoilt me rotten and life was very easy with them. When I look back now, even when my other brothers came along after me, they had nothing to do with them, it was just me. It was wrong but at the time, being young and for once the centre of attention, it never occurred to me that it was unfair.

Aunt Jean was another fantastic singer. Unfortunately, she had a terrible accident as a child and underwent brain surgery and suffered with fits and poor eyesight. It was quite strange because she and my mother hated each other bitterly, but the only thing they would concede about the other one was the ability to sing, as both had fantastic voices. My mother's voice was very sweet, whereas my aunt Jean had a powerful voice and was able to sing opera, jazz or any other genre. You name it, she could sing it effortlessly with fantastic range and never needed a microphone.

When my grandmother and aunts came to take me away, my mother would argue that she didn't want me to go but they would overrule her totally. Literally holding my mother at bay, they would pack a suitcase for me and off I would go. However, I enjoyed my time with them. My first watch and brand new pair of shoes were bought for me by them, which I was very happy about. The problem was that they would feed bullets for me to fire at my mother and as a kid I didn't understand their battle plan.

My father suffered badly with tuberculosis and they blamed this on my mother making salads and eggs for him to eat. Arriving home, I repeated a lot of what they had said and ended up getting a good hiding. I always felt I was on the wrong side of my mother and in truth never felt that comfortable with her. Now I can understand why because it was wrong of me to repeat those critical comments to her. But I was a kid caught up in the crossfire and what was I to do? Would a child refuse to go with people that spoil him? Did I think about my brothers left behind? No, of course I didn't, but that's how kids are. It did cause a very unpleasant situation for my mother and I felt the atmosphere boiling up. Being unhappy in that environment, I couldn't wait to return to the comfort of the countryside.

Not far from my grandmother's house in Tiptree, halfway down the High Street, there was a duck pond. Going back to the early 1960s when there were severe winters, my cousin Jeanette and I would walk along to the village, with our coats and wellies on. One time, when I was no more than seven years old, we noticed adults skating around the pond. It was too tempting and I decided we were going to join them. Taking just five steps, with Jeanette only three feet away behind me, I fell straight through the ice. I was sucked in by the freezing water, my wellies filled with liquid and I was dragged down. For what seemed like an eternity, I felt immobilized. Then my survival instinct kicked in, I put my hands up and my fingers caught onto the ice. Jeanette held onto my wrist for dear life but she was too weak to haul me out. Luckily some adults saw what had happened, quickly laid on their stomachs and dragged me out. The Martin family that owned the pond, and who were big landowners, came over, took me into their house, stripped me off, washed me down and then took me home to my grandmother. That was one of two times when I hadn't gone looking for trouble but fell into it instead.

Eventually, when I was about ten years old, our family made the move to Leytonstone. Again, my father caved into my aunt and uncle, who had brought him up. They lived at 125 Richmond Road, Leytonstone, and we moved into 63 Richmond Road. We were literally a hundred yards up the road. It was a miserable house. I did feel sorry for my mother because they badmouthed her constantly and made it very difficult for her. My father kept on gambling and then life hit an all-time low when the tuberculosis came back with a vengeance. He was admitted into what was then known as a sanitarium, where we would visit but be restricted to viewing him through the window. In those days, tuberculosis was a killer and it was very difficult to overcome it. My father was in a bad way and had already lost half a lung when it had flared up the previous time. Of course, my mother's salads were blamed yet again.

By then I had joined Norlington, an all boys school in the East End. Life was tough for a lot of East End kids in those days but it seemed particularly hard for me. Even as kids we always had to work. When we lived in Hackney, a man used to come round every week bringing many boxes filled with different types of glasses, such as whiskey glasses and tumblers, together with boxes of transfers. My brother Lee and myself had to work, the others were too young. I was about seven years old. Every night we sat around the table and soaked the transfers in a bowl of water to loosen them. There were lots of different transfers, such as vintage cars, derby winners and also some that were quite risqué at the time, ladies in bikinis with little crabs nipping at their toes or bikini bottoms. Hour after hour we would position transfers onto the glasses, making sure we removed all the bubbles out of them, as my mother had taught us. We didn't enjoy it but were made to do it. The man used to collect them from us in exchange for a small sum. I absolutely hated doing it and if I ever had the chance to get out that's exactly what I did.

I remember a few years later, when I was about ten years old, I literally had no shoes. My mother will own up to this and still feels bad about it. She went to the local secondhand stalls and there was nothing she could find that was suitable. Instead she came back with an old pair of suede ankle boots. They were black with a zip up the front and fur inside, the sort elderly ladies used to wear. When I saw them I had no idea what she had in mind. She took a razor blade to them and cut them down to try to make them look like a shoe. Cutting the zip out, she scraped out the fur that was hanging over the edges, so that it didn't show over the ends of the shoe, but it never really worked as there was still some there. Taking hold of a meat skewer, she made holes for laces, took the laces from my old shoes and threaded them through these cut-down boots. As you can imagine, at an all boys school in the East End of London they didn't go unnoticed. As the other boys looked down at my feet, shameful, scarlet embarrassment coursed through my cheeks.

Attack they say is the best form of defence. In order to protect myself from the jibes of others I became violent. There was a lot of anger within me, particularly at school. One outlet for this was sports, which I excelled at, and I made the cross-country running team with ease. Funnily enough, Graham Gooch was in the same year as me at school, although in a different class. Even as a kid, he was a fantastic cricketer. I did have some friends at school but it was a bit awkward as my brothers and I were never allowed to bring friends home. Nor were we allowed a bike or anything like that. Birthdays would come and go but they were never celebrated. Instead my father spent time in private celebration at the bookies.

CHAPTER 3
WORKING OUT

Hard graft has never bothered me, and even as a child I could pull my weight and a bit more. At the age of eleven, I managed to get a job at the local butchers. My best friend at the time was a lad called Paul Stanley and we were quite inseparable. Paul had a fantastic family, his mum was Irish, he had a brother and sister, and his dad Arthur was quite a character, who could do magic tricks. They had a little snooker table in their front room and I spent so much of my time with Paul and his family. His mum would feed me and obviously knew what was going on at my home, she was wonderful to me. Some of my happiest memories are the times I spent with them. Paul had a job in the butchers and managed to get me a job there too. Bear in mind that I was just a kid, I did Tuesday and Thursday evenings after school and all day on Saturdays. It really was hard work because the wooden blocks that they cut the meat on had to be scrubbed with a big, heavy wire brush, before being washed down. The blows from the cleavers used to dig deep into the wood and the blood and bits of meat would get right in there. We also had to clean the counters and windows. Saturday was the busiest day as we started at nine o'clock in the morning and worked right through until five o'clock in the afternoon.

I remember having to get rid of the entrails and also making sausages with sausage meat. The worst job for me was having to go into the big freezers with hot soapy water in a bucket and a set of steps to clean up all the blood, which was everywhere, all the while being surrounded by dead animals hanging up all over the place. The butchers kept us lads on our toes for the five pounds per week wage. For the entire time that I had that job, which was about a year, I handed over the money to my mother.

Paul had the best job as he rode about on the butcher's bike to make deliveries, which meant he received all the tips. He generously shared the tips with me and that was the only little bit that I kept back from my mum. I remember going down the lane to buy my first brand new shirt, this was when button-down collars first came out, in either dark green or blue denim. Anyway, I bought one and it didn't fit too well. I remember my mother doing her pieces because she couldn't work out where the money for the shirt came from and obviously I was holding out. That made her angry.

As a child I had some problems with my ears and was unable to take swimming lessons. I had always had a fear of deep water, a fear I still have to this day. Nevertheless, Paul and I joined the local sea scouts. Various groups of sea scouts went on The Discovery, the ship that Scott of the Antarctic had sailed in, where we slept in hammocks for a week. Of the more than two hundred sea scouts on that ship, I was the only one that fell into the Thames. From the ship we came down a ladder into a metal raft, then from that raft onto another ladder or stairway up to the street. Paul and I were playing on the raft and in I went. My little hat, which I had saved up my pennies to buy, went floating off down the Thames. As I was dragged out by some of the scout masters, I glanced up to see loads of foreign tourists snapping away on their cameras. That was my first claim to fame.

When my father recovered from his illness and returned home, he was unable to return to the printing business because the printing inks and other chemicals in the air were bad for his lungs. Again, my aunt and uncle, who had been publicans all their life, stepped in and decided that they would buy my parents a pub. We moved into The King's Arms at Tiptree when I was fourteen years old. Now we were in the local territory of my grandmother and aunt Jean, both of whom still detested my mother, who was now within easy reach of their venom.

The King's Arms was a lovely pub surrounded by a lot of land. The first thing my father did was set about building kennels, which he promptly filled with greyhounds. The pub was fairly near Clacton and Bury St.

Edmunds, which meant it was fairly near the flapping tracks. My father was quite the comedian and could tell great jokes but he wasn't one for work. He used to wake us all early in the morning and give us chores to do, such as cleaning the bars. Our time was spent either mopping up or bottling up. At the weekends, he would make us serve during the day. Living in a pub I became a very good darts player, at one point I thought about taking it up professionally. My mother enrolled me into Thurstable school but I hated it and rarely went. Instead, I used to play truant and visit my grandmother around the corner. After about nine months, at the age of fifteen, I was permanently kicked out of school.

Around this time was an event that literally shaped me for the rest of my life. Gordon van Sertima, a Guyanese bodybuilding champion and five times 'Mr. Guyana' winner, appeared at our local fete. He had stood on podiums with champion bodybuilders, such as Arnold Schwarzenegger and Sergio Oliva. At the fete I watched Gordon demonstrate his amazing lung power by blowing up a hot water bottle until it burst. He invited the audience to try to lift his heavy dumbbell above their heads with two hands. Nobody could, although one or two managed to get it to their waist height. With ease, Gordon bent down, picked it up and waved it above his head, as if it were a baby's rattle, and then did it with the other arm. Other feats included bending six inch nails and literally driving six inch nails through a scaffold plank with his bare hands. With his fantastic physique he resembled a Marvel comic hero. I was awestruck.

My big ears, long nose and incredibly skinny frame made me feel incredibly self-conscious. Although formidable in size, Gordon had a beaming smile and I summoned up the courage to speak to him. He turned out to be the most approachable man, a true gentleman. I asked him how he managed to get his incredible physique.

Bending down to look me straight in the eye, his deep, booming tone voiced the secret, "You train and you train hard."

It seems his words must have had a hypnotic quality because I was totally mesmerized and eager to learn.

Transfixed I asked him, "How do I train, how do I learn all of this?"

Gordon invited me to his gym, which was a garage he had converted into a training area. He showed me the exercises he used to become a mountain of muscle. That fuelled my ambition to become a bodybuilder. I'm now sixty two years old and still a regular at my local gym. No matter where I've lived, it's always been a priority for me to train. Like I said, that meeting with Gordon van Sertima shaped my life because the many hours spent sculpting my body would open doors for me. My larger physique and muscles became an asset in my later career.

Chapter 4
The Codfather

As I had left school, Cyril Smith, one of the chaps that frequented my father's pub, offered me a job at a company that converted old buses into shops or tour buses, like the open-top buses. Passenger Service Vehicles used to change them so that instead of getting on the left-hand side they would be accessed on the right-hand side, subsequently they were sold to American companies. There were some right characters that I worked with and they were a big influence in my life.

One in particular was a gentleman called Lee Armstrong, who had been a tail gunner in the war. At that time he was well into his fifties and wore a baseball cap back to front on his head years before it was fashionable. He was fantastic fun to be around and never stopped laughing, he used to sing and dance and was always entertaining. To begin with my work involved panel beating and I then moved onto the mechanical side of the business. I was a real handful but Gordon Little, the manager, and the rest of the crew really loved me. Buckets of water were thrown over me, I was covered in grease, you name it and I had it, but I still came back for more. It was a great job and the money was okay.

Lee was always raving about motorbikes, such as Ratley Rudge and other models, laughing with the lads about his escapades. With a way about him that's difficult to put into words, he was able to say the rudest things to anyone and just have them laugh, whereas anyone else wouldn't have gotten away with it. I can't explain it easily, he just had a fantastic way about him. I always said I wanted a motorbike when I was sixteen, so Lee and the lads searched through the local papers and ended up buying two scrap motorbikes, an AJS and a Matchless. They were basically the same identical motorbike and the lads brought them back to the garage. The mechanics stripped them down and restored the engines, the paint shop did the tank and between them they produced a great motorbike. Lee road-tested it and I've never seen anything like it. He flew up the road and came back past us at about eighty miles per hour on this old bike, threw it around corners and we were all astonished by his ability.

Unfortunately my motorbike riding skills weren't up to very much at all. Worst still, I never wore a crash helmet, despite having one, even though I came off the motorbike three times. The last time was when I rode back to Leytonstone to see my friend Paul. Coming up to the bridge by the bit of bypass that leads towards Leytonstone Station, doing around thirty miles per hour, I clipped the kerb on one side, which threw me into the road. I had no crash helmet on, the only protection from the tarmac was my tee-shirt. Luckily, the cars behind me managed to quickly stop. The skin on my knees was taken off and, as I put my hands in front of my face, I dislocated a thumb and a finger. Picking the motorbike up, I noticed the forks were a bit bent. I pushed it until I arrived at a house, where I knocked on the door, explained I'd been in an accident and asked if I could leave the motorbike in the front garden. My next stop was the local hospital to be bandaged up, after which I took the train home.

The next day, I was on the parking area of the pub and as Lee approached I stuck my thumb out. Pulling into the parking area, Lee asked where my motorbike was and I told him I had come off it yet again. After asking me if I was okay, he slapped me around the back of the head, grumbling that he had to sort me out about motorbikes. When we arrived at the garage, he had a word with the manager Gordon and the others. They decided there was a certain bus they had to road test. They road tested it all the way to Leytonstone, threw my motorbike in the back and brought it back to the garage for repair. Even so, my motorbike riding days were over. There had been too many accidents and the lads at the garage, led by Lee Armstrong, said there would be no more motorbikes. At this point, I was nearly seventeen years old.

The garage started to become a place that was frequented in the evenings by young girls from the village of Silver End. We always seemed to be working late on rush jobs and the girls, usually four or five of them, would all gather outside where the buses were parked and chat away. It was Lee who pointed out to me that the girls were coming to the garage to see me. I was really very shy about all of this, but Lee would grab hold of me and frogmarch me outside to speak with them. He was utterly convinced that he would match me up with one of them to lose my virginity. Eventually I started dating one of the girls, Barbara, who was my first real girlfriend, and things went along nicely.

The lads decided it was time to visit Jack Abercrombie, a car dealer, to buy a car. I wasn't quite seventeen years old and couldn't get a provisional licence. Undeterred the lads said they would buy me a car and teach me to drive around the back of the garage. That meant that once I had my provisional licence I could apply for my driving test. My lessons began behind the wheel of a Ford Anglia van. The lads drove it back and showed me how the gears worked. We drove around and around the back of the garage area and parked it up there, at night they parked it in the garage. Being my usual self, I decided one morning to reverse it back out into the parking area. I put it into reverse, let the clutch out and the van shot backwards into the garage doors, smashing up the back of the van.

There was another mechanic, Brian Lewis (who we always called Bub Lewy), who at the time had a little 1962 Mini Traveller. Brian offered to repair the van and do a swop for the little Mini. So there I was, having driving lessons from the lads around the car park, becoming more and more confident. I was seeing Barbara on a regular basis, as you do with your first love, but from Tiptree where I was living and with no motorbike, the cost of taxi fares was breaking me. In my wisdom and before getting my licence, I decided I would drive the Mini. I got away with this for quite a few weeks, although I think the lads had an inkling of what was going on but perhaps they weren't entirely sure. Barbara and I went courting in this little Mini.

One day, I was at the garage and the Mini van was there, the lads had left early and I decided I was going to drive back to Tiptree. I had left the garage in Silver End and was heading towards Rivenhall, where there's a big pit filled with water. There's a steep hill which comes to a sharp bend and then up again. I was bombing along at around fifty miles per hour. The road had just been resurfaced and, as I came onto the new tarmac, which at the time had no white lines painted on, an Eastern National bus came from the other direction. We met on the bend. I saw the bus looming up in front of me and hit the brakes hard because I was slightly on the wrong side of the road. The Mini went into a skid, I saw the bus coming at me and that was the last thing I remembered, other than sitting up in a ditch and hearing a voice shout "There he is!" and glimpsing what was left of the little Mini about twenty or thirty yards away before passing out. By the strangest coincidence, Barbara was actually on the bus that I hit.

I awoke in hospital to find my mum and dad sitting by the bed. It was very hard to see in the light and I had a burning sensation around my neck. Apparently, just before I hit the bus, I threw myself to the right as I wasn't wearing a seat belt, as in those days you didn't have to. The doors on the Mini were very flimsy and had a rope handle, rather than a metal handle, which meant I was able to pull on the handle and come out of the car, right at the point of impact. Everyone looked for me at the spot where the Mini had ended up, but I was about thirty yards away, face down in the ditch. The battery had followed me out and landed on my back, the acid had spilt over me but left no scars.

I think God was on my side because the Mini was a total write-off. The engine was actually pushed right into the back of the vehicle. The radiator of the bus was smashed and the axle was broken. Luckily the driver was uninjured but the accident caused an awful lot of damage. Even before I received my provisional driving licence, I had six points on it and a bill for six hundred pounds from Eastern National, which in those days was a huge sum of money. In time I recovered and went back to work and my old naughty ways. I was glad to be back at work with the lads. I thought the world of them, especially Lee Armstrong and Gordon Little, they were fantastic people and stood by me through the accident and everything else.

The company I worked for used to do buses up and turn them into shops or send them overseas. To be able to drive to exotic countries was exciting and all the lads wanted to do it, they all had a PSV licence. There were two owners of the company, one of which was Peter Newman. He had a friend, Mark Lucie, who was a very good looking, smarmy sort of man. We had just restored a bus that was due to be taken to the sunny part of Italy, everyone wanted to drive the bus over there. Gordon and all the boys had worked on it and it was decided that one of them should be the one to drive it over. Mark Lucie had been a stunt driver and had appeared in the television programme On The Buses. If you've ever seen the episode where the bus is driving around the park, it was Mark driving one of our buses.

Anyway, Peter Newman and the other manager, Roy Chappell, decided that Mark was going to take the bus to Italy.

We did have some laughs at that place. One of the owner's had a son-in-law, Alan Tween, who also worked there and was the next youngest one to me. I was just coming up to seventeen years old and Alan was about twenty five years old. He was a bit full of himself and loved talking down to me and telling me what to do, simply because there was no way he would get away with it with the other lads. Our lunch break was coming up.

Alan gave me my orders. "Right, go down the fish and chip shop because I want fish and chips for lunch."

I told him to get it himself but he kept on and bullied me into it. Fuming with anger, I went to the fish and chips and bought him chips. I then went next door and bought a wet fish, wrapped it up with the chips and returned to the hut, which served as our tea room at the back of the garage. Everyone was gathered in the tea hut when I arrived back. I handed the fish and chips, still in the bag, over to Alan, who was smiling and sarcastically telling everyone what a good boy I was. He opened the bag up to find the wet fish laid across his chips. He went ballistic but daren't hit me because otherwise the other lads would have grabbed him. As you can imagine, the whole place was in uproar, everyone fell about laughing their heads off, whilst Alan tried to slap me with the fish before eventually throwing it out the door.

I thought the world of these lads and anyone who upset them also upset me. They were all angry that Mark Lucie had been given the job of driving the bus to Italy. So, me being me, I climbed into the cab, took the housing off the heater, put the wet fish in there and replaced the housing. The next morning Mark rang in. He had arrived in Dover and mentioned there was a funny sort of smell in the cab. Roy, the manager, came out and asked if we had carried out any work on the radiator, perhaps with some radiator filler, as that could cause a smell. By the time the bus arrived in France, Mark could barely stay in the cab as the smell was terrible but he had no choice, he had to drive to Italy. When he arrived in Italy the smell was absolutely horrendous. He searched for the source of the pungent odour, undid the covering and found the fish, then phoned the owners of the company to tell them what had caused the smell. Of course, they didn't need to have Einstein's brain to work out who was the guilty party. Needless to say, I was remonstrated with and given my marching orders.

The lads pleaded with the management to let me stay, but I had gone too far this time, they had to let me go.

CHAPTER 5
DAYLIGHT ROBBERY

My next job was with a chap, Tubby Wright, who used to come and buy all the scrap metal off the garage. He had a massive scrapyard for used cars on the outskirts of Silver End aerodrome. There were hundreds of old cars there, it was a massive place. Strangely, Tubby was the one that towed away my old Mini, which he put on display and used to point me out as the driver. I worked for Tubby for about five or six months. In the meantime, I turned seventeen years old, applied for my provisional licence, which came through with the endorsements. After just seven driving lessons with the Ellis School of Motoring, I took my driving test and passed first time in Colchester. Finally I was legal on the road. My parents never funded me with anything, instead I saved up and bought my own car. The very first car that I owned legally was a Hillman Minx Convertible. Barbara and I were still an item at the time and I travelled to and from Silver End like a bat out of hell.

Eventually, I left Tubby's and managed to get a job in the building trade. At my father's pub there was about one acre of land at the back and a new housing estate was being built by Cadman Builders. I still lived at the pub, which meant the work would be right on my doorstep. I was put on the unloading team. As there were no forklifts, the building materials, such as pallets and bricks would come in, sometimes five to ten thousand bricks at a time, our group of lads would have to unload them by hand, which was really backbreaking work. That lorry would leave and then a cement lorry would arrive, to be followed by a plasterboard lorry or wood lorry. Unloading these lorries was my work for the entire day. It was seriously hard graft and the grit from the bricks would get into my eyes and scratch them.

Mind you, it was better money, which meant I could pay my mum and still have a tenner left at the end of the week, which was a few quid to have in those days. I started to buy clothes and other bits and pieces. Barbara and I drifted apart as she was quite a distance away and eventually I met a girl called Carol. We started dating, she was local to Tiptree, a nice girl with lovely parents, unfortunately her mother Doreen died quite young. I spent a lot of time at Carol's home and her family made me feel very welcome. We were just kids, young and feisty, most of our courting was in the car or driving about doing various things.

It was around this time that I began to drift into a life of crime and villainy. Jeanette, my cousin who I was very close to, was seeing a chap called Tim Jacklin, who was older than me. A real smooth character, he seemed to know everything that was going on and I became quite friendly with him. Even at an early age he would be described as a 'wide boy.' This was when credit cards very first came out. They were not as we know credit cards today with PIN numbers, instead they were cards with signatures on the back and the idea was brand new to the shops. The card would be inserted into a manually operated machine that made an imprint of the card onto a form, which you then signed and usually the credit limit was fifty pounds. Up until then I had never seen a credit card and had no idea what it was but Tim did. As I was driving legally, Tim asked if I fancied earning a few quid. I jumped at the chance and asked him what he wanted me to do. Apparently he needed me to do some driving for him, for which I would be well paid.

I drove him all over the place, literally all over the country. We would stop off and park in a town, he would go off, returning later to fill the boot of the car with bags of clothing, electrical goods, cigarettes and booze. We would offload the items elsewhere and then start again. Although Tim and I were friendly, in truth, I really didn't understand what was going on, as he didn't say a great deal about it. I had an inkling it might not be legal, although I didn't have a clue how he was actually doing it. At the time, it was like printing money really. At times, Tim would tell me to choose a nice pair of shoes, a good shirt, jacket and a pair of jeans. My wardrobe was filing up, it was continuously have this, have that. Tim basically slung all these items at me just for driving him around and that was it. Why would I say no to that?

Everything went pear shaped when Tim started seeing another girl and lavished gifts on her. For whatever reason they fell out and I believe she phoned the police. I'm not too sure of the exact details, perhaps he had told her what was going on. Needless to say, Tim was arrested and as I was associated the police came after me too. There was a knock on the side door of the pub and in my ignorance I opened it. On the doorstep were the CID officers.

"Ronald Buckingham?" they asked, to which I nodded, "Right, you're under arrest."

My mother did her pieces as they went into my bedroom and cleaned out most of the stuff I had. Luckily I didn't have a very big wardrobe and some of the items had been put in my brother's wardrobe, so I kept a little bit but all the aftershaves and other items just disappeared. Later, standing in the dock, I received my first conviction and was put on probation.

This incident had given me an insight into crime. The building work was back breaking, it really was and for about sixteen pounds a week, which by the time I had given my mum six pounds left me with a tenner. If I wanted a new shirt or pair of trousers I had to save for a month because I had to buy fuel for the car, pay for the car tax and that sort of thing. Being able to buy anything really nice was a bit of a slow process. Suddenly I had been able to have new clothes, shoes and lots of other nice things, although they had quickly disappeared when the police arrived. Not being a hardened villain, I had no idea how to get these things through crime myself.

Around this time, I had my eighteenth birthday, a big anti-climax. I didn't mention to my family that I was going to be eighteen years old, instead I hoped they would remember my birthday. They didn't. A couple of days after my birthday, I remember being in the kitchen of the pub with my mother.

"Oh wasn't it your birthday the other day Ronald?" she asked.

"Yes mum, I was eighteen," my tone was one of disappointment.

"Oh," she replied, "Many happy returns son."

It was about this time that I developed a desire for tattoos. Periodically I would travel back to Romford to visit Vic Shipton, a very well-known tattooist. It started off with a tattoo at the top of one arm, then the other arm, eventually covering the rest of my arms and my chest. My father hated tattoos with a vengeance. When I returned home I had my sleeves rolled down, even when they became infected, as they sometimes did in those days. I made sure they were completely hidden by my clothing. After Vic Shipton, in later years, I had other tattoos added by Skin Ink in Braintree.

One night, I had arranged to meet Carol and we were off out somewhere. Sharing a house with my parents and three brothers meant the bathroom was always busy. When my slot came, I dived into the bathroom, did my ablutions, slung a towel around my waist and had to make it to my bedroom door right opposite. This particular night, I opened the bathroom with a towel around my waist and standing there, waiting to use the toilet, was my dad. Staggering back wide eyed as he took in my tattoos, he shouted to my mum.

"Ethel, Ethel, come and see this silly bastard," he yelled, "He looks like a roll of wallpaper!" His quick quips were often amusing.

I left Cadman Builders when Carol's father offered me a job working with him on another building site as a painter and decorator. A little while went by and my cousin from London approached me to ask if I fancied earning some cash in exchange for doing some driving. He introduced me to a big Scottish chap called Jimmy, who shook my hand and asked if I was a good driver and told me there was some work where I would have to park up and wait for him and be ready to drive away quick. Together Jimmy and my cousin disappeared for a while, when they came back they slid into the car laughing and joking. I drove them back to where they needed to go and they gave me some money. It was more money than I could earn in a month or even two months, in the building game. One thing led to another and over time I became friendly with Jimmy and his brother Harry. Then the silliest part of my life began.

Together we did a few bits and pieces and I was considered game, meaning I would get stuck in because I had a lot of bottle. That was another way of saying that I was daft enough to do what they wanted me to do, which was a bit more than a driving role. Jimmy at the time was seeing a girl called Linda, who lived in Nelson Road, Hornsey. This was an area of really long streets with hundreds of houses. Linda told Jimmy that every fortnight the rent man would come down and collect all the money. I had been around her place with Jimmy a few times. Being young and impressionable, I looked up to Jimmy, who was quite a bit older than Harry and I, because he seemed tough. An ex-boxer, at the time I was knocking around with him, he was a doorman. Being very persuasive, he roped Harry and I into his next get-rich-quick scheme. The plan was to rob the rent man.

On the said day, we parked up the road, with a sawn-off shotgun, albeit unloaded, supplied by Jimmy. Waving a gun, rather than a stick, in someone's face is more likely to make them hand over the money. Jimmy was under the impression that there would be thousands of pounds to be handed over. What we didn't know was that the rent man used to drop money off at different places. As it turned out, there wasn't just one rent man, there was someone else with him. Pretending to tinker about under the car bonnet about five houses up from Linda's, we watched as the rent man and his associate went into the house before Linda's. We waited and waited, all the while with a holdall bag at the ready, stockings over our heads and the unloaded shotgun, together with rope to tie them up with. Linda was in on the whole thing, she wasn't going to scream but would let herself be tied up with them. The plan was to do the job, grab the money off the rent man and then scarper.

"They seem to have been in there a long time," I whispered to Harry.

"There's a house above," he replied. "Maybe they're having a cup of tea."

We continued to wait. And wait. And wait.

"This is taking way too long." I was getting jittery.

Harry agreed. So what did we decide to do? We went into the passageway, which leads to the two doors, one for the downstairs flat and one for the upstairs flat. Hearing voices on the other side of the door, we knew for sure they were in there. I had the gun between my knees, which began to tremble. Harry and I pulled the stockings down over our head. Right then the door opened. There stood the rent man, his associate and Linda. Instantly the men twigged what was going down and a fight ensued. At this point, we began to panic. I chinned the chap in front of me, who went over on his back, shouting and hollering as he took the stereogram down with an almighty crash. I waved the gun at them, told them to shut up and hand over the money, which of course they did. Little did they know, I was more shit scared than they were.

In the meantime, the woman from upstairs ran down, and other people began to run towards the house, in response to all the noise. Adrenaline kicked in and quick as a flash, Harry and I bolted, jumped in the car and drove away at speed. We dumped the car by Finsbury Park, which was daft as the place was crawling with police. Hopping onto a bus we escaped with the money. It turned out to be a few hundred pounds. The woman from upstairs told the police she had seen the two of us there before with Jimmy on several occasions. Really, how naive were we to think we could get away with it? All of us, including Linda, were in the frame, and the police were now searching for us. For some reason Harry and I ended up travelling to Crawley. We were in touch with Jimmy, who told us that the shit had hit the fan, both he and Linda had been arrested and the police were coming after us. Harry and I found a lodging house in Crawley, where we stayed for a week before travelling back to look for work.

With us we had what are known as a set of twirls, which is an old set of keys filed down flat that would open most cars. This is what we used to pinch an old Ford Anglia estate car, we threw our suitcases into the back seat and headed for London. Two young girls were thumbing a lift and being hormonal lads we decided to stop and offer them a lift. Straight away we realized it was a mistake. They were really mouthy, effing and blinding, but it was pouring with rain so we carried on driving to London. Around the Whitechapel area there was a roadblock. At the time the IRA were quite active and the police were checking people out. We couldn't turn around, we had to front it out. A policeman indicated for us to stop and wind the window down.

"Is this your car sir?" asked the policeman "Can I have your name?" I gave the name of my second cousin Johnny Harvey.

"Where are you from?" he questioned. I gave him an address.

"What are you doing?" his eyes scanned the inside of the car.

"Oh, we've just been up the road," I felt my voice quiver.

"Who are these girls?" he asked.

At this point the girls started to give the policeman abuse, effing and blinding, giving him loads of stick. I told the policeman they were hitch-hikers and that we had brought them into London. Keeping our cool, Harry and I thought we would get away with it. The policeman asked us to step out of the car, which we did. In those days, there was none of the computer access available to police forces now, it was quite backward then and we weren't known villains. The filed down keys we had would open the driver's door and start the ignition with no problem. The policeman wanted to know what we had in the back of the car and I told him just a couple of suitcases.

"Right, just open up the back" he demanded. "We want to look in the suitcases."

Harry and I weren't too worried as there were only clothes in there. The policeman walked round to the back with me, the girls continued to hurl abuse and he was quite put out by them. I put the key in the back and tried to open the boot but it wouldn't unlock. I tried it again and again. The policeman wanted to try it himself. He looked at the key and asked why it was filed down. Thinking on my feet, I told him I had only just bought the car and that I had been playing football over at Hackney Marshes, which a lot of kids did in those days. I made out I had lost the original keys and, as I had another set of old keys for another car, I had filed them down.

By now the policeman had put two and two together. Harry and I were arrested and taken to the Whitechapel police cells. Of course, the police found that the car had been stolen. We were banged up in the cells overnight and were sent to the Magistrate's Court the next morning, where we pleaded guilty. Straight away we were told it would be bail without surety.

"We're really in the shit now mate," I told Harry.

As we walked out of the dock, Hornsea CID officers arrested us. "We're charging you with robbery."

At the time, I was younger than Harry, nearly nineteen years old. As he was twenty one years old, Harry was taken to an adult prison. After questioning, we had to hold our hands up, there was no way out. I never mentioned Jimmy or Linda but they were in the frame nonetheless. Eventually Linda was bailed. I was on remand at Ashford Prison in Kent. Harry did his time along with Jimmy.

Some years later Harry was shot dead in Hackney by mistake. It was quite a famous case. He had a chair leg in a bag and was taking it back to his house, it had been repaired after it had been somehow damaged. Arriving back in Hackney, he went to the pub for a drink and the landlord mistakenly thought he was Irish. Because of the IRA troubles, the landlord phoned the police and told them he thought there was an Irish man in the pub with a gun. Harry was jumped by the police outside, who told him to drop the gun. Harry told them he didn't have a gun. Again, the police told him to drop the gun. Harry protested that he had no gun and as he put his hand in the bag to show them that it was just a chair leg, sadly they shot him dead. God bless him.

CHAPTER 6
DISHED UP

The 1970s were a strange time for me. My first time in prison made the local newspaper, my family were in uproar and my mother did her nut. The police were also trying to charge me with a robbery on a post office and another crime involving a gun in London, none of which stuck.

I was sent to the under 21s offenders unit at Ashford Prison and put in a cell with Danny Woods from Canning Town, who was quite famous as a robber and hard man. He was a fitness fanatic with an incredible physique, which suited me as throughout it all I had never stopped training. As we were on remand, we were allowed visits every day and to have our own food and treats brought in, although no alcohol was allowed. Danny received visits every day and whatever he received he always shared it equally with me. My family never came to visit me.

Mr. Porgy, was in charge of the kitchen. A big chap, he resembled the man from the 'Britain Needs You' poster. He always chose the bigger lads or those who had violence on their records to work in the kitchens. Danny Woods certainly fitted the bill and now, with the armed robbery charge under my belt, so did I. Danny, myself and a few other lads, such as Altez, who had stabbed a bouncer, and Frank, a Scottish lad who had also stabbed a bouncer, became the kitchen crew, along with others.

Lining us all up, he used to yell at us "Right, Mr. Porgy looks after his boys if they look after Mr. Porgy and Mr. Porgy is a very kind sir. What is he?"

Shouting back we would answer "A very kind sir, Sir."

Mr. Porgy was an out and out racist, it was quite endemic in prisons at that time.

"Right, I will look after you and you will have all the food you want to eat," he would bark. "You'll receive the best cuts, the best of everything, you'll get to play football in the afternoon but you'll do as you're told and you will respect me."

"Yes Mr. Porgy, Sir," we would chorus.

The inmates would go in for breakfast with a tray, onto which would be placed a rasher of bacon so thin it seemed as if it had been cut with a razor, a small spoonful of baked beans, porridge and as much bread as they wanted. Mr. Porgy let us know that woe betide any of us that let anyone, especially a black man, take more than they were entitled to. He pointed out that we would have a range of instruments behind us, such as ladles, pots and pans. If someone tried to take more than they were entitled to, we were to use the various implements behind us to hit them. Behind his strict façade, there was more than a hint of volcanic rage. A couple of days later, Mr. Porgy's lads all stood in the serving queue. I had the best job, which was the bread, as people could take as much bread as they wanted. It was pretty stale but they could take it. Just up the line from me was Danny, who was dishing out the bacon.

Gus Davies, was a big, black Jamaican guy, who I really liked, as he was always smiling and laughing, very funny with a great sense of humour. Just as Danny put a single rasher of bacon onto the tray Gus was holding, Gus slid a couple of fingers under the tray and hooked a couple of extra slices of bacon and tried to slide them on his tray. In a flash, Danny grabbed a huge metal ladle and cracked Gus right across the head with a bang. All hell broke loose, Gus and his mates went for Danny, the rest of us tried to protect Danny, and it all ended up as one big scrum. The screws came along and broke it all up. Mr. Porgy swore that Gus had attacked Danny Woods first, to ensure that Danny kept his job. Totally unfair but that was prison life.

After spending several months in Ashford Prison, I was moved to Latchmere House in Ham Common, which seemed like a breath of fresh air. In all I did five or six months waiting on remand before it was time for me to attend The Old Bailey. Police and prison officers came along to pick me up and I was given clothes to change into. What an experience. Having been bundled into a coach, I arrived at The Old Bailey. The coach drove down a slope onto a turnstile, which turned around in order that the coach would be facing the right way to move out. There was literally no room for the coach to manoeuvre around, hence why the turnstile was used. Handcuffed, I was surrounded by screws. I had never seen so many doors in all my life, they were every few feet. One door after another slammed shut behind me until I was finally placed in a holding cell. My solicitor came in to see me. I asked him what my chances were.

"You could be looking at five years easily," he told me. "What action do you want to take?"

I couldn't see myself getting away with it but wondered if I could ask for borstal. Thinking that was a strange request, he asked me why. I told him that borstal was six months to two years and that the lads on remand had put me wise. Some of the advice Danny had given me was that if I went to borstal not to let anyone mug me off, not the screws nor anyone else, just to steam in there. I thought I could look after myself but Danny gave me some good pointers. Jimmy, Harry and myself finally arrived in the docks. Jimmy ended up getting a three year prison sentence, Harry received two years. I asked for borstal six to two and that was exactly what I received. From there, I was transported to Wormwood Scrubs into the borstal wing.

I have often smiled to myself about this because borstal was a strange place. Filled with Jack- the-lads, everyone had a reputation, it wasn't in the least like a normal prison. It was all about ego, being a tough bloke and taking no shit from anyone, they were all shoulder rollers, but that was how it was. Upon arrival at Wormwood Scrubs, my hair was shaved and I was given a uniform to wear. The regime was one of marching and strict discipline. There were lots of borstals all over the country and outside of the Governor's office was a big map with pins stuck in showing where the borstals were. I was made to study the map. Hollesley Bay in Suffolk was the nearest one to my home. It was basically a working farm, where the inmates could work with horses, pigs and other animals, and where the inmates didn't have their heads shaved. In other words, it was the easiest of the borstals and everyone wanted to be moved there. Borstals to be avoided were Dover, Portland and Rochester, as they were really strict and hard and were where the really troublesome or problem lads went. I've never forgotten my prison number as it ended in 007, which made the others laugh. When the day came for a group of us to be allocated our borstal, the screw came out to line us up.

"Buckingham," he shouted "Stand to attention in front of the Governor."

I stood there poker faced as he turned to me and enquired "Buckingham, have you looked at the map?"

"Yes, Sir." I replied.

"Have you decided which borstal you want to go to?" he asked.

"Yes, Sir." I repeated.

"Which borstal is that?" His eyebrow raised quizzically.

"Hollesley Bay, Sir," was my request.

I explained I had chosen it because it was the nearest borstal to my parents, who lived in Tiptree.

"Hhmmnn" he sounded as if he was giving this his full consideration. "Yes, well I do think you need sea air," he replied. "However, I think we'll send you to Dover."

I felt totally gutted. Later, escorted by six screws, I was transferred to Dover Borstal, which was a very old building up on Western Heights, up on the cliffs and almost part of the castle with a moat around it. It was built during the Napoleonic wars by the prisoners to store arms and ammunitions and it had lots of old passageways running through it. Arriving at lunchtime, I was taken to the Governor, shown which dormitory I had been assigned to, before being given my kit, rain mac, coat, shirts and various outfits. I was the only new lad on the block at the time of my arrival. The houses were named Sandwich, Deal, Hastings and Romney. Once allocated to Sandwich house, I was locked in with around a hundred other inmates

Every morning, the lads woke, put on the grey shirt and trousers and tie ready for breakfast. After breakfast, we all changed into dungarees and boots ready for work. Each day we had physical training, the place was run on fitness and discipline, which actually suited me fine as I was incredibly fit, always doing press-ups, out running or in the gym. The physical training instruction Gordon van Sertima had given me as a youngster stood me in good stead, particularly as I was the only new inmate at the time.

On that first day, after being shown around, I was taken to the canteen, everyone was sitting down to lunch as I had caught the tail end of lunchtime. New inmates, known as saps, were given a new tie, which I recall was either red or green, and made to wear it for food breaks. Lining up for food, I was given a metal tray that was rounded on the corners and divided up for the various foods. Sausage and mash was my very first meal, along with a pudding and custard, and soup in another section of the tray. My allocated seat was right at the very back on a table with a Scottish lad, Alan Jamieson, along with Ozzie Hughes and Dave Baker. With my meal in my tray, wearing the tie, I began making my way to the table. All of a sudden, a short, stocky black chap, who was known as A.J. and had been a fighter or boxer, stood up and looked me straight in the eye. He was on the opposite end of a table I was walking by.

"Right sap," he snapped, "I'll have one of those sausages."

In a show of bravado, he said it loud enough for everyone to hear him. I just looked at him and laughed. A.J. put one of his hands forward to try and take one of the sausages. I tried to strike him with the tray and underhanded I swung the tray at his head. As a boxer he obviously knew how to avoid me, leaned back and the tray just missed him. The whole dinner, including the dessert, covered him. All hell broke loose, the screws were on us, that was it. On my first day there, I was nicked. I went without dinner and was dragged down to the Governor's office, who didn't think it was a good start at all.

"I'm not taking shit off of anyone," I told him. "I'll do my time and I'll do it the best I can but no way am I having anyone try and steal my food."

Neither of us were shipped out but all through my time at borstal we were wary of each other When inmates first arrived at borstal they were put into a reception dormitory. There were lads that had been there one or two weeks before me. In total, we did six weeks in this dormitory before being moved out into other cells. The dormitory was regularly raided by small gangs who swooped in to pinch cigarettes or sweets. Luckily for me, a few of the faces in borstal were familiar to me from the outside, which meant I rarely had any hassle, not that I would've put up with any hassle. For others borstal was too much for them to cope with. On more than one occasion I would hear dripping in the night, it was because one of the lads had slit his wrists.

I can't say there wasn't any violence in borstal because there was. There were grudges held and arguments but many a time the screws turned a blind eye. If you had a fall out with someone and a straightener was on the cards (meaning a one to one fight) it would always take place in the bath house, which had tiled floors. The thing to do was to wear a hob nailed work boot on the dominant foot, mine being my right side, and a plimsoll on the other foot, to make it possible to kick with the dominant foot without slipping over.

Often these grudges went on and it was imperative to have a good pal to watch your back, especially when you were stark naked in the shower with shampoo and soap in your eyes. Your mate would watch your back while you showered and you would do the same for him afterwards. The man who always watched my back during my time there was the Scotsman Jamieson.

Marching up and down was something I found difficult as I had never marched in my life. The day after the incident with A.J., we were taken down and told to line up, all turn to the right, which I did although a bit clumsily, and then by the left quick march. Having no real idea of what I was supposed to do, I just strolled off and was out of step with the others. I moved in the directions they told me but frankly I didn't have a clue. Mr. Doley, an ex-Coldsteam Guard, was a really tall chap, always immaculate with a trimmed moustache, a very politely spoken man.

"Okay Buckingham" he ordered, "Give a little skip and get in step."

I figured he wanted me to skip and look like a mug and had it in my mind this was how he was going to try to break me.

"Yeah alright," I replied.

He grabbed me, pulled me out of the line and explained to me that I was nicked again. Another great start. I was ordered to report to the office after finishing the plastering course I attended at the time. In the office stood Mr. Doley with the Governor.

"What you again?" asked the Governor.

I protested that I thought Mr. Doley was trying to mug me off in front of the other inmates.

"I just wanted you to get into step," he explained somewhat exasperated. Of course, I didn't see it like that at all.

The big thing at that time in borstal was a programme called Top of the Pops. After our tea at four o'clock, the lads would shower and get ready for the evening. We all looked forward to watching Pan's People, the dancers on the Top of the Pops show, cavorting around to the pop music wearing something nice, which sometimes meant not a great deal. My three hours of punishment work was in a very long corridor with a linoleum finish floor.

"Right, I want you to scrub all the polish off the floor and then re-polish with the big bumpers," ordered Mr. Doley, "And I want it polished so well I can see my face in it."

This was at five o'clock and Top of the Pops was due on at seven o'clock. With a huge bucket of water and scrubbing brush, I scrubbed away at that floor like a lunatic from one end to the other, dried it all, put the polish down and then polished with the bumper. When I had finished it shone so much I could definitely see my face in it and felt quite proud of my effort. Carefully I put everything away and dived in to watch the television, bang on time as Top of the Pops came on the screen. Right before Pan's People were due on, Mr. Doley burst into the room, grabbed hold of me and pulled me out.

"Your extra work was three hours," he yelled.

"You said polish off, new polish down and bumper it," I countered. "That's what I did and I think it looks really good."

He conceded that it looked fantastic. "But It only took you an hour and a half," he scowled, "Do it again."

And that was how I learned not to try and get around the rules at borstal.

It wasn't all bad in borstal, there were some high points. Even though I never had a great education, I loved crosswords and would spend hours keeping my brain occupied. Discipline was my forte, and I was able to focus on my goals with laser like intensity. Improving my physical fitness was a constant goal and one I applied myself to with great gusto. I enjoyed circuit training and was in the rugby and football teams. Basically I was pretty fit and, as a result, was never bullied by anyone. Plus I had friends in there, so it wasn't that hard to get through really.

As I mentioned, I went on a plastering course, which was down in the basements accessed via lots of steps from the main roadway. The plastering course was run by a civilian, Bruno Sockie, who I think was a Polish man. Each of us was given our own room that we had to plaster and we were taught as we went along. There was one lad in particular, Brownie Penge, who would do anything for a cigarette. A bit of a clown, he would sing and dance and we would encourage him, even Bruno Sockie would get him at it. The lads came up with the idea that Brownie would go stand outside the front entrance way and would sing 'Singing in the Rain.' The lads gave me a bucket of water and I positioned myself up on the adjacent flat roof, which was about five feet higher above Brownie's head. Of course, he didn't know I was up there. The plan was that once he began chorusing 'Singing in the Rain,' I would throw the bucket of water over him, then he would get his cigarettes. Sockie was in on the whole craic. Out comes Brownie, I'm perched on the roof with the big bucket of water, my eyes quickly scanned around and there, leaning on the wall looking down into the basement, was Mr. Doley. Damaging a uniform or anything like that was a nicking offence and that was the last thing I needed. Borstal was generally anything from six months to two years. If I behaved myself I might avoid having to stay any longer than I had to, but more nicking offences committed meant time added on. On average lads would do from nine months to one year in borstal. Having been nicked twice I didn't want to be nicked again. Swivelling my head back, I could see Brownie and the crew below me, but the lads in the workshop were unaware Mr. Doley was about. He was leaning nonchalantly with his arms folded, as Brownie crooned below. The lads were expecting me to throw the water over Brownie but I couldn't because Mr. Doley was watching. They thought perhaps I couldn't hear Brownie and told him to sing louder. And so he did, louder and louder, whilst I stood there with the bucket of water, glancing across at Mr. Doley, who was gazing down at Brownie.

Mr. Doley turned to me with a smile, "Well let him have it Buckingham."

Which I did with a whoosh. Along with the rest of the lads, Mr. Doley laughed and then sauntered away. Brownie took it all in good fun and was happy with the extra couple of cigarettes he had for his trouble. This incident showed what a nice man Mr. Doley was and because of this I truly respected him and it showed. I think he appreciated the change in my attitude towards him because he actually came to say goodbye to me when I left. A supporting voice in what could be a harsh environment, he told me that he thought I was something special. In a report that he wrote for my borstal record, he stated that I was a natural leader of people and had I been born in the time of the second world war, I would definitely have been leading people over the top and would have made a great sergeant. That was really encouraging and I treasured his words.

People surprise you at times, and Mr. Doley was no exception. Two Indian lads joined our dormitory and he came in to state the rules and regulations. As he was walking out, these two Indian lads started conversing in their own language. They were staggered when he spun round and answered them fluently in their own language with some home truths. It turned out he had served in India with the Guards and hence spoke their language. He certainly had my admiration that day.

I finished borstal after about ten or eleven months. Having completed my plastering course, I then went on to work on the houses outside with Mr. Jones, a fantastic man. He wasn't a screw but a civilian bricklayer and the kindest, nicest man I had ever met, who understood the lads. He knew we were young men locked up and that our girlfriends and family were on the outside and there was nothing we could do about it. Once when we were outside the prison walls during the last couple of months of our sentence, he spoke with us.

"You boys are fit, young, tough lads. If you want to run away then I'm not going to get in your way but please don't hit me," and then he cautioned, "But think about it because you'll only end up caught and brought back again and you'll be the worse for it."

Those were wise words indeed and our respect for him made sure we heeded them. Not everyone I met during my time in borstal had my respect. One such person that comes to mind was Mr. Linstrom, who was a brutal man. I used to play rugby but sustained a terrible knee injury whilst caught in a maul, my leg was caught under me and my knee went. It was strapped up by the medical staff. He forced me to play again the next week, even though I could barely run. The first time I was hit in a tackle, the crack could be heard all over the field. I was in agony for months.

At borstal we were allowed one visit a month for two hours. Carol, my girlfriend, was nicknamed Charlie Brown because of her big boobs. She had been coming down to see me with my best friend at the time, Gerry, who was married to Judy, with whom he had a couple of kids. He was quite a bit older than me, very laid back and a hippy type, quite the opposite to me but for whatever reason we gelled. When he brought Carol to visit me, he would sit with us for the first hour, then he would go off leaving Carol alone with me for the remainder of the time. She would often write to me and there were moments when I wondered if she had seen anyone else during my time in borstal, but she assured me that hadn't happened. We had been seeing each other for nearly two years and had grown very fond of each other.

My release date came and I was taken down from the borstal to the station, put on a train and sent off. Even at twenty-one years old, I wasn't much of a drinker, and even now I don't drink a great deal. However, there were about half a dozen lads going back to London and we decided to go and have a drink, just one or two. Eventually I arrived back and it had been prearranged with Judy, Gerry's wife, that I would meet Carol at Judy's house and we would stay over. I was greeted back home at my parents' pub with a frosty reception. My dad had only visited me once in all that time and my mum never bothered at all. As I had just come out of borstal I had no car, so I jogged round to Judy's feeling really excited about seeing Carol.

Judy greeted me with the words, "Ronnie, they've gone."

Confused I asked "Who's gone?"

"Gerry and Carol," her words echoed again, "They've gone Ronnie."

"Come again?" I could feel the turmoil within her but my mind resisted her words, "I don't understand Judy."

It turned out they had been having an affair and had used their visits to me in Dover as a cover. Apparently Judy found out about it and Gerry came clean.

"Why didn't you tell me before?", my mind was a pinball machine as the details slammed into my ears, "Why drop the bombshell on me now?"

Judy looked at me with sadness in her eyes, "Ronnie, we knew that you'd go over the wall and escape from borstal and get yourself in more trouble, so we thought it best to leave it until now."

As I walked away, I was totally guttered and shaken to the core. Not only had I lost my girlfriend but I had lost my best friend as well. For a very long time this incident made me paranoid about women and I felt I couldn't trust another woman again. Finding out about Carol screwed me up for quite a while. The crazy thing was that women threw themselves at me. It wasn't too long before I began picking up the pieces.

Chapter 7
First Impression

The jigsaw of my life began coming together when I started frequenting a nightclub called the Copford Windmill, which was to play a big role in my life in later years. It was owned by Bob Wheatley of Wheatley Taverns, who also owned the Circus Tavern and The Barn at Braintree and about twenty other clubs. I became friendly with the head doorman at the time, Mickey Caine, an ex-professional middleweight boxer, together with Johnny Harvey, who I later discovered was my second cousin, unbeknown to us at the time. As I was quite big and fit, I was asked to work the door now and then. I was still on probation at the time, and I wanted to settle down with a regular job and during the day I worked on building sites. I realized I had a lucky escape only getting borstal but I didn't want to return.

One Saturday night I was in the pub, my father came in and told me there was a big coach party from London and Teddy Enever's daughter was there. The Enever family were a big family from Manor Park, quite a feared family, with lots of brothers and a sister. Tommy Enever, Teddy's brother, was quite famous over the mini-cab shootings in Ilford as they went to war with the Blundell family. There were lots of shootings. It was quite strange because Teddy was a fighter more than anything else, not a villain but quite a handful.

"Cracking looking girl" said my father. "Come in and say hello."

I really didn't want to but my father coaxed me to go into the bar to meet Teddy's daughter, Susan, and we really hit it off. She was about three years younger than me, around eighteen years old, pretty as a picture and funny. Her cousins, Tommy, Billy and Johnnie Barney, together with various friends, all joined in on our conversation. Billy had been in borstal also, so there was plenty for us to gossip about and we all really gelled. The coach party finished their sojourn. Susan had taken a shine to me and decided to stay with her aunt around the corner. She had never had a serious boyfriend and was a bit naïve but a very nice girl. Her aunt Jean would bring her into the pub, we would have a drink together and chat. I never drank alcohol, just colas or juices as I was doing my bodybuilding training. As I had a car, I was able to take her out and we started seeing each other. Jean had a friend, Jack, who would run Susan and I back down to Manor Park to see her parents. At the time, her dad had a dry cleaning shop at the top of Third Avenue. He came from a travelling family and was a man of few words. Although not unfriendly, everyone always knew where they stood with him.

Susan and I fell in love and eventually married in a little registry office in Stratford, I was around twenty two years old at this point. Together we moved to Manor Park, first of all living with her parents in the spare room upstairs, later moving to a little bedsit in Ilford. Susan's nan on her mother's side Lil was a lovely old lady, who had been very ill in hospital and had to have her leg amputated. She had a flat in Jack Cornwall Street in Manor Park, it was a two bedroom flat. We moved in with her, whilst Susan was caring for her, as she needed help. Susan's dad wasn't happy about this situation, as he felt we were a young married couple and shouldn't be looking after her nan.

Susan's uncle offered me a job at his fruit and vegetable stall in Barkingside as a barrow boy. I loved getting there early in the morning with Tommy Ricks, who managed it, although it was long hours from six o'clock in the morning, when we pulled the stall out and set it up, serving right through until six o'clock in the evening. The money was really good and I worked there for quite a while. With working in the area and Susan's family being the way they were, I was introduced to a lot of other criminals. I used to see a lot of Roy Shaw, the famous boxer and bare knuckle fighter, who was always around Rosie Enever's house. I liked it there as I was friendly with Susan's cousins and we would all go over to the Wanstead flats to play football, after which they would be out on the booze. I remember my first argument with Susan, we were in the Blakesley pub one night and her cousin Tommy wanted to buy me a drink.

Tommy and Billy Enever, myself and a pal

"Great thanks, I'll have an orange juice" I said.

"No," he replied, "I said I'd buy you a drink."

Again, I told him I would have an orange juice and he told me he wanted to buy me a proper drink.

Susan turned on me "C'mon be a man, have a proper drink," she chided, "You're embarrassing me."

Sudden anger welled up like a flash and I turned to her. "What? You've got to drink beer to be a fucking man?"

I stormed out of the pub. Looking back, we married too young and didn't really have a sense of who we were as individuals, let alone have the maturity necessary for marriage. Love is blind as they say and at the beginning of our relationship we didn't notice our differing values. Little niggles became major issues over time. Susan smoked whereas I never smoked, I was always very anti-smoking. I used to screw her cigarettes up and chuck them out but she would just buy others. She was a bit of a social butterfly and enjoyed drinking, whereas I was the opposite.

Susan became pregnant with our first daughter Marie but at that time we didn't have a place to call our own in the Manor Park area. At the time my parents had rented an old cottage that needed a lot of doing up, for five pounds per week. It was halfway between Coggeshall and Kelvedon. Fair credit to my father because he was quite good at carpentry, probably from all the practice building his dog kennels. Together we worked on the cottage until it was ready for Susan and I to move into. It was very remote, about one and a half miles from either village, stuck in the middle. Marie was actually born on my birthday, 11th January.

A few weeks before Marie's birth, on New Year's Eve, Susan was heavily pregnant and instead of going out we watched television, as neither of us felt up to a night on the town. At around ten o'clock we went to bed. I relaxed on my back with Susan's head on my chest. I found it difficult to sleep, my mind was going round in circles, anxious about the forthcoming birth and the thought of being a dad at such a young age. Out of nowhere, I felt a blanket of cold air descend on me, the hairs on the back of my neck stood up. My sixth sense alerted me to the fact that someone was in the room. It was a creaky old cottage and in my mind I questioned that surely I would've heard if someone had entered our home. I was wide awake and surely nobody could be that quiet. Nevertheless, I knew that someone was in the room. Whoever it was, were they armed? Suddenly the feeling intensified, becoming so overpowering, I literally felt someone leaning over the bottom of the bed. Warrior instinct kicked in and I sprung up in bed, Susan's head fell off my chest, shocked she sat bolt upright. A large, fairly young man was standing at the end of our bed, bizarrely he was dressed in a suit. Susan and I froze.

"What does he want?" Susan could barely speak, "What does he want?"

As her questioning, terrified eyes looked to me for protection, he simply faded into the wallpaper. Since that time, I have seen a lot of spirits, but that memory stands out because he was literally embedded in the physical structure of the cottage, with his luminous hands there in the wall. I didn't know what to do. If it had been human flesh and blood, no doubt I would've punched his head in or thrown him out the window. But in this instance I was clueless. Susan jumped out of the bed and turned the light on quickly. He had completely disappeared. I had ceased worrying about the forthcoming baby, now there was just one thought catapulting through my brain. Who or what the fuck was that?

The answer to that question came to me in quite a roundabout fashion.

Ken Jolly, a chap I knew, managed to find me a job in a factory in Witham. At the time I had an old banger of a car that often wouldn't start and so I used to jog into Kelvedon and thumb a lift, or perhaps catch Ken on his way to work and cadge a ride. One night, when I was driving the car back from work, I spotted a young boy, probably no more than fifteen years old, hitchhiking. There were no pavements, it was getting dark and it was dangerous to be walking about like that. I stopped to offer him a lift. He wanted to go to Coggeshall to the local youth centre. When you think about it, I could have been a murderer or anything.

Concerned at his naivety, I turned to him and asked "Weren't you frightened walking along with no street lamps or pavements on a dark night, weren't you worried?"

"Well, there's a ghost that's meant to walk this road," he replied laughing, "But only on New Year's Eve."

He went on to tell me about the story when in the late 1950s or early 1960s, a young chap in a car was travelling along the road, which had many tight bends. On one particular bend there was a pond and evidently the chap was drunk, went off the road and drowned in the pond. Apparently his spirit used to walk up and down the road on New Year's Eve. My antennae went up because that coincided with the night that Susan and I saw the spirit of the young man in a suit. Well, that made me think. Now, as a working medium, I now know that pregnant women do attract spirits, in the same way that people attract spirits to them when they're dying.

Marie was born on my birthday, a beautiful blessing in my life. I wanted to provide well for my little family but felt frustrated as money was a bit of an issue. I had a car that was forever breaking down, an old Morris, and finding the money to repair it was difficult. I had too much month left at the end of my money and felt the lack keenly.

CHAPTER 8
FATE HAS WON OVER

Having been brought up in the pub trade, I was a good darts player and went on to play for Barking Super League whilst living in Manor Park. I continued playing for my father's team at the Kings Arm in Tiptree and one night we played a team in Kelvedon. The club was robbed, nothing to do with me, but the fact that I had previous convictions and had been in the club and signed the guest book, meant I was pulled in. Rob Booth, the CID officer in Witham, questioned me and I told him where I was but he was still very suspicious, as police officers are, but he had nothing on me and that was it. However, he took me over to view a map on the wall and I've never forgotten this.

"You see this area here and around there?" he indicated on the map, "That's my area and I think you're at it, leave my area alone and I'll leave you alone." He continued, "I don't care what you do elsewhere, just don't start committing crime in my area." "

If you do," he cautioned, "I'll put you away." At that, he shook my hand and off I went.

Funnily enough, someone from my dad's pub tipped me off about a factory that made automotive parts. I don't know exactly how but he had some connection to it.

"Look, I've been in there on a Thursday night, a lot of people work there and they're all paid cash," he whispered as he pulled me to one side. "It's kept in a safe on a Thursday night to be paid out Friday morning."

At this particular time, I knew a chap Groucho from Manor Park and I told him about it. We decided to pay this place a visit. Not a lot of people realize this but in the early 1970s, unlike today, the police were everywhere. Breathalyzers had just come out and people would often be pulled over. Today you don't see so many police, instead there are more speed cameras and people are only pulled over when they've been caught speeding. Because of the risk, I always made sure my own car was taxed and insured. We knew where this factory was and I parked in a lover's lane close by, where other cars would park. The police knew of it, no big deal.

We broke into the factory, which had its own oxyacetylene cylinder, Groucho cut open the safe, we nicked all the wages and it was a lot of money. I was elated thinking this was really going to help my little family, as we made our way back to the lover's lane, which was about half a mile away. To my dismay, stuck on the window was a sign 'Police Aware.' I couldn't believe it and to this day, I still have the feeling that somebody said something.

So, there we were, it was the middle of the night. My instincts told me not to move the car and to message home and tell Susan to report it stolen. I knew that wouldn't go down well with her but needs must. There were no mobile phones in those days, which meant the pair of us had to find a phone box and I phoned my brother Lee. He didn't have a clue what was going on. I simply told him I was stuck and really needed some help and could he pick us up, which he did and then took me back to my house. All the clothes I wore in that place, everything, I never took off. From there, Groucho and I went to pick his car up and he took me straight back to Manor Park to Susan's parents. I left word with Susan to phone the police and report the car stolen, I was in London on business and I would be back. Lo and behold, the police raided our home, asked where I was and Susan told them I was in London and that the car had been stolen. They questioned her on how I managed to get to London and she told them I had gone down with a friend. The police obviously didn't find any cash, as I had all the cash with me, instead they took some of my clothes and shoes with them.

And here's the strange thing. I had a complete change of clothes that I had taken with me, all the clothes I had worn were burned, including my shoes. Knowing the routine, I was going to return and hand myself in. I blew my nose, which is one of the things I knew to do, as with the safe being cut bits of metal would spark out and any bits up my nose could be picked up by forensics. Anyway, the police couldn't make anything stick other than my car was there, which we had said was stolen, thin story but that was it. However, the forensic test came back with a pair of shoes, there was grease from that factory floor, a jumper they took had little bits of burnt metal in the threads of the jumper. It was so easy for them to do. Simply go to the factory, take little plastic bags, scoop up a bit of grease and some other bits and pieces, the clothes are taken away, put a bit of grease on the shoes, sprinkle the clothes with something and forensics will find it. Rod interviewed me and informed me about the forensics result. I just laughed.

"I warned you" his voice lowered. "Unfortunately, it was just in my manor," he continued, "A couple of miles further on, Maldon maybe, you'd have been out of my area."

A very strange man but not unlikeable. Needless to say, I went to court and pleaded not guilty, because I had a young child I managed to receive bail. Rod then pulled me back in.

"What's all this about?" I demanded.

"Look, aren't you willing to work?" he asked.

"Yes, of course, I've had all sorts of jobs, I've worked on building sites and other places." I went on, "You find me a job that pays well and I'll work, what's the big deal?"

"Right, you've got a car now?" I told him I had. "Okay, go down to Pitsea, Basildon, there's a massive building site there, find a bloke called Dave, the site agent who's a good friend of mine and tell him I sent you, he'll give you a job."

I went to see Dave, who seemed like one of my own, tattoos and a big smile on his face.

"Oh you've been nicked then?" his grin crinkled his eyes.

I told him I was on bail. At the same time, a chap who was quite famous around that area was Micky McCabe, who was probably one of the hardest men I ever met. He went on to run all the doors around Basildon and the surrounding area. He had an amazing reputation for being a fighter and hard man. He had just been released from a twelve, so he was on license and he had also managed to secure a job at the site. Dave decided to pair Micky and myself together and we started work putting in concrete ground beams. The ground workers would dig the trenches, put the concrete foundations in and Micky and I would get the beams on our shoulders, even though they weighed around 300 to 400lbs, we would carry them and position them by hand in the trenches. Normally men doing that job would wait for the forklift and it would take ages, but we were so far in front there was no more work for us to do.

"I'm really impressed with you two!" Dave's smile was even broader than before.

He ended up making me storeman and Micky the ganger, what a combination. I was now in charge of the stores and everything that went in or out through the stores had to go through me. The store was huge as the housing estate comprised of hundreds of houses. Security used to go around on a bike it was so big. I really hit it off there and worked really hard. Then Dave called me into his office.

"Right, you're going to be the van driver," he informed me. You're going to pick up so-and-so in the morning and take them back at night."

This was a bonus as I was able to keep the van and use it privately, plus I received a wage increase, which turned out to be good money. Straight away my mind thought of a fiddle. There was a big Irish gang, who were sub-contractors there, the governor of them approached me and told me he wanted shovels and picks and that he would buy them off me. He bought around six picks and shovels and other bits and pieces.

At the time, I would sell new shovels, picks, and other bits to the Irish gang, then steal them back and burn the Union Jack pattern on them using a hot wire. When the Irish gang complained that someone had nicked the shovels and other stuff, I'd tell them to look around the stores and if there were any without marks on, they must be theirs. But of course, there were none without marks.

"Oh the thieving bastards," they were really pissed off, "Someone else on the site has taken them."

There were all sorts of silly scams going on. Micky and I earned really good money, he kept control of the lads and I kept control of the stores, and we both had money making fiddles going on. One involved some sub-contractors, big Irish chaps, who were diehard gamblers. Even when working on the building site, I made sure I did my fitness training, even if it meant using what was on site. Mickey saw me doing presses above my head with the mastic drums that weighed one hundred and twelve pounds but were very hard to grip. I could do twelve repetitions without a problem. That gave him an idea. Knowing the Irish guys would bet on anything, Mickey suggested that I get one the drums up on my chest in front of them and squeeze out two repetitions. The Irish guys commented on how well I had done.

"Right, we'll have a competition!" they jumped up excitedly, "You go against our big Connemara man and let's see who can do the most."

Immediately bets were made and fingers flipped through notes. Micky said as he was my mate he would back me. Of course, I backed myself and the Irish guys backed the Connemara man. The money sat in the middle of the crowd. The Connemara man went first, he managed about five repetitions. The Irish chaps whooped it up thinking it was a strong start. My turn came and they elbowed one another's ribs and mocked me in order to put me off. I stood in front of the drum and stared at it. They continued to make fun of me. I picked up the drum and slowly, carefully, pushed it above my head. Then without any apparent effort, I breezed out a total of ten repetitions. The look on their faces was priceless and they moaned like mad as they knew they had been had. But hats off to them because they coughed up the money.

Another scam involved a digger driver, who was pornography mad. At the time there were cine projectors and some of the chaps on the building site would deal in these films. I told Micky I had a plan. At lunchtimes, all the men on the building site would meet in a big hut, which held around eighty people, to eat their lunch. At the time there was a painter and decorator there, a Cockney called Arthur. I nailed a full sheet of Gyprock onto a wall and Arthur painted it white. Dave didn't take any notice of what was going on. The actual site foreman, a chap called Giffy, liked porn films as well. I persuaded another chap to come in with his projector, Micky was on the door and it was two pounds per head. The lads would come in, eat their sandwiches and watch some blue films. We did two sittings per day and were probably netting forty quid each a day and giving the projector guy a cut of the profits.

Eventually, the time came for me to attend court in front of Judge Greenwood in Chelmsford. To be fair, Rob Booth went up and asked for a non-custodial sentence because Dave had told him how well I was doing and that I was really grafting. Dave knew I was doing some fiddles but he turned a blind eye to the little bits going on. With the money for the van, the wages and the little bits of fiddle on the side, I didn't need to go out and do anything else. However, Judge Greenwood wasn't having any of it. I ended up receiving eighteen months in prison.

It was a shame because Judge Greenwood was given good recommendations. It was only me that was nicked, Groucho didn't come into the frame as I never put his name up. That didn't go down well as they knew there was someone else involved. I couldn't have done it on my own and they probably realized I had no idea how to use oxyacetylene. Fair play to Groucho, he only took a percentage of the money, the rest was put by for when I was released.

Just before the time when I received eighteen months for cutting the safe, there was quite a funny incident involving Groucho. He was a cat burglar, who could silence any alarm and break into the most complex places and quite frankly, as burglars go, he was amazingly skilled and nimble. In contrast, I was far too clumsy for that game, burgling homes would never have been my thing. However, there was one skill that Groucho hadn't mastered - he couldn't drive. Therefore, he always relied on someone to drive him around. I did feel quite sorry for him, as he had been a bit used by certain people and they would drive him somewhere, drop him off and pick him up hours later and want their share of the money or goods.

Through another man called John, a bit of inside work came up and, as usual in these cases, it was given by the family of someone, which is really sad when you think about it. There used to be a racing stadium in Essex and the inside information was that on a Saturday night the owner used to take all the takings, which was a lot of money, and would lock it in his safe at home until he was ready to bank it on the following Monday morning. The work was outside Essex and Groucho asked John and myself to take him, which we did. We booked into a hotel and met up in the bar and had a drink, chatting with some of the locals. Behind the bar was a stunning blonde barmaid, very flirtatious and Groucho rather liked the look of her. John on the other hand hardly noticed her as he was a happily married man who wasn't into any shenanigans with other women.

A couple of strange things happened. I told the others I would pop up to my room to shower and change and would be back down later. This wasn't a problem as Groucho wasn't interested in doing the burglary until later and we wanted to rest up after the long drive up. I asked the barmaid if it were possible to borrow a hairdryer, and she advised me to knock on the door of No. 13, which was the other barmaid's room, who would probably have one to lend me. I knocked on the door of No. 13 and an absolutely stunning redhead answered, a silk kimono style dressing gown draped around her, clearly she had just finishing bathing. What a gorgeous sight. To cut a long story short, she took a shine to me and moments later we were downstairs with the others in the bar having a drink and chatting away.

John indicated to me that he wanted a quiet word, "We've got a problem."

"What's that?" I asked.

"Groucho's holding a few quid," John grumbled as he rolled his eyes upwards.

The strange thing about Groucho is that if he had money there was no way you could get him to work. He could be taken past a place that a blind man could break into and if Groucho had a few quid in his pocket, he wouldn't be interested. On the other hand, if he was skint, he could be dropped outside the Royal Mint and he'd give it a go. That was him all over. He was a drinker, not an alcoholic but he liked a drink, but his downfall was gambling, he was a serious gambler. Groucho should have been a multi-millionaire with the amount he had stolen in his lifetime, but instead he spent his money on horse racing. I only grafted with him occasionally but I knew the antics he got up to.

"He's got about two hundred quid on him," John cautioned me, "That means we need to get him to spend it quick."

At the time, two hundred quid was a lot of money. So there we stood in the bar, chatting away to the lovely barmaids. I went straight for the redhead as she was lovely, but I have to say Groucho wasn't really a ladies' man, he liked to think he was but he didn't really have what it took.

"C'mon Groucho, get some champagne in," I encouraged.

Quietly, on the side, I told Groucho that the ladies probably didn't get that sort of attention in such a small town and with any luck we could be on it. Naturally, he saw the sense in what I said and ordered champagne, but that hardly made a dent in the money he had in his wallet. In a flash of genius, John remembered seeing a bookmakers further down the road. He told me that he would pretend to go to the bookies and make out that he's met some Cockney lads who have recently moved into the area and who had given him five absolutely certain racing tips. What he actually did was walk into the bookies, pick out a couple of favourites from a few races, plus a few outsiders, and then made his way back to the hotel an hour later.

"'Ere Groucho, I've got something interesting for you," John beamed.

Intrigued, Groucho asked him what it was.

"Can't believe this mate, I've just met a little team down the road, right in the horse business, they work in the stables in Newmarket," John carried on with Groucho's ear glued to his every word. "They've given me some inside tips, they're not bumpkins like this lot, they're London boys like us and they've given me these five horses as certs."

Quick as a flash, Groucho grabbed a newspaper and began looking at the racing pages.

"Two are favourites, three are outsiders," he pondered, "I don't think they've got much chance."

"Listen Groucho, all I can say is these guys reckon those horses are going to walk it," John sounded totally believable, "Those guys have put plenty of money on those horses themselves."

At that, Groucho leapt into action and galloped around to the bookies. John winked at me and we started laughing. Needless to say, Groucho banked virtually all of his money on these horses in some sort of accumulation bet. With just thirty quid left in his pocket, he made his way back to the hotel.

"We'll soon get him to part with that thirty quid," I told John. "We'll get him to spend that and then he'll be up for doing the burglary later."

We all stood in the bar, chatting and flirting with the two barmaids, asking them where the best places were in the area and promising to take them out later. Our plan was to look at the job on the Saturday night to decide on how we were going to rob the place, then come back and take the girls out.

In the late afternoon Groucho mentioned he would quickly pop out. "Right, I'm off down to the bookies to see how the horses got on."

John volunteered to go with him, flashing a quick smile at me as he did so. Groucho walked into the bookies to study the results on the boards.

"Blimey John, the first one's in," Groucho said quietly. "The second one's in… the third one's in… the fourth one…"

With trepidation John leaned in to listen further.

Groucho's eyes were on stalks as he scanned the boards for the last result. Finally he found it.

"Fuck me John, they've all come in, your mates were right!" he hollered with delight.

Well, he won an absolute fortune, thousands of pounds. The bookies had to give him every single penny they had in the till, which at the time was about six or seven thousand pounds and an IOU for Monday morning as they didn't have enough money to pay him. He arrived back at the hotel, pockets stuffed with cash. Needless to say, Groucho didn't fancy working that night. Being the decent bloke that he was, and knowing that John and I would be going home empty-handed, Groucho shared his winnings with us, but still managed to return home with around twelve thousand pounds in his pocket.

Groucho has since passed over, he may have been a thief but he had his good side too. What a character, there was no way he could be kept out of heaven because he'd soon pick the lock on the pearly gates. God bless him.

CHAPTER 9
PICNIC IN PRISON

So I was off back to prison, Wormwood Scrubs. In those days, when you received eighteen months you had to do a year. Nowadays you might do six months out of it but in those days you had to do a minimum of a year. When it came to being allocated, because I had the armed robbery on my conviction list, I was actually Category B. They wanted to send me to Camp Hill on the Isle of Wight but I explained I had a wife and young child. Nevertheless they insisted they wanted to send me to Camp Hill.

"You do that and either I will chin a screw, one of you lot, or an inmate," I warned, "And you'll ship me back so don't waste your time."

The governor came up with a proposal. "Are you willing to work?" he asked. I told him I certainly was.

Scratching his chin, he made a decision. "Right then, Brixton it is."

Brixton Prison was a remand prison used where people had not yet been convicted, they were awaiting trial but the authorities feared runaways. There were one hundred and ten convicts that ran the prison, they cleaned, made the food, tidied up, did the reception. They basically ran the prison supervised by the officers. That's where I ended up in F wing.

There were quite a lot of men with mental health problems and other issues, such as drug addiction. They were in the hospital wing lower down and F wing was above it. There was always lots of noise going on below and

I would be awake most of the night because of it. The majority of inmates would be banged up for most of the day. Rising early, I was normally on reception by six o'clock, worked all day apart from lunch and sometimes worked until nine o'clock at night waiting for all the coaches to come in. Baths had to be run, food had to be cooked and other preparations made for the new inmates. It was at the time that John Binden, a film star and gangster was there. I got to know him quite well through training with him in the gym, where he was allowed to train for remedial purposes for stab wounds he had sustained in the famous fight with Johnny Darke. At the same time, the notorious Chainsaw Gang were there. Strangely, they weren't that intimidating and I wasn't in fear of them, they were a heavy crowd but really nice men.

On the contrary, on the landing below F wing was one of the biggest, hardest men I had ever seen, a great big Irish man. He had this way about him, which meant you just moved out of his way as he was really menacing. Late one night, I was stretched out on my bunk. There were three of us to the cell, we were near the wall and life was on the other side. It was perhaps one o'clock in the morning. Faintly, in the distance, I could hear an Irish voice singing 'It's a long way to Tipperary.' Anyone who was asleep at the time probably wouldn't have heard it but I had sharp ears in those days. All of a sudden, like a fog horn sounding in the dark, this intimidating Irish man below us started bellowing through his window.

"Will you shut the feck up yer bastard," he yelled, "There's people in here trying to sleep, you're a disgrace to the homeland yer feckin' eejit."

Well, it was so funny the whole place erupted in laughter. Like a scene from the Flintstones, the F wing woke up, we set off the floor below and it was bedlam for the rest of the night. It was a crazy place.

Mind you, I added to it at times. I've always had the ability to mimic a West Indian accent. I used to shout out the window at night, using my best West Indian accent, insults to the huge Irish man, who was convinced I was the West Indian in the cell along from him. I'd shout out all sorts of insults to the Irishman, to which he would scream back me, thinking I was the real West Indian, all the terrible things he was going to do to my body, like ripping off my head and shoving it up my arse.

Another funny incident involved me putting my liberty at risk. I possess an actual drawing to prove this, a cartoon. In the cell with me were two chaps Dave and Tim, who was a fantastic cartoonist. He would grab a pencil, a piece of paper and bang, he could knock out a cartoon just like that, producing caricatures with lightening speed. The screws cottoned onto this and would have him do drawings of the other screws, giving him tobacco in exchange.

There were the three of us in a cell with a bucket, one single bed and one set of bunk beds. The cell was only eleven feet by seven feet and we were stuck in there with each other. At one point during our time in F wing, there was a gun scare, the result being that for twenty three hours a day, every day, for about two weeks we were banged up together. We were only let out to get meals to bring back to the cell and for twenty minutes of exercise a day. Most of the time was spent reading books, but let's just say things could get strained and it was easy to get wound up over silly things. The job of emptying the pee bucket was taken in turns. One time, I was convinced that I had done my turn and it was Dave or Tim's turn and they were convinced it was my turn. Male pride in prison can get a bit insane but I wasn't going to empty it, nor were they. The pee bucket was brimming and getting fuller and fuller.

Towards the end of a prisoner's stint in prison, he could often get a job as a yard's red band, sweeping up, etc. A red band is someone with only weeks remaining of his sentence. Often remand prisoners charged together would be kept in separate parts of the prison, so they couldn't converse or work anything out. A chap Davey from Manor Park, was a face, a real smart, good looking chap, who earned a lot of money. He organised a message for me to give to someone in another wing, which I had to do on the quiet. Working my way around with the broom and cleaning up the yards, I arrived at the right wing and asked a chap in a cell what number he was and in which direction the numbers ran. I finally worked out which was the right cell and carefully pushed the note through the cell window. That's what happens in prison, we help our own. A couple of nights later, Davey was on the twos, I was on the fours. Leaning over the rail, Davey was waving me down. Obviously, we weren't allowed to go down and mix with the remands.

"I've got something for you," he gestured me down.

Some of my mates created a diversion and the two screws on our landing were dealing with that. I quickly shot down the metal staircase down to the twos.

"What can I do for you Dave?" I asked.

"Have this," he shoved a pillowcase stuffed with something at me, I had no idea what.

I ran back upstairs and into my cell, hid the pillowcase under the bottom bunk and waited for dub up. Jumping up to the top bunk, which was mine, I undid the pillowcase. There was a bottle of wine, expensive caviar, meat, lobster, tins of crab. You name it, it was in there. Davey was a wealthy lad and he was used to the best.

Tim decided he couldn't stand looking at the full pee bucket a moment longer and with a lot of moaning and expletives directed at me, he emptied it. When he returned, you could cut the atmosphere in the cell with a knife.

"Okay you boys, you've got one guess at what I'm eating," I teased, "If you're right I'll share it with you."

To begin with they told me to fuck off but there's not much to do in a prison cell and so they started guessing. Was it a Mars Bar?

"Nope, c'mon give me a few guesses," I ribbed, "You'll be glad you did."

They gave a few silly guesses but in the end I gave in and told them I had caviar and other food from Davey. Of course, they didn't believe me until I jumped down to the bottom bunk and revealed my wares. As prison food had been the only food available for ten months, I shared what amounted to a banquet, along with a bottle of wine on top, with my cellmates. We were in bloody heaven, although we had to get rid of the evidence the next day.

Whilst I was in Brixton, the pop group Squeeze released the track Cool for Cats. Part of the lyrics were 'In and out of Wandsworth with the numbers on their names. It's funny how their missus' always looks the bleedin' same.' Eventually I was released from Brixton and returned back home to find those lines were remarkably prophetic.

Chapter 10
Running Out Of Luck

Micky McCabe had been very good throughout my time in Brixton bringing my wife to visit me. I never had any worries about Micky as he was as straight as a die, very old school. When I returned home he treated me to a few quid. By then, Micky had started branching out and had taken over several doors, putting his own doormen on certain doors. In 1980, I started working virtually full-time at the Copford Windmill, later to become The Kings. It was a fantastic club, it was the most popular one at the time, although now it is no longer except as part of a housing estate. People would come from miles around to be at The Windmill. Bob Wheatley, who owned it, was a colourful character. Tuesday night was the soul night with Craig Royal, Wednesday night was Grab A Granny night, which was a term used for Over 25s night, Thursday night was Hen Party night, Friday night was Party Night and finally Saturday night was Cabaret night. Bob Wheatley knew lots of acts, such as Tammy Wynette, Cliff Richard and Shirley Bassey.

Lots of comedians had their start in life via the club. Saturday night was the night a lot of the big and popular bands would play, or comedians such as Bernard Manning and Jimmy Jones would be on. It was a great club right from the early days and one where you had to arrive suited and booted. The doorman were smart with bow ties. Micky put me on the door there although I knew a couple of his lads were quite dubious about me. Ted in particular, who has now passed over bless his heart, said to Micky that I didn't look the part. I was very youthful looking and suave and the ladies seemed to like me. Micky reassured him that if anything kicked off, I could handle it. Of course, a little while later it did. It's difficult to explain the camaraderie between doormen, it's all about 'us against them' and I had some fantastic times there and worked with some great people. When I first started there, the door was covered by Peter Bedford, Barry Glen, Kevin Keeshan, Ted, Ken (who we called 'The Thug') and myself. Micky would come and work sometimes, although he also covered other doors too. Sometimes I would rotate and work at The Barn. Five nights a week I worked, earning really good money in hand. I was doing other bits and pieces, ducking and diving, so Susan and I were living a bit easier.

Some years later, Micky McCabe was tragically killed in a road accident. It was the biggest funeral that Basildon had ever seen. When I say there were hundreds there, I mean there were literally hundreds of people there. Because Micky was an ex-con, and with hundreds of doormen on the march, the police closed off all the roads for the funeral procession, which was absolutely massive. With Micky gone, there was a big opening for someone to run all the doors and take over from him. Paul Smith, who was known as Smut, took over and I started to work for him. To be fair to him, he increased the business and expanded into all sorts of door work, with occasional stints for repossession companies, which I did for him during the day now and then. That was a big turning point for me as Smut put a lot of work my way and made me head doorman at several clubs. Also, because I could talk and was always very smart, he would often send me to represent him in business meetings.

At The Windmill there was a new manager in town, there had been several managers who hadn't lasted long, but then Dennis came along and brought one of his own doormen along with him. At six foot four inches tall and heavily built, Roy Stewart, a Jamaican living in Tottenham, became a lifelong friend of mine. There are many stories involving this chap, who was a gentle giant of a man, unless you were on the wrong side of him. We got on really well together. The Windmill was a crazy club at that time. With Dennis in charge, we started a football team, we had all the cabaret nights, wear as little as you dare nights, Miss Wet T-Shirt nights. Dennis had such a big following and it was the most popular club in Colchester for years, it really was something else and I had some really good times there.

Life became a bit more settled and I dropped into a routine, which included training. There was a brilliant gym in Witham at the time, called The River Gym. The owner was a chap who turned out to be one of my closest lifelong friends, Andy Reid. I used to train there really hard and also go out running.

During my time at The Windmill, I met a chap, who could best be described as too good looking, called Carl. Anyone who knew me at the time would know who I was talking about. With blond hair and a square jaw, game for anything, naturally great physique, the ladies would virtually swoon at his feet. He also trained at The River Gym. Carl was a trained butcher and was doing well for himself. Because I had been in prison, people in the nightclub would put work my way. They all seemed to want to befriend me, as everyone wants to be the friend of a doorman, or they wanted a few quid. Blokes would come in and tell me they had seen a safe somewhere or whatever. Carl and I started doing bits and pieces together and we were getting a few quid. I managed to secure Carl a few nights on the door. Life was looking up, I even bought myself a Jaguar, although I was always under the watchful eye of the police and was pulled in by them once or twice, although I was let off again, it was no big deal. Carl and I became like brothers.

In 1981, my second daughter, Vicky, was born. We nicknamed her Magoo, she was a tiny, beautiful child. Sadly our marriage started to go wrong, which was nothing at all to do with Susan. As I said earlier, we were totally different people who had married and brought two kids into the world at a very young age. By then I was just twenty six years old and I hadn't been overly confident with women even though I had girlfriends before Susan, but up until that point there hadn't been many women in my life. However, on the door it was unbelievable. It was a standing joke amongst all the other doormen, and any doormen that happen to read this book will add weight to this, as I'm sure there are enough of them who have experienced the same thing. Women literally threw themselves at me, it was ridiculous because it was all the time, all night long and every night. They were on my case and blatant about it. It was just put there for the taking. They would arrive at the nightclub in ridiculously short skirts. There was one particular girl, who looked like Koo Stark. She was around nineteen years old with dark hair, very fit and good looking, always wore a pony tail and a very sexy sort of girl. Every night the club was open, she would be there, always pursuing me, trying to draw me into conversation, telling me she was wearing stockings and no underwear, that sort of thing. What can I say? It was on offer and I caved in.

One particular night, I was standing by the wall and I had an inkling something was about to go off on the dance floor. This girl kept walking past me, slowly backwards and forwards. I was concentrating on the dance floor as I thought a fight was about to break out. After three or four times of doing this, she stopped in front of me. Looking at her, I noticed her blouse was undone almost to her waist.

"How many more buttons have I got to undo before you notice me?" she teased.

That was literally how it was with these women. I was given phone numbers by the score and used to pass them to Kevin Keeshan, whose partner used to laugh at him when he produced them, as she didn't think they were his anyway. He used to keep the numbers for me. Of course, a man gets away with it for so long, starts to take liberties, getting in late and suchlike, but Susan was never a fool. She caught me out a couple of times and there was hell to pay. It isn't something I'm proud of. She threw me out and then had me back, again and again. I would be given another chance and I would blow it, again and again. It's difficult to explain, I felt like a kid in a sweet shop. I didn't go out of my way for anyone but they all went out of their way for me. I know it's absolutely wrong and I'm not trying to make excuses for myself or anyone else. I suppose when Susan had the kids, things started to go downhill a little bit. It wasn't the same between us, I would go home, the kids would be crying in the night, and she was exhausted. There I was on the doors, suited and booted with women in their finery, wearing short skirts and the rest is history. Like I said, I do regret this part of my life, particularly as there were my children to consider.

It was around 1982, I had yet again been thrown out by Susan, when a chap came into the club and gave me the wink about a bit of work. There was a warehouse that he used to deliver to that sold videos, colour televisions and other electrical goods. He told me the doors were alarmed but it would be easy to get around that. Videos in the early 1980s made really good money as they were expensive. The warehouse was within a big wire compound, with large metal gates fitted with a massive padlock and high wire fencing surrounding it. Everything was floodlit at night, basically you were never in the shadows. The alarm bell could be seen on the side but from what I had been told, it was only if the doors or windows were opened that it would be set off. Backing onto the warehouse was a boxing gym. We checked out the padlock before setting off to buy a similar one. Carl and I, together with this other chap, prepared to break in.

Beforehand, we stole a furniture lorry, we dumped the furniture and then parked the lorry close to the warehouse. One of the lads stayed with the lorry, the other two cut the padlock, put the new padlock on and we locked ourselves in. The other chap took an air rifle with him and blew out the lights at the back. If anyone drove past the warehouse would appear lit up as normal but the lorry was parked in the shadows. We entered the gym that wasn't alarmed and broke through the wall into the warehouse. Using the forklift, we lifted the pallets of video players, televisions and car radios up to the doors. Communicating via walkie-talkies, we let our driver know it was time to bring the lorry up, opened the doors and let him in. Forming a chain, we loaded up the lorry. When we had finished, we let ourselves out, padlocked the gates and headed off.

We knew a farmer based in the middle of nowhere, who let us take the load there. In the early hours of the morning, we unloaded the lorry into a barn and then dumped the lorry quite a few miles away. We whipped out the whole dashboard out because if the dashboard was left in, it could be reckoned against the log the lorry driver kept of the miles done, the distance could be worked out and the police might work out the radius from where the goods had been stored. The police actually commented on what a smart move it was.

To all intents and purposes, the goods were already sold to a team in London. The value of the goods to buy new from shops would be around eighty thousand pounds. In a gentlemen's deal, we settled on a figure of twenty thousand pounds, which was a fair price given the huge haul of goods on offer and the added extras, which we threw in as one big deal. The team from London came to view the goods. As they say, money talks and shite walks. They wanted to buy it but they only wanted to give us ten thousand pounds. No deal as far as we were concerned, so off they went. In the meantime, we had to get a bit of money together. Carl knew a chap who was a butcher and between him and one or two other friends, we sold some of the items individually in order to drum up a few quid.

I worked with a chap called Peter on the door, who was a sound bloke and told him that we had been let down. His dad worked with a chap who had a tyre company and who had a lot of money. After having a word with him, Peter confirmed he was interested. Carl and I drove down in my car, a big Citroen that I had just bought off a school teacher, to meet him in the prearranged spot. Peter's dad met us and introduced us to this man, who was there with his wife. Instantly my back went up, I didn't like this man. There was an uneasy feeling swirling in my gut. He asked us how much stuff we had and could he see a sample. I knew this would happen, so we took him to the boot of my car and showed him some goods. It was over a Bank Holiday, which meant he had to get the money together. We agreed to meet up again on the Wednesday morning to do the deal. As he had his own lorries, he would work out the transport details, although obviously we never told him where the goods were. The feeling of unease continued to spin inside me. As we made our way out of there, I looked in the mirror and saw his wife writing something down.

"She's taken our registration number," I said uneasily. My next words became our fate. "This is going to be on us."

The following Tuesday, Carl and I were arrested by the police. Later, I bumped into the school teacher that I had bought the car off.

"Mr. Buckingham, I was raided by the police the other morning," he bristled, "I told them who I had sold it to and when I produced the paper with your name on, they said that made sense."

To cut a long story short, what probably happened is that the chap who owned the tyre company had been caught buying a bent load before, the police may have told him they wouldn't charge him and that they would let him off, possibly over something quite trivial, but perhaps told him that if he was offered anything else that he owed them the information. Of course, he turned us in.

Unfortunately, Carl did some work for a butcher and the butcher paid him by cheque. When they raided Carl's place they found the cheque. Even though it was payment for straight work, the police didn't know this and they probably thought that Carl had sold the butcher some goods, so they raided the butcher's place and found the video. This is how luck can turn against you.

We were both pulled in. Carl was as sound as a pound, neither of us said anything but it didn't look good for us. Everything just started to unravel. We were given bail on the condition that we returned the goods, which we agreed to but there was no way on earth we were able to return it all. Funnily enough, despite making several trips, we were given the green light by the police not to be stopped because we were returning goods, which at the time gave us the chance to do other bits and pieces. In all I think we returned a dozen or so but kept the rest, making out they were sold off and we couldn't get them back. It was our money but we knew we were going to be put away. To give Carl his due, he held his hands up with people unknown to doing the actual theft and that I was just a fence, I just helped out. The police didn't like it but that was what happened. At court there was just Carl and myself, I still tried to plead not guilty, but because of the cheque and other bits and pieces, Carl had to put his hands up. Sadly, he received three years and for the lesser charge of handling, I received two years. We started off at Wandsworth together and then were sent to different prisons. I think Carl went off to a semi-open prison somewhere in Berkshire. I went back to Wandsworth Scrubs and was subsequently transferred to Norwich Prison, where I served the two years.

Whilst in Wandsworth, I was on reception one time when Charlie Richardson was being released for a few days out prior to his full release from prison. I made him a cup of tea and sat in the reception with him for about an hour. He was entertaining and told me lots of stories about him and Frankie Fraser in the old days. George Dixon also served time in Wandsworth, he had worked for the Kray twins and I became quite friendly with him. He had some amazing stories, one that comes to mind was about John McVicar, where he was up in front of the judge and had been found guilty of numerous armed robberies and carrying guns.

Apparently the judge turned to McVicar to ask, "Before I pass a lengthy jail sentence on you, have you anything to say for yourself?"

Without hesitation, McVicar calmly put his hand in his pocket, pulled out a box of matches, pushed the centre of the box about three-quarters out, put it to his ear and said, "Beam me up Scotty."

The whole court fell about laughing, even the judge. "You know I can't help but admire you, I was going to sentence you to fifteen years but I'm going to reduce it to twelve years." That is exactly what the judge promptly did.

The old time villains were not like the thugs of today. Another story involving McVicar was when he had robbed a bank and had left his getaway car on the other side of the bank. This meant when he fled the building, he had to make his way through a tiny alley down the side. Of course, all the bank alarms were going off at full pelt and the people milling about wanted to chase him. As he ran down the tiny alley in order to make his way to the next street and his car, there was a little, old lady making her way down the alley. Being the man he was, even though he was having it on his toes and was in a hurry, he wasn't about to knock over an elderly lady. Instead, when he reached the point where the lady was shuffling up the alley, he stopped and pressed his back to the wall in order to get by her.

"What a way to earn a fucking living," he quipped as he squeezed past.

After Wandsworth, I was moved to Norwich Prison, which was a strange place. I was in the main prison to start with and that was where I met the infamous Frankie Fraser. He wasn't an actual friend of mine, just someone I met in there, quite an interesting character and very polite. From there I moved to the dormitories on the other side of the prison. There were a few people there that I already knew and because of my reputation working on the doors, they told others about me and generally I was left alone. To be honest, it all went fairly smoothly there.

The only blight was that during one of the break-ups with Susan, which was quite lengthy, I had taken a flat on in Coggeshall. A bit before that there was a lady there, Sue, who owned The Cricketers pub, a very good looking, attractive lady. I ended up seeing Sue, who had been married and divorced, and ran the pub on her own with staff, she was a real big character. We had been seeing each other a while in a 'no strings attached' relationship, whilst I was on bail. It was around the time that the Dr. Jones case hit the headlines and the police actually set up their centre on the parking area of the pub, which meant the police were using the pub for meals and rest times. They weren't keen on the fact that I was seeing Sue and on the other side of the bar, they knew I had been in and out of prison and was on bail. Neither did a lot of the locals like it, they were on her case as she was a good looking woman with a pub and they didn't like me around her.

"I'm pregnant," her words were a total bombshell.

"Hold on, I thought you couldn't have babies?" I was shocked.

From a young age, she had been told she would never be able to have children, it was medically impossible.

"Neither did I," she answered, "I was told I couldn't have babies but I'm definitely pregnant."

Unlikely as it seemed, Sue had returned to Tottenham to see her family doctor to tell him she thought that perhaps she was pregnant as she had all the signs. Apparently he laughed and told her there was no way she could be. She begged him to give her a test, which came back positive. The doctor informed her that the tests could be inaccurate and the only way to be sure was to have a test at the hospital. Going straight to the hospital, she refused point blank to leave until she had the result. Again, it was a positive result. It was literally a miracle. Sue came back to me to give me the news but wanted to make it clear that there was no pressure on me, she was wealthy enough to bring the child up on her own. Although it wasn't a planned pregnancy, she wanted me to understand there was no way she would consider anything else but keeping the baby. In time, I ended up going to prison and our relationship was over.

In a strange twist of events, she ended up marrying a policeman who had been working on the Dr. Jones case. Sarah, my daughter, was born. Susan, found out about the birth whilst I was in Norwich Prison. At this point, we had made up, after numerous break-ups. She threw me out and took me back numerous times, in between I had flats in Witham and Coggeshall that I rented. I was all over the place.

Andy Reid was still a big part of my life, he had his own place in Maldon and I always had a key so I could seek refuge as and when needed. He often came home to see my suitcase in the hallway and would shout up the stairs "Have you had another row Ronnie?" Throughout everything we were the best of friends.

To give Susan her due, Norwich was a long way to travel but she never missed a visit. Finding out about Sarah broke her heart. I felt terrible about it but the cork had come out of the bottle and the genie was out. She didn't visit or contact me for a few weeks. Eventually she visited me and this was how strong and loyal she was.

"What do you want to do?" Susan asked. "I'll wait for you, we can give it one more try but I want you to promise me that you'll have nothing to do with that child."

From what I knew, Sue had sold The Cricketers, moved away and was with somebody else. I had to agree to what Susan asked. Some years later, when I was back on the door at The Windmill in the 1990s, a car pulled up and two women came out. Sue came over to me and introduced me to the other young woman, my daughter Sarah. In March, 2016, Sarah gave birth to her own little girl, Aurelia, and now we couldn't be closer and have been in contact since that first meeting at The Windmill. My other daughters accept her as their sister and Susan accepted it, so there was a happy ending there.

Getting back to Norwich prison, it was quite weird being in the dormitories, there were some characters in there but I had no trouble and to be honest, I dominated it a lot. I played in the football team and also did a carpentry course there with Dave, a mate of mine in the prison. Our tutor was a smashing chap, Mr. Jones.

I do remember one particular wheeze in there. You could get in and out of the building, there were fire escapes down, and although there were no bars on the windows, there was barbed wire fencing around. The screws would patrol the perimeter. I had seen a few people use coat hangers to try to make grappling hooks in an effort to get over the wire, as other inmates cheered them from the windows. There was a chap there, Big Pat, who was a local, wealthy man, he was in there for tax avoidance or something like that. In any case, he wasn't a hardened criminal but he had a few contacts. One day, Pat asked me what I liked to drink and I let him know that I didn't normally drink. He insisted there must be at least one tipple, so I settled on Baileys as it wasn't too strong. As he was the librarian he had his own key to the library, so he could lock himself in or out. There were a few inmates, three or four of us, fairly sensible people, that he liked. Pat used to get his friends on the outside to fill hot water bottles up with booze because they wouldn't break easily, they would throw them over the fence in a particular area, towards the fire escape. We would then get one of the mugs doing a short sentence to slip down the fire escape, nipping out between the screws patrol runs. Sliding down, the mug would gather up the hot water bottles and bring them into the library, where we would enjoy an alcoholic beverage. Surprisingly we were never caught.

There were quite a few dormitories with about eighty lads in our wing. One strange occurrence happened one night when I was fast asleep on the top bunk. Out of the blue a voice woke me up.

"Ronnie, Ronnie, quick mate, wake up!" the voice insisted.

"What's going on?" I was dazed.

"We've just screwed the canteen!" the voice answered.

It turned out some inmates had broken into what we called the canteen, which was the shop where we could spend the wages we had earned by doing the laundry or whatever. Of course, mostly the money was spent on tobacco or sweets, perhaps peanut butter. A jemmy bar had been smuggled in from the workshops and the padlock on the canteen was broken off. All the tobacco and sweets were nicked Now wide awake, I found myself surrounded by lads piling Mars Bars, Marathon bars and God knows what else on me.

"What am I supposed to do with all this?" I was pissed off. "You know they're going to be crawling everywhere looking for this lot."

I figured I could get away with a bit of chocolate, as it was on my record that I didn't smoke, but nothing like this amount. I ended up giving it away, even to cons that I didn't really like, just to get rid of it. All the wrappers were chucked out onto the hardstanding outside. We ate so much chocolate we literally felt sick. This time, although I wasn't the one to blame for the crime, I did enjoy the fruits of their labour.

Chapter 11
Beware the Dangers Of Alcohol

Whilst I was in Norwich Prison, Susan managed to get a council exchange and moved from Witham to Collier Row, as she wanted to be near her family. The house was in Charlotte Gardens, Collier Row, which was quite nice. When I finished my time at Norwich Prison, Susan picked me up and took me back to the new house. The area was the place to be as it was near to London and somewhere we both fancied living. Obviously I didn't know many people there but became friendly with a chap who owned a gym in his house and I started training there with him. Cleo, our Staffordshire Bull Terrier, joined us and I was happy as I had always loved dogs. We could walk in virtually any direction and be in the countryside or around by the Pinewood pub. Life carried on at an easy pace, Susan did well working on her uncle's stall, the one I used to work on, but somehow it was never the same between us. It wasn't her fault at all, it was mine, but we gave the relationship another go, which pleased the kids.

My brother Lee was seeing a girl called Debbie, who had a lovely grey horse stabled in Witham, which she used to ride around to see us when we lived in that area. Marie, from when she was just a tiny kid of two years old, was absolutely smitten with horses. Debbie taught her to ride and it has since been Marie's lifelong hobby and she now has horses of her own. Later on, Vicky also learned to ride and became another good horsewoman. I bought the girls their first horse, a beautiful Palomino called Barnaby. The woman who sold it to me guaranteed it was safe but nobody could ride it. We stabled it at my parent's land and there were travellers living next door, who were great horse people and even they gave up on it. That was sold and eventually I went down with her uncle to a place in Hertfordshire and bought a Welsh cob called Rag Sallyanna and that became Marie's first horse. She went on to win some gymkhanas on it. The horse was able to run and jump well and would go wherever she wanted it to, as biddable as a dog. We brought the horse down and kept it at the Ports Stables in Collier Row as both the girls were riding then, which was around 1984.

I still travelled back to Colchester to work the doors at The Windmill and other clubs, such as Kings in Canvey Island. Then I was made head doorman at Piers in Southend, and would also work in Basildon, as well as The Flying Bottle in Pitsea. After this, I worked at another pub in Enfield, my cousin's pub, and The Bricklayers Arms, also called Mr. B's.

Unfortunately, I slipped straight back into villainy again. It was a way of life really. Carl was out of prison and we met up again like old times. I started knocking about with another chap Ray, so there were sometimes the three of us, although it was mainly Carl and myself. We were put onto something that sounds really daft but it was to do with cigarette vending machines and the vans that delivered the cigarettes. It might seem strange but the vans had safes in them. The delivery vans would empty the machines, which only took pound coins. The pub landlords would often swap the pound coins for notes, which were put into the safe in the delivery van. The usual case was that the front passenger seat would be removed and the safe was put there. It had a rolling lid into which the money went in, once it had fallen to the bottom it was impossible to take the money back out, and it was sealed with a big padlock. However, it was possible to snap the padlocks off. Of course, we found out about these and how much money was in them. We drove around and when we spotted one, we would follow it from pub to pub, knowing that they would generally be finished by three o'clock, by which time they might literally be holding thousands of pounds, often as much as five thousand pounds. So, it could be quick and very swift. Cars were bought, although we never gave our real names, they would be taxed but not traced to us and we either wore gloves in the winter or wiped them down whenever we used them. Much of our time was spent following these vans about. Carl would normally be driving, we would pull up next to them, I would jump out and do the window with a centre punch, go through with a jemmy, break the lock, grab the money and go.

We became quite good at this and did take some liberties. One of the cigarette vans used to deliver to a social club. The driver would drive into the building, unload the cigarettes out the back and go off to get the money. This particular time, a group of young men were there. One was walking about wearing a cowboy hat and six toy guns, others pretended to be knights. Carl and I arrived and, as it was wintertime, we wore peak caps and scarves and carried our big holdall bag. We saw the van pull in and waited a few minutes for the driver to get out and go off to the social club or the cigarette machine, which was further away. With this particular cigarette van, the safe was in the back. It was alarmed up and the back was locked up. The young men were milling about right up to the pavement area outside. We just acted as if we were part of their crowd and the people passing hardly noticed us.

When the coast was clear, we positioned ourselves at the back of the van. I pulled out the jemmy bar from under my coat, then prised open the back doors and climbed in. There were still boxes of cigarettes in there. Without warning, the young man in the cowboy hat and six guns started firing the toy guns at us, we thought he was about to make a citizen's arrest. Suddenly he stopped, his eyes widened as he stood there staring into the van. Within moments, he was joined by the others. They had spotted something. There I was, crawling in the back as the safe was right behind the driver's seat, breaking the padlock off and getting the money out. Carl, who was standing behind me, was pushed aside as the lads jostled one another and started grabbing the boxes of cigarettes, ripping them open, totally ignorant of the money that was there.

We couldn't believe what was going on but quickly pinched the money and as many of the cigarettes as we could get hold of. We were out of the van in a flash but they were now in it. The guns were back in their holsters, the cowboy was grabbing boxes of cigarettes, whilst Carl and I hot-footed across the road to where our car was. I've no idea if the lads were still in the van when the driver returned or not and wasn't about to stick around to find out.

One other thing I will talk about, which was quite funny, was when the three of us entered into a department store in a high street, we discovered it just by chance and made an entry. We had a large Luton transit van parked in a car-park up the road. Two of us went in and the other one stayed with the van for a while. This was at a time before mobile phones, so we just had walkie-talkies to communicate with each other. The department store had a big loading bay and we decided that we would sort out stuff that would sell the easiest. Cigarettes were the best thing apart from actual cash because they were light and easy to sell. Alcohol was less profitable because the bottles are heavy and clumsy and they would only sell for half-price. So, it was cigarettes first of all, then videos were big sellers, portable televisions and various other boxes. We took it all down to the loading bay and stacked it by the doors. The plan was that one of the lads would bring the van to the loading bay. This was the amount of front that we had, we thought it was just a case of loading it up and away we would go. This was late one Saturday night, around one o'clock in the morning. The other lad, who was driving the van, popped in to see if he had any ideas about what to make a load up with.

In the massive double shop window there were cardboard cutouts of people and families, all pointing down at their feet to where there were video recorders. In those days, you could still get two or three hundred pounds for a video recorder, plus they didn't take up a lot of room. One of us decided to be the lookout, while the other two crept into the window. Bear in mind this was in a main street in the town, we planned to grab the video recorders and take them to the loading bay. As we were about to start doing this, the lad who was keeping lookout warned us someone was coming. Quickly we shot back into the shadows, hiding beside the washing machines.

A chap was staggering along the pavement, with a brick in his hand. Clearly drunk, he stood swaying in the moonlight, looking through the big shop window at the video recorders. He was about to brick the window. What could we do? If he did that then the alarm would go off full pelt. Only parts of the shop were alarmed but that was one of them, the noise alone would bring people out of their flats above the shops opposite. To say we were cursing this chap was an understatement. We would have to jump ship and leave the treasure we had found behind.

Waving the brick about above his head, he leaned one way and then the other, swinging like a pendulum in a high wind. His eyes squinted as he fought to locate his target, then he took aim at the window. Like a scene from a Charlie Chaplin movie, he threw the brick back behind his shoulder but the momentum spun him around because he was so pissed. As he wobbled around like a spinning top, despite his alcoholic stupor, he somehow spotted the off-licence store across the street. Rotten drunk, his head swiveled between the department store window with the videos and televisions, back over towards the off-licence with the alcohol in the window, then back to the store window and then rotated back to the off-licence.

"Please, please, please, choose the off-licence," we were on our knees silently pleading with him.

Game on. That was exactly what he did. Staggering across the road, he aimed the brick straight through the window of the off-licence, grabbed a couple of bottles of booze and off he stumbled down the street. The flat windows above the off-licence were flung open, a woman screamed and it was like something out of an electricity advert with lights being switched on everywhere. Of course, within two minutes the police arrived, swiftly followed by a glazier, who had been summoned to replace the shop window.

The police were everywhere, one had a dog. Hidden behind the shop window, we were laughing so hard the dog's ears pricked up. I hissed at the others to be quiet because I was sure the dog could hear us, but we were locked in and hopefully nobody could see we had broken in. For the couple of bottles of booze that had been pinched, the police activity was enormous. Police were in the street, patrolling in cars, they were in the off-licence and also outside it to make sure nothing else was stolen, while the local glazier carried out the repairs to the window. As soon as it was safe to do so, we scarpered.

Chapter 12
No Comment, Ma'am

Unbeknown to me, I was coming to the end of my criminal career. I had broken up with Susan yet again and had moved into a flat in Witham. Although I saw the kids regularly it was really hard being away from them. Ray, who had been out of the game for a while, came to tell me he was having a hard time and that he needed some work and a vehicle, so I gave him Susan's car. I promised her I would get another one and I told Ray he could have it and pay me for it when he had some money. Ray and I had been friends for a lot of years and I trusted him.

In the meantime, there was another incident where Carl and I were pulled in. Some antiques that belonged to a well-known and titled man had gone missing, something like a grandfather clock. To be honest, I can't remember taking anything like that but because this man was titled and very well-to-do, all the stops came out. The policemen handling the case were Snowy, who had arrested me a few times, and Roger Corbett, who subsequently became a very good friend. He was a big lad, who liked to play rugby and as the old bill go, a nice enough bloke, we'd had a few run ins with him and he wouldn't do us any favours but, by the same token, he wasn't a stitch-up merchant. Carl and I were always smart and up for a laugh and, to be truthful, didn't give a sod really. We were taken to Chelmsford police station and questioned. As usual, we said nothing. I explained to Carl that the police didn't want to waste time. If they had to ask questions, then they didn't know the answers, but if they had enough evidence then they would nick us. It was as simple as that.

Whatever their questions were, our answer was always the same, "No comment."

Nothing was going to be said and we were going to maintain that we weren't guilty all the way. The police were about to give up, when out of the blue this woman, who I can only describe as not the prettiest woman, came in. She outranked all of them, perhaps a newly promoted Chief Inspector or something like that.

"Right, leave this to me," she glared at each in turn, "I'm going to sort this out."

She sank into the chair opposite to me. "You'll answer my questions, we believe you've taken this stuff." She tried her best to sound authoritative. "Hold your hands up, we've got loads of evidence on you so don't go wasting our time."

My eyes widened as I stared into her eyes. "You know what? Have you ever been told just how sexy your eyes are?"

Perhaps she thought I was serious because she answered, "I don't want any of your old flannel, just answer my questions."

"I can't," I answered as a slow smile formed on my lips.

"What do you mean you can't?" she spat.

"You're mesmerizing me, I'm getting turned on," I taunted. "I think I'm getting a bit of a hard on here looking at you."

"Don't start that game with me," she glowered at me.

"Well, I can't answer your questions. Is there any chance you and me can go out for a drink later on?" I goaded.

"I wouldn't go out for you with a drink," she stared angrily back at me.

"Why not?" I countered.

"Forget all of that, you're here to answer questions on this crime," by now she was beyond angry.

"I don't want to talk about any crime, I haven't done nothing but I want to take you out." I continued, "I actually think I could take you to bed."

Well, that was it. I looked at the policemen behind her, who were biting their thumbs trying not to laugh. In the end, she threw the papers and everything else up in the air.

"Get him out!" she yelled, "Just get him out!"

The police had picked us up from Witham and we were now in Chelmsford.

"How are we supposed to get back?" we protested.

"That's down to you," they chorused.

"No, that's down to you," I retorted.

"Off the record, I'm driving back to Witham nick, if I see you en route I'll pick you up," one of the policeman conceded.

Anyway, Carl and I were walking along and saw him coming towards us in his car. I rolled my trouser leg up and stuck my leg out along with my thumb. He stopped and we hopped in the car.

"I still think you bastards had something to do with it," he laughed, "But that was one of the funniest things I've ever seen." He dropped us off and away he went.

Getting back to the cigarette vans, we had followed one particular cigarette van for miles. It was his last port of call and the driver had to leave the van and walk hundreds of yards to the machine. There was nobody else about, it was absolutely deserted. We thought this was fantastic, a dream come true, as we popped the window, undid the safe and filled the holdall with cigarettes and mainly pound coins. It was a lot of money, a few thousand quid. The holdall was bloody heavy but we lumped it into our car and sped off, heading for home.

About five miles away, we were travelling through a little village, when the car started to swerve. Carl swung the car into the kerb, he had no choice, the wheel had buckled under the car. There we were, stuck in the middle of nowhere, knowing that the police would be out looking for thieves and there was our car, completely useless. As we climbed out of the car, we noted curtains twitching as people watched us. Having grabbed some rags, we started wiping the car down, cleaning anything we might have touched. Carl had the boxes of cigarettes, I had the holdall with all the money in it, ready to walk away with it. But where were we going to head to? We quickly decided to go in the direction of the woods, where we hid the money and cigarettes, hoping nobody would find it. Returning to the road, as luck would have it, a lorry was going by and we stuck our thumbs out to hitch a ride.

"Where are you guys headed to?" asked the lorry driver.

"We just need to get somewhere civilized mate, our car has broken down back there and we need to be somewhere," we replied.

Bury St Edmunds was his destination and from there we took a train back home. Obviously we weren't going to leave all that money in the woods, taking a chance we returned the next day but this time in our own car. 'Police Aware' stickers were plastered all over the abandoned car, together with finger print dust. We parked our car, quickly dived into the wood and luckily our stash was still there.

One time, we stopped at a car park to check out another van and there, in the car parked right next to us, was a courting couple in the car. They looked up and blatantly saw me face to face. Slightly embarrassed, they were obviously up to no good. If we were caught, they weren't going to come forward as witnesses!

Another time there was a lorry full of cigarettes parked near a working men's club, which we decided to have a go at. Positioned at the back of the lorry, crow bar at the ready, we were about to break into the back when the driver came out, saw us and realized what was going on.

"Oi" he shouted.

"We don't want a confrontation mate or to hurt anyone," we told him, "We just want what's in the lorry."

But the driver decided he wanted to be a hero. Carl and I decided to scarper and leave him to it but he came running after us. Obviously we weren't keen on him seeing which car we were getting into, so we were going along at a pace, wrapped up in hats and scarves. However, the hero decided he was going to intervene. I stopped dead in my tracks.

"Listen mate, do yourself a favour," I cautioned, "Fuck off."

He stood his ground.

"We haven't had your load or dented your motor," I warned him, "You're just the driver, just go away,"

He wasn't having any of it. "You're a thief!" he exclaimed and started running after us.

More as a threat than anything else, I ran towards him with a crow bar and threatened to smash him across the head with it. This time his bottle went, he scarpered. And so did we.

Chapter 13
Sold Up The River

Around that time, two things happened. Firstly, Carl went to do a bit of work on his own. One night, unfortunately for Carl, someone very artistic was watching and sketched a picture of him. He was an attractive man yet very distinctive, with an unusually square chin, and this person drew him to a tee. Secondly, Ray used my car to do a bit of work, which I had warned him not to, as it was my own car and in Susan's name.

"I've compromised the car, it's on top and I'm going to burn it out," Ray alerted me, which he promptly did. Of course, the car number was traced to Susan and, by default, to me.

Carl was pulled in for the bit of work he had done, along with whoever was with him, and the police had him bang to rights. I was arrested for association and both of us were taken to the nick. The police questioned me about the car. Now, the Romford police stated that the car was outside my house when they passed it but it definitely wasn't. The reason why they said that is something I will reveal as the story goes on. They made out that they had five different people who had identified us at each scene of crime. One of them was the lorry driver I had threatened with a crow bar. He wore glasses, which is nothing but it was five months from the time I had chased him until the alleged identification, which was a long time. Of the five identifications, two of them picked out other men in the line-up, two others said that nobody in the line-up could be identified. Just one bloke picked me out. I recognized the couple who had been canoodling in the car and they actually winked at me as they went along.

So out of five people I had been put in front of, all good witnesses, only one had picked me out. The police were annoyed by that but for me it was a welcome relief. Carl put his hands up and I was considered an associate of his, hence I was being charged with conspiracy to an attempted theft with persons unknown. Ridiculously silly charge but the police were desperate to get me. As the court case loomed, my solicitor advised me that a good barrister would be needed.

My barrister was a man I would never forget, I went to meet him at The Temple. He was a very tall man, who seemed to really know what he was doing. In hindsight, I believe you're sometimes sold down the river when the police want you badly. Bearing in mind I drove a nice car, had horses, perhaps he wondered how I had obtained the money, or even thought I was a public nuisance, but anyway he started to question me. He was dismissive of the police claims.

"If the car was there, why did they not arrest you with the car?" he asked.

Of course the police could claim that I might have been violent so they went for reinforcements and when they came back the car wasn't there. But I maintained the car wasn't there even though the police maintained it was.

"This is fantastic. You've been put in front of five witnesses and only one has picked you out and two of them picked out innocent people," he said. "If they could make that mistake then so could the one who picked you out."

He deliberated further, "Plus it's been five months from the time the driver saw you at the back of his van until seeing you in the line-up, he could easily have been mistaken."

My barrister told me he admired my police cell technique, as he referred to it.

"You've said nothing and given them absolutely nothing," he stated. "It must be very hard to sit there whilst you are being questioned and questioned and just say 'No comment' I can't believe they're taking this to court - you'll walk it."

I felt relieved, it was just what I wanted to hear. Carl was staunch and would not put me in the frame but he had to put his hands up for different reasons. In any event, we were going to court together.

I have a theory as to why I think this happened with the Romford police. As I mentioned, Susan and I had the town house together, but due to a humdinger of an argument, Susan had thrown me out. I had a little flat over in Dagenham to stay in. I had taken up golf and wanted my golf clubs back. Anyway, we were in the middle of an argument, there was a lot of shouting and hollering going on. I just wanted my golf clubs, Susan was yelling at me to go away and that I wasn't going to have them. At this point, I threatened to kick the garage door in to get the golf clubs as I had a golf match to go to. And so it went, back and forth. Unbeknown to either of us, one of the neighbours had called the police. Cars pulled up and three young policemen got out, they had their uniforms on with civilian jackets over the top.

"What's going on here?" they questioned.

"It's alright mate, it's just a domestic, I just want my golf clubs and she won't give them to me," I told them.

They completely ignored me and just then Susan came down, it was about eight o'clock in the morning and my golf match was in an hour. She had her dressing gown on. One of the policeman looked at Susan.

"What's the matter sweetheart?" he asked her.

"Whoa, hang on a minute," I was agitated. "Let's get something straight, she is not your sweetheart, this is nothing to do with you, I just want my golf clubs back. Tell her to give them to me and I'll be gone."

Again, he completely ignored me. Talking across me he spoke to Susan.

"Is he threatening you sweetheart?" he questioned her.

"Now listen, I'm her husband and once again she is not your sweetheart," by now I was really pissed off. "I'm not threatening her, I just want the golf clubs."

Again he ignored me and asked her if I had been threatening her. Susan told him no.

"If he's giving you any aggravation, we'll sling him in the car and take him down the nick," he advised her.

Now, I've always been quite strange in that I'm normally very mellow in many ways, but there's something that when I rage, I really rage. I glared at this policeman. Having been a doorman for years, I can suss people out quite easily.

"What you three think you can throw me in that car? You couldn't throw me in that car you three clowns," I squared up to them. "If you want to rock and roll and make a row of it, let's go. C'mon big man, let's go."

Susan had been brought up around that sort of thing with her family. To give her credit where it's due, she was very shrewd and stepped between us. His bottle had gone. I was weighing him up and I knew I could've gone through him and his colleagues like a dose of salts, which of course wouldn't have done me any good, as I'd be back in prison again. Susan knew that and she didn't want to see me in trouble.

She put her arm around me, "C'mon I'll give you your fucking golf clubs."

The policeman asked her if she was sure everything was okay and she reassured him she was fine, so the police returned to their car and went.

"You idiot, what have you done? You know they're going to have it in for you now," she was furious with me. "You can't go about threatening the police."

I told her I thought he was being an arse. At that point, I think my card was marked but the police weren't going to put that in writing.

There was still a lot going on in my life and eventually I made up with Susan but our relationship was very temperamental. It was on and off constantly. There was a lot of feeing between the two of us but too much water under the bridge. She wanted to love and be with me but she couldn't let go of the past and I can't blame her. Other things were going on around me, I felt quite bad but I had done my best.

The day of the trial at Chelmsford Crown Court came and as far as I was concerned, I was going to walk it. Carl was sure he was going to prison and I felt gutted for him but I would make sure that I grafted so there was a few quid ready for him for when he was released. That's the sort of people we were. I remember at the time I had a really nice Granada Ghia, which was the car at the time, it was a couple of years old and I drove it to the court with Susan and parked it up. It was a baking hot day in July, so I left the sun roof down, ready for me to drive home after the hearing. I stood in the dock, whilst the witness for the prosecution was being questioned.

"So you say that Mr. Buckingham threatened you with an iron bar," my barrister questioned the lorry driver. "I see you wear glasses?" he asked.

"Yes, I do," replied the eyewitness.

"Is your eyesight good with your glasses?" the barrister continued, "Is your memory good? You're sure it's him?"

"Yes, it was definitely him," answered the eyewitness.

"Okay, you couldn't have forgotten him over all those months?" my barrister queried.

"No, it's definitely him," the driver stated.

I waited for my barrister to ask the police how many identification parades I had been put on, to which they would have to reply five, and then to ask how many people picked me out. Just the one? Did any of the other people pick out innocent people? To which the police would have to answer yes two, and of course the other candidates didn't pick out anyone from the identification parade. That would go well in my favour. Unfortunately my barrister didn't ask any of those questions, instead he just questioned the one eyewitness and no more. He was my barrister and I had no option than to trust him. I asked him about the others and he told me that we would get to that later on. Next up for questioning were the police.

"So, you say you saw this car and registration outside the house in Charlotte Gardens?" My barrister stood with his thumbs perched in his pockets as he spoke.

The police affirmed it was definitely that car and they had noted it because it was a known criminal's car, albeit in his wife's name.

"Okay, thank you." replied my barrister.

At this point his questioning stopped. Concerned, I asked him why he had ceased with his interrogation.

"No, let them continue and fire their bullets," he reassured me. "We'll be down in the trenches, let's keep our head up and in the end we'll come up and in our closing statement, we'll blow it all away."

I trusted that this man knew what he was doing. In fact, he was selling me down the river. We had only been in court a short period of time, Carl had put his hands up. He received a two year prison sentence.

The judge turned to me, "Due to all the evidence against you, you'll be remanded in custody."

I was taken away and had to return to court the next day for the jury to sum up. I couldn't believe it. My barrister didn't even show up the next day, instead he sent someone else.

"Look, you've got to tell them that there were five eyewitnesses and only one picked me out," I pleaded.

"We can't do it," he replied, "That questioning is gone."

Stunned, I asked him "What do you mean that questioning is gone? The car was gone, it was burned out, it wasn't there."

"It's too late," he informed me. "The only thing I can do is try and help you out in the summing out."

I thought it was diabolical. He would never admit it but he said to me "He sold you down the river, these are mistakes that even a novice wouldn't make."

I stood back in the dock in front of Judge Watling. When I was previously convicted and given a two year sentence by Judge Greenwood, he would deliberate back and forth but wasn't known to be heavy with his sentencing. However, Judge Watling was a totally different kettle of fish. In his summing up to the jury, he reminded them there was a good eyewitness. The jury were never informed that I was put in for five identification parades, which was a crucial piece of evidence. The stance of the police would be that my barrister didn't question them about it and therefore he was admitting that it was true. I couldn't believe it. Whilst the jury were deciding on my fate, I was taken down to the cells. Within half an hour I was brought back up to find the decision was that I was guilty of conspiracy, which meant four years. Although I was taken aback, I wasn't about to let the judge know that I was shocked.

"Thank you very much Sir," I quietly answered.

I didn't show any emotion as I was led down. But inside of me, it was a different story, I felt totally gutted.

Sooty came down to see me, "It's ridiculous, you've got to appeal against this mate, we wanted a conviction of course we did, but we would've been happy if you had probation or suspended sentence," he went on, "If you had one year that would be more than enough but four years? It's madness, he's gone right over the top."

Flabbergasted he questioned me, "Your barrister, where the hell did you get him from?"

“Your people chose him for me,” I answered.

“You’ve got to appeal,” he replied, shaking his head.

This is how strange life is. As I sat in the cell a couple of hours later, a man was pushed into the cell with me. Long, greasy hair, leather biker jacket with patches on, hobnail boots, filthy jeans, dirty coat, he looked like a dirt bag. He continually moaned that he had received eighteen months. Together with other men, who were unknown, he had beaten a man almost to death with baseball bats or pickaxe handles. For that he received just eighteen months.

“Mate, do yourself a favour and shut up,” I was becoming angered just listening to him, “I’ve just got four years for conspiring to an attempted theft, you’ve done GBH and just got eighteen months? Shut the fuck up.”

When the sweat box came I had been in the cell all day. To make matters worse, Susan came down to speak to me, her heart was breaking. I had been given four years, that meant I was definitely going to have to do at least two years and she knew it. She drove the car home, her face wet with tears.

It was a beautiful summer’s evening, I’ve never forgotten it. I had been put in the sweat box and was driven through Chelmsford and onward. By the time the van had arrived in the city, the pubs were full, people were standing outside having drinks, or walking around basking in the beautiful sunshine. I sat on the driver’s side of the van, the sweat box stopped at the traffic lights and this lovely BMW convertible sports car pulled up alongside us with a stunning looking girl sitting in the passenger seat. A real ‘Jack the Lad’ was driving, he obviously knew what a sweat box was, perhaps he had done a bit of time himself.

“Oi lads!” he shouted up to us, at the same time lifting up the girl’s skirt up so that we could see her knickers. “You ain’t gonna get any of this for a long time boys, good luck.” After those few kind words, he roared off up the street.

Chapter 14
Currying Favour

In Wandsworth, after the shock of the four year sentence, having gone through the routine of reception, being stripped naked, I was handed the prison uniform that included two pairs of pants, two pairs of socks, two shirts, a jumper and a pair of jeans. Those clothes had to last a week. I had been used to being spotlessly clean but was now back to having just one bath a week. They even used to come round and measure the water, six inches was all that was allowed. Sometimes the inmates would get away with a little more water but ten minutes soak was the maximum time. No chance of relaxing or unwinding, just in, scrub, and get out again. Inmates would be queuing up for a bath. As usual, I was taken up through the system, down a corridor and into a cell. The cell was just eleven feet by seven feet, with two bunk beds, a single bed, a chair and a small table. It was full of smoke. Two blokes were laid on the bunks reading books, there was a full piss pot in the corner and the place absolutely stank. Four years suddenly felt like a very long time.

Okay, perhaps I knew I wouldn't do the full four years but it did mean at least two Christmas Days would be missed, all for a totally stupid charge. As soon as I went into the cells, the other inmates were on me, asking if I had cigarettes. They wanted to know where I had come from and generally chat, because it's so boring in prison, banged up virtually all day long.

There was no work to keep occupied with in Wandsworth Prison, it was an old Victorian prison. It took weeks to get used to the food and for the first few days I suffered diarrhea and stomach upset, which was the norm. In prison it's accepted that in the cell the bucket is purely for peeing in, only in the most dire circumstances, when we couldn't possibly hold it, did we defecate in the bucket. In such a small cell, with two other blokes, only bathing once a week, a little window eighteen inches square with bars on and a small Perspex section that slides open to get some fresh air in, the stink if anyone had to defecate in the bucket was awful.

Early morning was 'slop out' time, which was when we took turns to empty the bucket and queue up for the toilets. There could be as many as a hundred inmates on one landing with just three or four toilets. When we finally reached the toilet, our head and shoulders would be above the toilet door and our knees downwards would be on show. Whilst in there, the other inmates would tell each other to hurry up, especially if they were desperate for a dump. One funny thing I will always remember was when a chap was sitting on the toilet and he had run out of toilet paper. There was always a screw nearby to the toilet to save arguments.

"Hey Governor, pass us some toilet paper over," he called out.

Now, the toilet paper was Izal, the shiny stuff that resembled tracing paper. The screw handed him just three squares.

"Three squares? What am I meant to do with that?" he demanded.

With a wry smile the screw answered, "One up, one down and one to put a shine on it."

We all burst out laughing. That was Wandsworth.

During the twenty minute exercise break, we went down into the yard and everyone walked around like zombies in a three hundred yard circle. For some strange reason everyone would walk clockwise. Rain, wind or shine, that was it, then it was back to the cell. Breakfast at seven o'clock, lunch at midday and dinner at four o'clock. From four o'clock in the afternoon until seven o'clock in the morning that was it. I always ended up losing weight. Inmates would be in Wandsworth for several months waiting to be allocated. It was a horrible prison, very Victorian and depressing. Time went on and I just had to settle in and do the bird. Luckily, I was eventually allocated to Highpoint Prison, which is in Suffolk.

Coincidentally, years later whilst working as a medium, I returned to Highpoint Prison with Steven Treadaway, another well known medium from Norfolk. One of the screws there had a son with an eye condition and needed to go to America for specialist treatment that wasn't available in the U.K. Steven and I did a fundraising event in the prison grounds. Lots of the screws and their families were there, along with a crowd of local people. All the money we raised was given for the young lad's treatment. Strange how life comes around.

I had a lucky break as I was sent over to Highpoint North, which was closed in with three different houses there and because I was doing four years, which was a longer sentence in that particular prison, I was given my own room. It was very clean in there, a totally different type of prison, with baths and showers that could be used day and night. I wasn't locked in my room, although of course there were rules and regulations, screws would be about and inmates were told to come out of each other's cells. However, the inmates could let themselves out to use a proper toilet in the night or to use the showers. Being able to keep clean made such a difference. In Wandsworth the inmates were allowed to take a bowl of hot water and wash in the cell, they would rip a towel up to make a flannel out of it to enable them to have a strip wash. At least the clean ones did. As a non-smoker I could buy a roll-on deodorant with my wages, along with a few sweets or peanut butter.

While in the Highpoint Main, I trained in the gym and the top physical training instructor, Mr. Johnson, who was a senior officer, a weight lifting fanatic and a professional referee, he had even been a referee at the Olympics. Being able to lift weights meant inmates would be on his good side and I could certainly lift weights. I was given a job as the gym orderly, which was fantastic, along with a short Afghan chap called Ismet, who we nicknamed Izzy. He was a tiny, immaculate and funny chap. To me, being the gym orderly was the best job there. Okay, I had to clean football boots and rugby boots, give kit out and stuff like that, but at least I was in the gym all day long, apart from going back to have lunch or tea in the dining hall. It was a time of continuous weight lifting, football and rugby. Being a sports fanatic it suited me and I ended up being the captain of the rugby and football teams and discovered I was a good badminton player too.

Luckily, one of the officers there was a county standard badminton player and he would call us out for practice, because we were in the gym all day it was our job. He showed us the moves and encouraged us to be good in order that he could practice. Izzy was a brilliant badminton player, so quick and nimble, but I also became quite good and in the end Izzy was only just beating me. I actually broke several Suffolk county records in there, became a member of BAWLA (British Amateur Weightlifters Association) in the prison and gained silver and bronze awards, which Mr. Johnson encouraged. Also, In total, I think I broke five county records for odd lifts. He used to referee them and I still have the certificates for the Highpoint Weight Lifting Club, which sounds quite funny now.

The main physical training instructor there was a young bloke called George Trotter, who came from Newcastle and had a real Geordie accent. A smashing chap, very competitive, we could give him some stick and get some back, he was a character, a nice man. It was one touch football, badminton, all sorts of sports, because he was sports mad. Along with Izzy I would practice all the different sports but we still kept up our duties in the gym, cleaning the boots and keeping the place tidy.

Highpoint Prison had two football pitches and two rugby pitches. One time, on a freezing winter's day, Izzy and I had to repaint the white lines. With only our thin prison coats as protection against the elements, I argued it should be the garden party's job but no, the screws told me it was a job for the gym orderlies. Of course, I soon wangled myself out of it. I told Izzy to leave it to me. My knee problem had flared up again at the time because of the rugby and I walked with a limp, which I still do to an extent. Izzy and I had to mix up the lime white paste and off we went to begin painting. However, it looked like the lines had been painted by a drunk, as they were all over the place. Mr. Johnson came over and did his pieces at us. I explained it was to do with the knee and that it hadn't been done of purpose, all the while keeping my straightest face. He appeared to accept that excuse, although I think he was doubtful. Needless to say, the job was passed onto the garden party lads, who called me out on the episode and a few other names besides.

There was always a sense of mischief with me, I always wanted to cause the screws problems but without getting into trouble, if you see what I mean. As I said, I was the captain of various teams, including the volleyball team, and outside teams would come a play us. There were some real characters in those teams. We had an education block as a lot of inmates were illiterate, so civilian teachers would come in to teach. There were language courses and various other courses, in order to help the inmates try and make the best of their time in prison and leave a better person than when they went in. The education block also housed the store room, where the table tennis bats, ping pong balls, dartboards and all sorts of stuff was kept. In each house there were dartboards and perhaps a pool table. Of course, things would be ripped or broken, so every month or so George would take Izzy and myself into the education block. In there was what resembled a large blue bin on wheels and we would pick up all sorts, such as new dartboards, table tennis balls and other kit. One day we were in the education block, George had just gone off to talk to someone and we had several bits in the blue bin already. We were standing next to the kitchen, where the civilian teachers cooked and ate their food. There was a hotplate there, which I told Izzy I was going to nick.

"Why do you want a hotplate?" his eyes widened with alarm.

"I'm going to have it," I muttered as I dived in quickly and stuffed it in the blue bin under some other bits and pieces.

Back in the gym, I hid the hotplate in the false ceiling above us. Within five minutes, the prison was in uproar, with everyone searching for the hotplate. They never found it because they never expected it to be in the gym. The prison was turned upside down. In the dining hall we were all told, in no uncertain terms, that it must be returned. Izzy's eyes pleaded with me but I replied to them with a po-faced stare. I wasn't having any of it.

After about six weeks, everything had calmed down regarding the hotplate. Being a non-smoker and quite a shrewd bloke, I had a lot of tobacco around me that could be sold for jewellery or other stuff. Tobacco was the currency in prison and I exchanged some for curry powder from the lads in the kitchen. Izzy was a brilliant cook and curries were his thing. We scrabbled together the best bits of meat, butter, vegetables and the curry powder. The kitchen hands were sneaking it all out to me and I was quietly sneaking it into the gym.

"Right Izzy, I'm going to get that hotplate down so you can do us a nice curry," I beamed my most persuasive smile at Izzy, who was somewhat concerned and none too keen on the idea.

I told him not to worry. I wet a towel and then shut the boot room door with the twist down handle (there was no lock). The wet towel was placed along the bottom of the door so that the smell couldn't get out and I wedged the door handle up with a broomstick so that the handle wouldn't turn. Although not entirely happy with this arrangement, Izzy set about making the curry. Bloody hell, it was amazing. As prison food went, I have to say Highpoint wasn't too bad, but Izzy, now that man could really cook. He cut up all the meat, popped it in the pots I had acquired from the kitchen staff and cooked it on the hotplate. The aroma was absolutely tantalizing as the curry bubbled away and my stomach was rumbling big time. Just as we were about to dish up, the door began to rattle. Someone was trying the door and that someone was George Trotter. Oh shit.

"Buckingham, Buckingham, open this fucking door," boomed George's voice. "I know it's you, what are you up to in there? It's me, I'm the fucking screw, I lock you in, you don't lock me out. Open this fucking door."

Izzy's face paled, "What are we going to do?"

"There's only one way out, we can't hide it," I was thinking out loud. "Quick! Put some in a bowl, get a spoon ready and leave the rest to me."

I pulled the towel back and opened the door. George stepped in.

"It's the fucking hotplate, fucking hell it's the hotplate!" Disbelief etched itself on George's face as he staggered back.

"George, it's old news mate, it's been in here for a while," I informed him. "Get in here."

George's head swiveled back and forth from the door to the hotplate. He didn't know what to do.

"'Ere George, have a try of that," I put the bowl of curry and rice under his nose. "Don't worry about the hotplate, it's done and they've got a new one up there, all's good mate. Just get your gums round that."

With great gusto he scoffed down the curry.

He looked at Izzy and gave him his assessment, "Well alright Izzy, I've got to say it's a fair ol' curry."

"Now look George, now that the hotplate's here nobody's going to find it mate, so you don't have to suffer Mrs. Trotter's sarnies anymore do you?" Clearly, my invention knew no bounds as I suggested more. "Bring in some eggs and bacon and Izzy will cook you a great breakfast."

That was exactly what he did. Of course, I suggested he bring in more rashers of bacon and a few more eggs for the boys, and luckily he obliged. So that was the saga of the hotplate. It was really funny because George gave us the nod when the board of governors came round one day. We had cooked another curry and the odour, although tantalizing, was really strong. Quickly we hid the hotplate and all the evidence. All the while, the visitors sniffed the air. Mr. Johnson would have nicked us if he knew. He was sniffing too and asked what the smell was. George told him it was a mulligatawny soup his wife had given him in a flask. Nobody twigged what had happened.

George was a good man. I remember I made an appeal and it took some time to be heard. Susan still visited me on a regular basis, which was lovely of her but it was hard when it came to the end of the visit. If I had used a different barrister in the first place, I would've walked from court and wouldn't have received a four year sentence, that's for sure. Giddens, the solicitor was really good and came to see me in Highpoint. I told him it had to be sorted out but he wasn't able to help. Although he knew my barrister didn't do his job properly, novices wouldn't have made the mistakes he did and I should have walked, solicitors won't go against their own kind. He wouldn't take the matter further. I was left to try to appeal against the sentence by myself. One evening I went to the gym and George was there with a piece of paper in his hand. He asked me to pop into the office with him.

"Look Ronnie, I hate to break this to you mate," his words held a strong note of disappointment, "But your appeal has been turned down." Fair play to him, he was really upset for me.

Evidently, the appeal judges considered that because I had violence on my record, in their opinion, had the lorry driver pursued me in the chase, they considered I might have seriously hurt him with the crowbar. The sentence would remain at four years. George was also the bearer of bad tidings when, after sixteen months, with a possibility of release, he told me it had been turned down. Full credit to him because he did it in a gentle, civilized way.

"Don't worry about working tonight, I can see you're gutted," he told me. "Go back to your cell if you need to and just reflect on things and take your time, there's no problem with that."

George would always give me glowing reports when the time came every six weeks. If you ever read this book George Trotter, you are a true gentleman and I owe you one. I cracked on with prison life because what else could I do? If I had to do time, then Highpoint Prison wasn't a bad place to do it.

At the prison we had a big board up for various sports and my name was up there for weight lifting as I broke both house and prison records. This was going really well until a new physical training instructor came into the block to work with George, a little Scottish man called Drew

Agnew. We took an instant dislike to each other. Whereas George was an easygoing chap, Drew was full of himself, quite new on the job. He would dig me out in front of everybody at every single opportunity. My temper had its limits and one night he really started giving me some stick in a really sarcastic, nasty way. I committed the cardinal sin of telling him he was a typical jock, all mouth.

"How about you and I have a straightener?" I challenged him. "C'mon, forget your uniform, you're the big man, let me and you go for it."

He was all for it at the time, or at least he made out he was, but nevertheless declined my invitation. Of course, George had to step in and asked me to step into the office. He told me he had to get rid of me. Luckily, he talked Drew out of nicking me, which I'm sure he would've done. I was transferred from there to the worst job, which meant the laundry rooms.

Strangely enough, a couple of years later, when I was back on the door at The Windmill, who did I see at the bar, waiting for a drink with a couple of his mates? It was Drew Agnew. I went and rounded up the other doormen and surrounded them. I tapped Drew on the shoulder. His face when he turned and saw me was a picture, his jaw nearly hit the ground.

"Hello Ronnie, how are you doing?" he inquired. "Do you know your name is still on the board at HIghpoint for your weightlifting records?"

I cut straight through all that and asked him that now he was on my turf, did he want to have that straightener. I looked at his mates faces and you could see them thinking 'Oh shit what has he brought us into?' He obviously didn't fancy his chances. To be honest, I couldn't keep a straight face, a couple of years had gone by. I burst out laughing, put my hand out to shake his hand, which he accepted with great relief and a big sigh.

"Let's just let bygones be bygones." I laughed. "Forget it, I was in a different mindset when I was there, you were a bit new to the job, let's have a drink and put it behind us."

He was happy to do just that but I shall never forget the look on his face.

Because of years of watching cabaret and my dad being a bit of a comedian, I've always been able to tell jokes and always had that sort of personality. Bill, the civilian that ran the laundry department, just happened to like jokes. For my punishment, I was sent into the laundry room, which was a hot, sticky and dirty job. Straightaway I sussed Bill out, went into the office and started telling him a few jokes. He was crying with laughter. Literally, I did nothing, I would come in, make some tea for us both and tell jokes. None of the other lads would say anything, I had a bit of a reputation, they just got on with their jobs. If Bill gave me any jobs they would be the best jobs, such as sorting out the different colours, but that was just now and then, as most of the time was spent drinking tea and telling Bill stories.

I managed to get through my time at Highpoint quite well and about three months later my next chance of parole came up and luckily enough it was granted. Susan had stuck by me throughout the sentence, she visited me regularly and sent me letters. In the meantime though, I think she had started to find her feet, had met friends and was going out clubbing. Luckily her mum lived around the corner, which was handy for babysitting duties. Susan was making up for all the lack of socialising when the girls were small, but she still visited me and was very loyal to me. She always made the effort and looked nice when she came on visits, she always drove up and it was a long way for her.

All things happen for a reason and I realize that now. I met a chap in there, Georgie Strange, who was a nice bloke and had turned to God after he found religion in prison. Even after prison he stuck by it. In his time, he had been a merchant seaman and had some really funny stories about women being smuggled onto the ships and all the escapades they got up to. A few of us would sit in Georgie's room in the evening and get him to tell us the stories.

At the end of telling them he would say "Please God forgive me for what I've done," and we would fall about laughing.

Georgie was older than me and had a brother, Mickey Strange, a very wealthy man, who lived close to my home. Georgie told me that his brother bought and sold items and always had stuff, he told me to visit his brother, as he might be able to help me out a little bit. When my sentence finally came to an end, George and a few of the other screws waved me off. That was it for me, the four year sentence had made me realize that I couldn't win any battles, the authorities could tie me up and spit me out. Determined to make a real go of my life, I returned to Charlotte Gardens to Susan and the girls. The next few years were to be a strange mixture of success and failure.

CHAPTER 15
'BOUT A SHARP DRESSED MAN

Back on the outside, life appeared settled and I seemed to have a relatively charmed existence. But life has a way of pulling the rug from under your feet doesn't it? After a year of being home, having been out golfing for the day, I returned back to the clubhouse to find there was an urgent message for me to return home quickly. I drove home like a lunatic to discover that Vicky had suffered an epileptic fit, totally out of the blue. My precious little one was just four years old. It ripped me apart, there's nothing worse than seeing your child suffering. For many years after she endured terrible fits until she was fourteen years old. Her education suffered as she hardly went to school, she gained weight and had a bad skin condition. She really was in a bad way. Vicky has since gone on to have four children of her own, is a qualified hairdresser and was able to pass her driving test. Although she still struggles with her reading and writing, she manages to get by. When as a parent you first experience the pain of watching your child suffer, feeling like a helpless bystander, unsure what the future holds for your child, whether your child will eventually get better or not, it can send you into a tailspin of worry and upset. More determined than ever to do what I could for my family, I knew that I had to be strong and absolutely had to develop some stability for my family's sake.

After coming out of prison, I was still on parole and had been looking for a job. Luckily enough, through our next door neighbour, I met some lads who did industrial cleaning at The Sun newspaper in Wapping. This was at the time when Rupert Murdoch had just taken over The Sun and all the pickets were outside. It was a tough call as we literally had to go through the picket lines to get to work. It was night work, which I wasn't used to but at least it was work. The company was called J & D Cleaners and the offices at The Sun spanned a huge area. It was quite a big job but because of the fact that the work meant having to go through the picket lines, a lot of people were put off working for them. The pickets would bang on the roof of the car, scream and shout at us, even though we were nothing to do with the newspapers, we were just cleaners but we still endured the treatment. Nevertheless, I was desperate for a job and nothing was going to stop me providing for my family.

The initial interview was with Joe, an older chap that owned the company. I confessed to him straightaway that I had come out of prison and was open about my life and what had happened. Joe loved a villain, he listened to my stories before telling me I had the job. It was really good money. He asked me if I knew anything about cleaning and I explained to him that from what I had seen it was very much like cleaning in prison, electric bumpers, polish on, polish off, no complicated chemicals or anything like that, cleaning floors, toilets and cracking on with whatever needed to be done. Having always been a clean and tidy person, I wasn't worried about getting down to cleaning. Straight away I got stuck in.

Three weeks later, I was called up to see Joe, who told me he was so impressed with my work and my attitude that he was making me foreman over everyone else on the night shift. There were some lazy sods there but I kept them on their toes. There were certain jobs nobody wanted to do, such as cleaning the toilets, but they had to be done and I made sure everyone, including myself, took their turn. There were some arguments about certain jobs but I gave them the option of doing them or leaving. Normally, they would buckle up and get on with the work.

I took Georgie Strange up on his offer and went to see his brother Mickey, who turned out to be a fantastic chap. At the time, Mickey did all the cabbage for Pierre Cardin and he had boxes of shirts. Although absolutely legal, they were basically overruns. I could buy a box of twelve off him at five pounds each. At the time they were the shirt to be seen in, selling in the shops for between twenty five and thirty pounds. Other brands Mickey dealt in were Coconut Club and Favre Leuba watches, which were not well known but you couldn't buy one of those watches in the shops for under three hundred and fifty pounds. I was buying the watches from Mickey for fifty pounds. When I say I was buying them from him, Mickey knew the score that I had just come out of prison and didn't have a lot of money. On the strength of Georgie's recommendation, our transactions were on a trust basis. The very first time, I loaded up my car I asked Micky how much I owed him.

"Don't worry, sell them and then pay me," he said, "And anything you can't sell just bring it back, not a problem."

I used to go into work with a holdall, get the lads on the job, do my fair share of work and then I went all around the printing works, which was a huge place and I would catch people in their breaks. Now, you have to understand the newspaper presses stop and start, and there was often a lot of people standing around idly waiting for the machines to start. For instance, in the loading bay, the papers would come down the carousel and when the carousels weren't operating, the lads would be standing around waiting. I would introduce myself and just had a way of selling. I was known as 'Ron the Shirt' because I always had stuff with me. There were pairs of shoes, trainers, all sorts of t-shirts, suits - you name it, I had it. It was all good quality stuff and I was able to double up on the prices. I would carry a little book to tot up the sales, and at the end of the month, when they were paid, I would collect the money. Frankly, I was making a fortune. Along with the wages I was earning, as Joe had given me a couple of raises, I was raking it in.

At the time, a job with News International was something else, with full BUPA cover, the wages were phenomenal, the shifts were so many days on and so many days off. Having made myself familiar with the entire enterprise, the only place I really fancied working in was the loading bay. This was where the papers came down the carousels, the lads would load the lorries, then late at night what we called the white mice, the little white vans, would load up before heading off to the newsagents. The manager there was a chap called Jim Newell and I found out he was into golf, sold him a few bits on the cheap and also treated him to a few bits. I asked him if I could put my name down for a job there and thankfully he put my name at the top of the list. Within a very short space of time, I was offered a position. I thanked Joe and Derek for all they had done for me, but they fully understood that it was a better move for me and more money. My time with News International was great, I worked with a brilliant bunch of lads there, we had so much fun on the work floor. Most of them were Canning Town boys and very friendly. I managed to get my brother Lee a job there too, which was great as he had always been a grafter.

"Ron, get your brother to slow down, he's making us all look bad," the lads pleaded.

Again, I went around selling my bits and pieces and did well. Unfortunately, there was an under-manager there, Derek Weeks, an alcoholic who was always half cut, a nasty and vindictive piece of work. The head of security there was an ex-policeman and because I went around with this bag of stuff, he looked into my past and through associates that he still had in the force, he found out about my sentence. With a big smile of his face, Derek Weeks came up to me and told me I was wanted upstairs with Reg Lym. Now Reg was an Australian gay man, an older chap, who always wore leather trousers. He was the top man there during the night shift, nobody was higher than him. The minute I arrived in his office I knew something was afoot. With a big cheesy smile on his face, Derek asked me to go in. Reg Lym had a folder in front of him that he was flicking through.

"Sit down, Mr. Buckingham," he instructed. I sat down.

"Right, it's been brought to our attention that you have quite a prison record," he said as he leaned back in his chair.

To be fair, a lot of stuff went missing at The Sun, but I was far too sensible to nick anything and always kept my nose clean. Besides, there were cameras everywhere. The stuff I sold was legitimate.

"I haven't lied to you, I wasn't given any questionnaires or asked to declare anything, I went through the picket lines and now I've got a job. So, what are you going to do? Sack me?" With bated breath I waited for the axe to fall.

"No, not at all. In fact, I've spoken to Jim Newell," Reg answered, "He says you're a top lad and he has you in mind for the cage job."

I think his answer pissed Derek off, as the cage job would be a promotion. Reg asked me if I was selling stuff and I told him I was, but it was legitimate and I was only selling to the lads during their break times, as often the lads didn't have time to go out to do any shopping. I offered to show him the receipts I had for the goods. He told me that it wasn't to continue. Fair enough, I returned to work and Derek said nothing, he just pulled a few faces. The money I made was good, so I thought sod it, I wasn't going to turn the money down.

A couple of weeks later, I pressed the lift button, the doors opened and there stood Reg Lym. I froze like a statue, holdall in my hand. What was I to do?

"I don't suppose you're interested in buying a shirt Mr. Lym?" I smiled.

He shot me a funny glance and told me to piss off, then he just smiled and let it go. In truth, I don't think he was bothered.

In the meantime, I applied for my first ever mortgage and because I worked for the News of the World and the wages were good, Susan and I managed to buy the town house in Collier Row, which was great news. I started the cage job, which meant I worked from midnight until eight o'clock in the morning. The job entailed mostly sitting in an office, there was a forklift truck and a cage that contained the newspapers. We would wait for the vans to load them up, sometimes with one bundle or they might be just twenty papers short. I would give them the papers, they would sign for them and away they went. Basically it was a doddle of a job and extra money.

Derek Weeks continually made digs at me. Although I often worked at weekends or on special shifts to help out him out, he made a few comments about thieves pointed my way, in front of others. As I said, the lads would have stuff off me and I was able to get virtually anything at the time, but it was all legit. I made friends with a smashing bloke Roy, who worked in the dark room. He would show me the archives with all the old boxers, Henry Cooper, Joe Lewis and more. The News of the World had been about for years and all the original photographs were kept there, including the page three girls, all in beautiful black and white images. Money was pouring in and life was going well. Until Derek overstepped the mark and made a really cutting remark in front of the lads once again referring to me being a thief. It was the straw that broke the camel's back. I waited until he went into the toilets and followed him in, pinned him to the wall, got right in his face and told him what I thought of him and what I was going to do to him if he carried on digging me out. It was a silly move but he had pushed his luck. Of course, he ran whining to Jim Newel, who called me up into the office.

"Look, I can understand he really rode you," he said, "But I'm having problems with this."

He didn't sack me. Instead I let my hot head get the better of me.

"Jim, you know what?" I blasted, "I'm jacking it in."

A silly move to make perhaps because the money was good, but I might have ended up giving Derek a good hiding and getting nicked for it. There were no witnesses to me pinning him against the wall but frankly it wasn't worth my while losing it with him. I had my family to consider.

I continued making money from the items I bought from Mickey and luckily also managed to get work as a doorman through my cousin Glen, who owned a nightclub called Mr. B's, as well as stints at The Windmill. On a Sunday morning I would go to Glen's, who always had strippers in there and the place would be packed with men. In the corner I set up a little stall and sold the shirts, earning a week's money in just a weekend. I learned I could earn a really good living ducking and diving.

Meanwhile, on the home front things weren't going too well. Susan had found a life of her own and started to go out a bit more. I had left the job at the newspaper, which she thought was a bad move, so there was a bit of friction there. Although she stood by me, I was working really hard, getting in at eight o'clock in the morning and then immediately I would shoot straight over to Mickey's to see what was available. After that, I would be at The Kings working on the doors, selling stuff there as well. I was earning good money but didn't have the same security. The tension meant that Susan and I were falling apart. Too much water had gone under the bridge, she had found her feet and now had her own friends. We had the kids and for their sakes we did our best to stick together but she couldn't let go of the past. Who could blame her?

Chapter 16
Would You Adam And Eve It

Earlier in our marriage, after I had come out from doing the two years in prison, Susan had bought me a fantastic Staffordshire Bull Terrier, who we called Cleo, a darling little dog. I always felt better when I was away that she was around the house. She was very protective of the kids and gave them something to love. Marie still had her horse and she would ride it down to Charlotte Gardens and Vicky being a little tot would have a go, but it was mainly Marie who was the horse riding girl. She started doing gymkhanas and loved her horse to bits, she moved on from Rags Sally Anna up to a larger horse called Holly. Unfortunately, some time later there was a knock on the door. There had been some sort of horse flu that had affected the stables and sadly Marie's horse was the only one to pass. I had to break the news to Marie and God forgive me I have never seen pain like it on a kid's face, she really adored her horse. Eventually we bought her another horse. Now, as an adult she has two horses.

Susan and I worked hard on the house and had a new kitchen put in and new big bay windows fitted. I was really playing a straight game at that time, working and then coming home, loading up the car with all this stuff to sell. Working nights was very hard for me but then I would have to pick up the shirts and other bits to sell on. All the time I would think about what was going on with Susan. It was really hard going in the summer months. During the day I would try to sleep, but lawnmowers would start up and the noise was aggravating. It was very difficult and sometimes I would take some Night Nurse just to try and get some kip.

It was around this time, the late 1970s, that I met another man who turned out to be a lifelong friend. At the time, his partner Helen, who was a Greek Cypriot, became great friends with Susan. As I said, Susan was developing her own life, going to the country clubs and catching up on her life. Life had been difficult for her, Vicky still suffered the epileptic fits and she had a lot on her plate. The arguments between us became worse and eventually I moved out, although Susan would still come and visit me.

During the winter, I worked the doors at The Windmill. One night, a couple of days before Christmas, it had snowed and was freezing cold and we had to clear the parking area, which nobody really wanted to do. Everyone would leave the club a bit after two o'clock in the morning and because it was a residential area we had to get everyone out and away from the club as quietly as possible. Not that they always listened when we asked them to keep the noise down. The staff would take it in turns and this particular night it was my turn to clear the parking area. At three o'clock in the morning, I was the last doorman to leave in my blue Sierra estate car. My thoughts were on my divorce, which was going through, the house in Collier Row had been sold and I had my little bit of money out of it, the rest went to Susan, who ended up buying a flat in Collier Row. All the ins and outs were tumbling around in my brain. Like the crazy relationship it was, I had yet again moved back in with Susan. I was driving down the A12, not particularly fast as I was aware of the weather, although the road appeared clear and I was probably doing around sixty miles per hour. I reached a point not far from The Windmill, at the flyover at Kelvedon Bridge when, without warning, I was a ball caught in a pinball machine. Immediately my mind questioned why this was happening. The answer was black ice. I hit the bridge, the car went over and smacked into the central reservation barrier. All rational thought stopped, to be replaced by a sense of peace, as in slow motion the car then spun back over and then hit the bridge again. From there, it spun itself back into the reservation barrier. Spinning around and around, silent emptiness filled my brain to be replaced by a calm acceptance of what was to be my fate. Suddenly my conscience snapped to and I found myself facing back the way I had come. Miraculously, I was alive. What should I do next?

Calmly, I eased myself out of the car to survey the damage. The bonnet was up, the windscreen and windows were still intact, both headlights were blown out, both front and back wings were completely dented in, only one back light was working. This was before mobile phones were commonplace and there was no traffic on the roads. Enveloped by a sense of tranquility and certainty that the car would respond, I started the engine up. It was stuck in second gear but luckily there was enough room to turn it to face the right way. I pulled the car into the side of the road, tied the bonnet down with some string I had found in the boot, tested the wheels and pulled the wings away from the tyres, which luckily were still intact. Jammed in second gear, I drove the car all the way back to Collier Row, up to Susan's flat and parked outside. It was really late by now, well past four o'clock in the morning. Susan was awake. More than that she was ready for a row. Who could blame her? She started on me immediately.

"Look, I've had a terrible journey," I resigned myself to yet another quarrel.

"Yeah, I've heard that one before," she was beyond furious.

"I've written the car off," I answered.

"Oh so what did you do, walk home?" she snarled.

"No, I drove the car," I replied.

"Well how can you drive the car if it's a write off?" obviously Susan didn't believe me.

"Before you go any further, look out of the window," I sighed.

There was no mistaking the fact it was smashed to bits. Strangely, throughout the journey home, I wasn't pulled in by the police. Susan's face crumbled when the realization of what could have been hit her. She was very apologetic and concerned that I could be hurt. And here's the really strange thing, I wasn't in the slightest shocked or bothered, but I could so easily have been killed. Yet again, I had walked away unharmed without a scratch. Why was that?

Within a short space of time, Susan and I split up yet again and I moved, from one place to the next. I rented a little one bedroom house from my cousin Glen and this was followed by a flat over in Dagenham. After that, one of the lads that worked at the printing works wanted to rent out his council flat in Canning Town. I basically bought the rent book off him and he bought a nice house out in the sticks. I had the flat redecorated and it looked really good. Susan would turn up and stay the night there.

There was love between us and I still went back to see the kids. Unfortunately, the lad who I was renting the flat off decided he wanted it back. As he was a mate I sold it back to him, he paid for all the work that had been done and took the flat back on. It was quite unsetting moving from one abode to another. In the meantime, Carl had disappeared off the scene. We had always ended up getting into trouble together and I think there was pressure from his parents, who were slightly older. I still think the world of Carl and I class him as a top man but we really didn't see much of each other after that and now I haven't seen him for years.

As they say, one door closes and another one opens. I became great mates with a chap called Mickey, who was an exceptional man and still a good friend. A real character, he owned a video shop. Without doubt, he was the most immaculate man I have ever met. He had two Staffordshire Bull Terriers, Gucci and Ferruci, who would run everywhere with him. Mickey and I were inseparable friends and trained together, especially on a Sunday, when we would run for ten miles around Victoria Park. We also ran around the Eaton Manor racetrack from time to time.

Mickey started copying videos but made sure they were always in the proper boxes. He rented a big house somewhere, had machinery put in and found someone to run it. The holograms and printing were made but they were a fraction of the shop price. The films weren't old movies, they were new box office releases. It was around the time of The Terminator. In those days a film would cost Mickey sixty pounds to buy and two pounds to rent, but he was able to sell them for ten pounds. Mickey asked me to do the rounds every Saturday morning delivering the videos, he always looked after me.

One of his friends had a shop with a large frontage in Canvey Island, which he had shut down and there was no electric. He suggested that Mickey and I sell stuff from there. As I was also buying and selling bits and pieces, it seemed like a good idea. Mickey knew everyone, everywhere, and they all liked him, that was the sort of chap he was. He had a short fuse and was a bit feisty but I really liked him. Anyway, we went over to Hackney to buy tee-shirts at cost from someone he knew. Lo and behold, there were tee-shirts printed with matchstick men carrying surfboards on their shoulders, the Canvey Island Surfers. Mickey and I couldn't believe it, we bought every one, took them to Canvey Island, where they sold like hot cakes. It was uncanny how the money kept coming in from all different angles.

At this time I met Debbie, who was one of the gym instructors at the gym in Dagenham. She was unbelievably fit, had a fantastic figure and had trained all her life and was able to do sit-ups by the hundred. Being a training fanatic she suited me and we trained together and got on well. My relationship with Susan collapsed and we finally called it a day.

Debbie rented a little flat and I spent a lot of time with her. It was very off and on with Debbie. There was a lot of stuff coming up about her past that I didn't like, she didn't trust me and I didn't trust her, but somehow we just kept getting back together. We would go out jogging and training together so there was a bond there. It was a very physical relationship and I suppose that was a draw. Although she was a really nice girl, I couldn't get over certain rumours I had heard, which was daft as I had lived quite a life myself. She always denied it but I always knew it was true. We would split up and then get back together continuously.

Debbie worked at a gym in Dagenham called Adam and Eves, then moved over to the one in Leytonstone. The Adam section was upstairs and the Eve section was downstairs. Because the Adam section didn't have a gym instructor, the gym was struggling. Debbie put a word in for me to her boss George, who ran the two gyms independently, one look at me and George realised that I knew my onions when it came to fitness and hired me on the spot. It was a great job and I met loads of people, there were all walks of life in there. Together Debbie and I found a little flat in Dagenham and after training, we would shut the gym up and go home together.

One night I finished a bit earlier, just before nine o'clock, as it had been quiet in the gym. I closed up and came down, opened the car door and threw my bag in. My parking space was to the side of the gym, it was in an unlit alleyway and barely wide enough to squeeze in my tiny car. It was fairly long, about twenty feet, and I used the first ten feet of it to get the car in, keeping it tight to the left-hand wall so I could squeeze out the driver's side. In the pitch black I heard a sound, as if someone had landed on their feet. I sensed someone there in the dark, running towards me at full pelt. Straightaway, I thought I had upset someone on the club door and that whoever it was had decided to settle their score. Even in the inky gloominess I could make out a fairly tall man running straight at me. Bad move. I pushed the car door fully open, waited for him to run into it, then I threw a sharp right hook around the side of the door that connected with the side of his head. His legs buckled as he collapsed onto the bonnet of the car, slid down over the wing and ended up a crumpled heap on the floor. I quickly slammed the door shut, jumped over to him, had him by the scruff of the neck and lifted him up from the ground ready to whack him again. The man started to scream and shout, making a terrible fuss.

"Please don't hit me, please don't hit me," he wailed, "I'm sorry, I'm sorry."

In an instant I realized this was no thug plotting to set about me, he was far too wimpy. Then it dawned on me. At the alleyway where I parked the car was a brick wall and on the other side of the brick wall was the ladies changing rooms that lead off the downstairs gym. It had a flat roof and a skylight on the top. He had positioned himself on the flat roof to look through the skylight at the ladies changing. Needless to say, I dragged him up and shook him about a bit and went through his pockets, found his driving license and read out his name and address. I frogmarched him into the ladies gym, where Debbie was.

Posing at Adams gym.

"Ladies look at Tom the Peeper here," I announced, "He's been on the roof looking through the skylight at you all getting changed. What shall we do with him?"

It would be an understatement to say they were a bunch of characters in there, those ladies could be scary. Surrounding the man like a pack of wolves, they taunted him that he must have a little winkle, what a sorry sight he was, what a pervert, and suchlike.

"Please, please, call me what you want," he sobbed, "But don't tell the police, my wife will leave me and I've got a young child."

I actually felt a bit sorry for him, it was pathetic really. The ladies hurled abuse at him, right up to his face, as I hauled him out of the building. Holding him at arm's length by the scruff of the neck, I kicked his arse and away he went.

One of the chaps who used to come into the gym was Tony Dempsey, an Irishman with a Irish pub somewhere. Mickey and I ended up doing the door there at weekends. Tony pointed out the troublemaker to us, who was his potman, Mannox, an old fellah with a glass eye. Mickey and I couldn't believe that this old, one eyed man could be any sort of problem at all.

Tony smiled at us and warned, "You'll see."

Mannox was a heavy drinker, whose wages were spent on alcohol as soon as he received them. He tended to cadge drinks off other people and when he couldn't cadge any more drinks his party piece was to stand next to someone, remove his glass eye and drop it in their drink.

"You won't be wanting that now will you?" he'd say whilst sliding the drink away.

This behaviour normally resulted in Maddox getting a hefty slap, and Mickey and I would have to intervene to calm things down. But Maddox enjoyed the drink anyway.

On other nights I still worked at The Windmill, and also sometimes worked in Clacton with friends there, Reggie and Kenny Shorter. The Shorter brothers worked at the Cockney Pride and the Hydro Club in Clacton. Basically I hopped in and out of work as and when needed.

One particular chap, Som, was a big Indian chap, who had a printers opposite. He owned a disco and dressed the part, with outrageously big floral ties and shirts. He called himself the Wacky Paki and was fantastic fun. Along with some other Indian gentlemen, he started Cosmopolitan Promotions, and put on some big shows that were popular with the Indian community. Som would buy major venues such as the Ilford Palais and other big halls, and he asked Mickey and I if we would do the security, along with another stocky Jamaican chap who trained in the gym. I laid down the law that I wouldn't allow any ceremonial daggers in, and if any of the younger generation came in looking for trouble, I would ban them and wouldn't be overruled. They came in traditional dress and would dance and enjoy the wonderful food and curries. Sometimes the younger Indians would be rude and arrogant about the other people there. I would stop them coming in and they would shout over their shoulder in their own language to others inside to go and get their uncle or whoever, and a chap would tell me it was okay because it was his nephew, but I wouldn't budge. To be fair, the management always backed me to the hilt with my decisions and they paid us very good money. This was the time when Mickey and I were running around Victoria Park with the Victoria Park Harriers and we were mega fit.

Instructing in Adams gym with Som lifting weights.

Yet again, I had broken up with Debbie. Mickey was living over Woodford way and was in a relationship and his partner had a child. He was earning good money, even bought a Porsche but basically he was a straight runner, who introduced me to a lot of nice people, putting work my way. A flat came up opposite the golf course in Chingford Road, Woodford, and Mickey went straight in and furnished it for me, he even paid the rent for me. We started training in a gym called Physicals, where I met a really nice girl, another Debbie, who was part owner of the gym. I was still connected to the other Debbie in a way and would be backwards and forwards. Looking back now, I can see the people who would have been really good for me. The new Debbie was a lovely, generous girl, who had been a dancer at the Moulin Rouge, ran marathons and was massively fit. But I walked away from her and returned to the original Debbie. We decided we would give if a proper go and ended up moving back to Tiptree.

Chapter 17
A Doorman And A Diplomat

Everything in my life felt turbulent, yet it was simply a reflection of the confusion that I hid inside of me. Looking back, I wasn't sure what it was that I was searching for. Without a clear plan, I was headed in no particular direction. Debbie and I bought the place in Tiptree and set about creating a home. Door work was my main source of income, along with buying and selling bits for Mickey, and doing the odd bit of work with Smut, who always kept the door open for me and I can only speak well of him.

Smut worked the door on Piers at Southend on Sea, right next door to the Westcliff Casino. The club had experienced a lot of aggravation with a group of local lads, who terrorised the club door. It's always very hard to work on a door in an area that you live in. You could be out with your family and bump into people you had thrown out of a club the previous night, get outnumbered and it might turn out to be a problem. One particular chap, John, was a known face down there. I did my homework and discovered he was one to be reckoned with and had a bit of a team behind him. At the time, I was the head doorman at the club, which was part of the Brent Walker group. It was an immaculate nightclub on three floors, big Chesterfield settees, a real classy place with the casino next door to it. There were quite a few doormen there, all good lads. My car at the time was a little red XR2. The doormen would take it in turns to pick each other up for work sharing one car. It was a lovely door to work, we could go upstairs and have a three course meal and use the gym and swimming pool if we wanted to stay on.

Jan White, who ran the club, marked my card about this known face and the trouble he caused, throwing ice cubes at the barmaids and causing rows. No way did she want the man in the club. I checked him out and he was one to be handled carefully. I told the lads to point him out if he turned up and I would take it from there. A couple of months later he turned up with a mate.

"Are you John?" I asked.

"What's it to do with you?" instantly his stance was aggressive.

I indicated that I wanted a little word with him. He was obviously ready for a fight but I quietly informed him that I just wanted to talk to him. You have to understand this man had a gang behind him, and although we had a lot of doormen, it's possible the club would have been wrecked and it wouldn't have ended there. In all likelihood he would have returned with yet a bigger gang behind him, and so it would continue. Diplomacy was always my strong card.

"I respect this is your manor, I respect that you like to use this club, I respect that you are a man to be reckoned with, I understand that," I chose my words carefully. "I'm going to make an offer to you."

John looked at me quizzically as I continued. "If you and one of your mates and a couple of girls, even up to three mates come in with your girlfriends, I don't mind. If you get one of the doormen's attention and come to the front of the queue, you'll get a handshake and made welcome, if you look the part. In return, you don't give any of my doormen abuse, you don't cause fights, you don't throw ice at anyone, you respect us as I'm showing you respect."

He took a moment before replying, "You know what, I like you mate, you're a proper fellah," he offered his hand.

Regardless of his words, I was ready for him to pull me into a head butt but he didn't. After that, I can honestly say he was brilliant and came to the club on a regular basis with his mate Kevin. I ended up quite friendly with both of them. They were never any trouble, in fact if anyone started any trouble, they would stop it before the doormen got to it. It's funny how if you keep your cool, everyone else cools down too. Many people think doormen are all brunt and no brains, but the truth is they have to know how to stop trouble before it starts. That takes a combination of logic, diplomacy and intuition in equal measure.

At the end of one shift I was ready to go home but couldn't find my XR2 car. What I did find was broken glass. It had been nicked. Talk about karma, I had to laugh, after all I had stolen cars in the past. Leanne, one of the barmaids, offered me a lift back to my flat in Witham, where I was living at the time. I rang up my mate, Andy Reid, as we always had keys to each other's place. He wasn't married but if he had any aggravation with a girlfriend, he would move into my place and likewise I could just turn up at his.

I reported the car stolen and about a week later, I received a phone call from the police in South London. They told me they had found the car and where it was, the window had been popped and the barrel had been dragged out but it would start with a screwdriver. Andy and I went to the address in Mitcham but couldn't find the car. We returned to the police station and told them the car wasn't there but they insisted it was. I asked them if they had secured it in any way, but they hadn't and had just advised me of its position. Quite sure we had looked in the wrong place, the copper radioed a colleague to check and of course the car wasn't there. Andy took me all the way back to Witham.

Yet again, a few days later we had another call. The car had been used in an armed robbery. A Securicor van had been robbed, the car had been rammed, the radiator had been blown and basically it was a mess. Back again to Mitcham, the car was loaded up and taken away. However, it had been fingerprinted. The police didn't suspect me obviously. Sitting with the copper, he asked me if I knew a certain name that he revealed and asked why that person would be in my car. I told him that as we worked together as doormen we often shared rides. He gave me another name, and another, and another. In all, five sets of prints came up, including my own. Based on the evidence that day, I would surmise that the majority of doormen have done time! The guys were all killing themselves laughing back at the club when I told them the story. Luckily, the police were as good as gold and didn't try to pin anything on me.

On the work front it was going well. On the romantic front it was a different story because Debbie and I kept breaking up. Entering into the 1990s, Susan had remarried. At one point, the kids had played her up a bit and she brought them to me and said that Debbie and I would have to look after them. I didn't have a problem with that and to be fair to Debbie she was fine with it, so they came to stay. It would never have lasted, I think it was just that the kids were giving Susan's new husband Larry a bad time. Vicky's fits were easing off a bit, which was good news, and eventually they stopped completely, thank God. In all, I think Marie had a week with us but missed her horse and all her friends and she returned back to Susan, who welcomed her home. Vicky stayed with us for a few more weeks, I did a bedroom up for her and registered her with the local school. Debbie helped Vicky with her diet and fitness because due to epilepsy Vicky had put on a bit of weight. Vicky then started going back to Susan for the weekend, who now had a new house with Larry in Harold Wood, and soon after Vicky returned to live with them full-time. Susan was cracking on with her life, which was great, enjoying wonderful holidays and a bit more financial ease. She was a wonderful mother to our children and deserved to be happy. I felt really pleased for her.

Chapter 18
Lies and Damned Lies

Big changes began to stir in my life. I was still working at The Kings in Canvey, also The Kings at Seven Kings, The Windmill and The Barn, there was a flood of door work, five nights a week. However, I had experienced many house moves in a short period of time, which was really unsettling. I felt all over the place, physically and emotionally. My relationship with Debbie had reached rock bottom and fallen apart. In my mind I had wanted the relationship to work, trying to make her the right person for me but it didn't out. I left Debbie with the house, she sold it and moved away. I never saw her again after that. It was time to move on.

It sounds crazy but straight away I met someone else at the club, who I thought was absolutely perfect. Really petite and beautifully spoken, with big blue eyes and a butter wouldn't melt in her mouth face, to me she seemed so classy and different from anyone else I had ever known. I'm someone who prides himself on being able to suss people out pretty quickly and easily, but I have to admit this time I didn't see it coming. To say she caused me a load of grief is an understatement. It turned out she was one of the worse people I ever went out with. She was someone who could out cheat me, seeing loads of other men at the same time as she was seeing me. Living in a beautiful cottage, impeccable in her dress, immaculate around the house and a beautiful cook, she seemed adorable. But a wrong 'un as they say.

In fairness, people did try to warn me about her, but despite the rumours, I never caught her out on anything. Instead she completely convinced me that I was losing the plot and told me I was delusional, nuts and paranoid. But still the rumours continued. One of which was about a gamekeeper she was supposed to be seeing. Her cottage was in the middle of a farm on an estate, so it was plausible. Of course, she completely denied it but others were insistent it was happening. I knew she had been married and had an affair behind her husband's back with someone close to them. She told me right at the start of our relationship, which made me think she was honest. I was playing a straight game with her but let's just say weird things were happening with this girl. At nights I would go to her place, other nights she often came to the club, where she was very possessive and didn't like me talking to other women, but was happy to flirt herself. One night after work, I drove over to her place. I tried the door but it was locked. As I said, the cottage was in the middle of nowhere, I stood there banging on the door.

Her head popped out the window, "I'm really ill, go away."

I told her if she wasn't feeling too good I could look after her.

"No, I don't want you seeing me like this," she said, "I feel ill, go away."

I continued to reassure her that it wasn't a problem, I would look after her.

"No, I don't want you seeing me like this, just please go away." She was insistent.

I decided to head back to Andy Reid's and let myself in there. Yet all the while, a feeling of unease continued to wash over me. Something felt off, but I couldn't quite work out what.

After a while of seeing this particular girl, I felt a continual niggle rising up from inside of me. Mind you, she was clever and no matter what we spoke about, she would drop in comments insisting I was paranoid and whatever else. As cool as a cucumber, she could lie her way out of anything. Boy was she smart, way out of my league and I've been around, as you can tell by this book. One night, I had been on the door since eight o'clock. Turning to the other doormen, I told them I would be out for an hour or so and asked them to cover for me. A flash of intuition told me there was something going on and I decided to act upon it. I drove to her cottage, pulled up very quietly, walked round and found there was a strange car there. As it was the summer, I went round to the back of the house to the living room window, it was wide open. There she was sitting on the settee drinking wine with another man.

Sticking my head and shoulders through the window, I asked "Who's this then?" It was my turn to be as cool as a cucumber.

"Oh, he's a family friend, just called by on the off chance," she answered smiling, not at all ruffled by my appearance. "Ronnie, this is Nick," she introduced us.

I made my way to the front door and, as I did so, the window at the back closed with a loud thud. Her head popped out of the bedroom window, a favourite trick of hers.

"I want you to go away," she demanded.

"I thought you were going to introduce me to your friend," I answered calmly.

"No, you'll beat him up," her calm and collected mask was beginning to slip.

"If he's just a family friend, why would I want to beat him up?" Instinct screamed at me that she was lying.

"Well, I want you to go away," she tried to regain her composure.

I suggested to her that I meet him and we sort it out but she wouldn't agree. I turned around and made a note of the car registration number. She was still hanging out of the window and I was still waiting for her to let me in. Eventually, this tiny, little blonde, woman, who had once been married to a policeman, threatened to call the police on me, an ex-con and doorman. Knowing what would happen, I decided to leave.

The next day, I called in a favour and had the registration number I had noted checked out. Now I knew who the man was. At least I knew I wasn't paranoid. A mutual friend warned him that he was playing with fire and that if I caught him, I would do him some serious harm. Luckily common sense kicked in and I asked myself what would be the point of doing anything?

There was other stuff that came up about this woman. As often happens in these cases, there was another chap who frequented The Windmill, who I knew fairly well because he was a regular. He was known by a nickname. I never thought of him as a threat, even though he was always around her.

She always took the mick out of him behind his back, the fact that he wore a vest under his shirt and the way he talked. It was a constant stream of negative comments about him. This turned out to be another rouse.

Unbeknown to the man, a friend of his was a very good friend of mine, but of course the man didn't know this. He bragged to my friend that he'd had a very close brush when he was round the cottage one night with her and I turned up. He told my friend other stuff and it turned out he was sleeping with her. Luckily for him, this was quite a time after I had finished with her, but I couldn't leave it like that. Months later, whilst working on the door, he came into the club all cheery and smiles. During the evening, I moved up to the side of him at the bar.

"I know the answer to something, yet I'm going to ask you the question, but I do know the real answer." My voice was eerily calm. "If you tell me the truth, I will shake your hand and there will be no hard feelings and you can walk away." I looked straight at him and continued, "If you lie to me, they will have to carry you out of this club."

His face blanched and he started to fidget. Barely able to speak, he nodded and told me he would answer the question. I simply asked if I went to her house one night when he was there.

"I'm sorry mate," he answered, "Yes, I was."

Lo and behold, I wasn't paranoid after all. I knew a hundred percent that for all her sweet façade she was a liar and cheat. But I suppose that's another way of saying my sixth sense was being fine tuned by the events in my life.

Chapter 19
Never Judge A Book By Its Cover

Even before my involvement with the woman who lived on the farm, even way back to the late 1980s, I had often pulled myself to bits, trying to dissect the reasons why I couldn't settle, why I felt the way I did. Woman were attracted to me for sure, but there was still a feeling inside of being the ugly little kid, the scruffy one at school that people couldn't take to. I suppose in a way, much as I would try to deny it to myself, the business with Carol, even with my mum to an extent, and my early family life, had left me with a sense of not being good enough and not being able to fully trust that I was loved.

Looking back, I can see this was compounded by unconscious anger and resentment. Back when I came out from doing the two years, around 1982, my uncle George, who had brought my father up, had passed over, and my father had the pub at that point, but then my aunt Mil passed. Again, my father was left a small fortune, which included a house in Leytonstone, a lot of money and a few other bits. My parents went on a holiday spree, they visited America and all around Europe, the Canary Islands, the Channel Islands, you name it, they went there. Yet they never thought to treat any of us kids to a holiday. Were we in some way undeserving? Somehow, my father would always get in debt and was always on the phone to me, asking if I could help him out. Yet he had gone through absolute fortunes without a thought for anyone else. For all the money he received, neither myself nor my brothers received any birthday treats. Birthdays came and went with no celebration. Did my parents resent or regret having us? I have no souvenir, no keepsake, nothing was ever given to me to mark a special occasion. It just didn't happen, they were very much into themselves. The pub had been earning good money but for one reason or another it went pear shaped, and my parents were always on my case for money.

It's funny how events affect and shape us. With my children and those closest to me, I always saw giving money or buying gifts as a sign of love, because those things had never been done for me. In my subconscious it was important to me to buy my wife and girlfriends things. I was always generous with money and still am, it was always a sign of affection. It wasn't until Nicky, my now wife and love of my life, explained it to me and said that she didn't want presents, she just wanted me and my love, that I began to experience clarity around the whole issue.

Back then, I tried to make sense of why I was going through these relationships, why I just walked in and out of things. It was me doing most of the leaving, ninety per cent of the time and it was mostly my fault. But the episode with the woman in the cottage happened and it really made me sit up and start thinking. I didn't play around behind her back, I thought that was it, I loved her. It seemed that everything was right about the relationship. Except of course for the fact that she couldn't seem to stop putting it about.

It is through relationships that we learn and although at the time it was awful to be on the receiving end of her lies, what she did do for me, in terms of growing as a person, was immense. She was completely different from anyone else I had been out. Very in control, she appeared very smooth, enjoyed fine wine and superior dining and had good manners. Not that I've ever been rude with women, I had always been articulate and very old fashioned, always remembered my please and thank you, would always give my seat up for a woman or someone elderly, if someone was struggling to carry bags, I would always offer to help. That was the sort of man I was and still am and always will be.

Yet she showed me a different side of life and, in a sense, I'm sure I did the same for her. She had been married to a policeman, and then she was in a relationship with me, an ex-villain and doorman, which she knew I was, at the time it was a bit of a thing for her. I was a bit rough and ready, heavily tattooed, and totally different to what she had experienced in her life. However, she was a player and very clever, astute at getting through situations. But I do owe her a lot of thanks because she continually put me down about being a doorman, asking me if that was all I was or all that I had ambition for. It was true that I couldn't do the doors forever but what were obviously her own inner torments meant that she felt the need to constantly go on and on, running me down. Some people can't help themselves, they think that by putting others down they'll feel better about themselves. It doesn't actually work and deep down they know it, and until they gain clarity about themselves and their behaviour, they continue in a loop of projecting their insecurities onto others. She was caught in that loop but still her putdowns continued to ring in my ears.

At the same time as our relationship screeched to a halt, the desire to make something of myself started to bubble up. I decided to go on a sales course, which was a bit of a joke because I could sell better than the people training me, but I completed the course and looked for a job. There was an advert for a company in Burnham on Crouch called the Furber Collection. I rang for an interview and presented myself suited and booted. Ian Lindsey, the owner of the company, interviewed me and straightaway we clicked. He was cocky and laid back with a big grin on his face, quite a character and had been a fantastic salesman all his life. He had worked for Wilson Golf Clubs and had taken out all the best golfers for lunch. Basically he knew his stuff. He asked me if I had a resume, which I didn't, so asked me what sales experience I had. I told him I had been a barrow boy and was good at selling stuff. Laughing, he told me that didn't cut any ice as he had proven sales people coming for interview. I told him I knew there would be paperwork and I could do that, but at the end of the day selling is selling and I could sell anything. Obviously I had piqued his interest because he looked at me oddly and asked if I thought that was true. With that, he left me in the office and ten minutes later came back with a big cardboard box. It was full of various sample goods.

"So, you can sell? he asked grinning.

I told him without a doubt I could.

"Right, go and sell this lot," he challenged.

That suited me, it was right down my alley. I took the box around a ten mile radius and after three hours returned to the office. I had sold everything. Handing over the cash, I told him I had orders for more if there was more stock. His face spoke volumes, he was gobsmacked.

"How on earth did you do that?" he was incredulous.

"I told you I can sell anything," I smiled broadly.

Suited and booted for the Furber Collection at the NEC

On the spot, he offered me a three month trial on a wage and told me if I passed the three months and proved my mettle, I would be given a bigger wage and would be part of the team. True to his word, after I sailed through the three month probation period, he wrote a letter to me confirming what an asset to the company I was and how proud he was of me, welcoming me on board with a decent salary and commission. I still have the letter to this day.

It was great, sometimes I would be out making sales, other times helping on the factory floor, or even driving the lorry to make a delivery. We would all pitch in with various jobs but my priority was sales. Whatever task he set me I did, even when he thought I might not be quite up to speed, but wherever I went, I came back with orders. In total I worked there for two years and loved every minute of it, they were great people. I was in my element, sometimes I would be suited and booted working at the NEC in

Birmingham doing the shows with him, which was fun as he was such a great laugh.

Throughout my time with the Furber Collection, I still worked as head doorman at The Windmill. We used to have a guest book into which we would sign people in, such as Mr. Whoever plus one. There was a chap there who we named 'The Clough,' a bit of a face in Colchester. The Clough was accused of aggravated bodily harm on a certain person on a certain night. His alibi was that he was actually in the club and his name was in the book to prove it. Being the head doorman. I was asked to go along and be a witness to the fact that The Clough was at the club. I went along to Chelmsford Crown Court and it was quite strange for me to not to be in the one that faced going to prison. Judge Greenwood walked in, who I had been up in front of before. It was my turn to enter into the witness box. I wore a smart blazer, nice trousers and a tie and looked the business. The prosecutor was a smug chap and because The Clough's defense had questioned some of the witnesses against him who had prison records, the prosecutor was allowed to bring up my criminal past.

"Mr. Buckingham, would you say you're an honest man?" he questioned.

"Yes, I like to think I'm a honest man, so yes I would," I replied.

"Ah, I have quite a list of offences here and see you've had quite a few terms of prison, which makes me think otherwise," his tone was somewhat self-righteous.

"Well, if that's the case, then the judicial system doesn't work does it?" I answered, "Because here I stand," I continued, taking a piece of paper out of my pocket with a flourish, "With a letter here from my employer, who I've worked with for about eighteen months, which says I'm a credit to the company, earn good money and pay my taxes. So if you're saying I'm still a dishonest man, then clearly the prison system doesn't work. The very system that you and Judge Greenwood are part of is a waste of time."

The prosecutor became very red in the face. Quickly he made reference to the case where I stole the videos many years before and for a lot of money.

"Mr. Buckingham, you were sentenced to two years for this crime," the prosecutor persisted, "Would you mind telling the jurors how much was involved please."

He stood back with a big smirk on his face. Most of the jury were quite young and a lot of them were female. I stood there, chin in my hand, scratching my head.

"Well Mr. Buckingham? Do you need us to refresh your memory?" he went on.

"Oh no, I know exactly how much it was, thank you," I responded.

"Then why so long?" he was becoming impatient.

"Well, we're going back so far it was pre-decimal and I'm trying to determine if these young jurors would understand it in pounds, shillings and pence," I countered.

The whole court sniggered. The prosecutor's next form of attack was that The Clough had given me a back-hander, that he had paid me money to give him an alibi.

I looked the prosecutor straight in the eye, "You obviously haven't done your homework have you?"

Perplexed he responded "I beg your pardon?"

"Well, you haven't studied the man you are trying to prosecute have you?" I retorted, "Because if you had then you would know he is the tightest man in Essex. If he was a ghost he wouldn't give you a fright. What on earth makes you think he would give me money?"

The jury desperately tried to stifle their laughter, even Judge Greenwood smiled.

Butting in, Judge Greenwood asked "Mr. Buckingham you received two years for this crime?"

I answered "Yes I did, Sir."

When he asked me where I was sentenced and by whom, I replied, "In this very court by your goodself Sir, and may I say what a fair sentence it was Sir."

On a roll I continued, "Not like that Judge Watling, who gave me four years for conspiring to an attempted theft, which was an outrage. If that had been you I wouldn't have had anything like that sort of sentence, it would have been eighteen months or a year. You're a very nice man, Sir."

Judge Greenwood grinned, everyone else laughed. The judge questioned me on The Windmill guest book, asking what the 'plus one' meant.

"Now, we've got to have a bit of a scenario here, Judge Greenwood," I explained, "Let's imagine you're visiting a nightclub."

He quickly interrupted, "No, I don't think that's very likely."

"Now hold on a minute, you've got to hear this, you're a judge and you have to be broadminded," I answered.

"Okay Mr. Buckingham, do continue," he said.

"So, you're going to a nightclub," I carried on, "Who are you going to take with you? A couple of floozies. Now when you get to the door, I would recognize you. I'm not going to put in the book Judge Greenwood plus floosies or the names of the young ladies am I? Because if Mrs. Greenwood comes up the club and sees it, then you're bang in trouble and I'm not going to do that to you. So, I'm going to put Judge Greenwood plus two."

Well, even he laughed. In the end, the jury were struggling to contain themselves and The Clough was laughing so much his false teeth popped out. The prosecutor hadn't much more to say and anything he did say I made fun off. In the end he ordered me out of the box. I took a bow to him and out I went. The Clough was found not guilty, which was against all the odds.

Evidently one of the jurors, a young woman who was the foreman for the jury, said that if he was found guilty his witnesses would be in trouble. Judge Greenwood apparently affirmed that yes, it would be perjury. The jury came back with not guilty. To this day I still have the letter that The Clough's barrister at the time sent me, describing me as an absolute star in the witness box and also mentioning that now that Judge Greenwood knows he can go to a nightclub with a couple of floosies, hopefully he'll be a nicer and gentler man to deal with.

CHAPTER 20
NEVER BREAK A PROMISE

In the early 1990s, my daughter Marie met an American chap, fell in love and moved out to America. I think she was only seventeen years old at the time.

"What do I do Dad?" she asked.

"Look, I love you to bits and have always loved you," I told her, "But do what you want to do and if that's what you want to do then go for it."

She did exactly that, starting off in Memphis for a few years and then North Carolina. Vicky's fits had come to an end, life was settling down a bit for my two girls, I felt proud of them both and I wanted them to feel proud that I was their dad.

My previous relationship had, in its own way, pushed me on to make something more of myself. It had also sparked my interest in older properties because I loved the cottage she lived in although she only rented it. In Sible Hedingham I saw a house called Swan House, built in 1729. It had been dilapidated but had subsequently been completely renovated and split into three. I bought the middle cottage and easily secured a mortgage because I had steady employment. The house had big bay windows with leaded glass, it was full of beams, big open fireplaces, log burners, a small courtyard garden with private parking around the back. It became a huge project for me. I bought books detailing the style of the era it was built, and had a winding staircase and red carpet put in, which was fashionable when it was originally constructed, even the carpet on the stairs had brass rods going across. I treated myself to a grandfather clock for the cobblestone hallway and furniture that complemented the décor and style of the cottage. Everyone raved about my new home. It made me feel good because I felt I was beginning to make something of myself and was climbing back up the ladder.

It was around this time in 1995 that I met another girl at the club, Anita, who lived in the Dovercourt area. The relationship was a bit up and down but I had a thing about this girl, she seemed quite different. Fate has a strange way of intervening sometimes. We started seeing each other and I popped over to Dovercourt a lot. In the meantime, before completing the purchase of the cottage, I stayed in Maldon with Andy Reid and then rented a little flat whilst the house in Sible Hedingham was being finalized. I had started seeing Anita in Dovercourt but it was a long drive backwards and forwards. We had an early break-up but made up again and decided that she would move into the cottage with me. Everything had been arranged for the moving in day and I was looking forward to it but, at the very last moment, she called it a day. That was an unexpected blow to me. By now, I was sick of relationships, it was the last straw.

At the same time, my father was diagnosed with lung cancer and was told he didn't have very long to live. I had always had a strange relationship with my parents but at the end of the day he was my father and the pub they were in, The Kings Arms at Tiptree, was a cold place and due to his illness he really felt the cold. I told my parents to move into my cottage, which they absolutely adored. They enjoyed listening to the stereo system, playing Nat King Cole. My father was never one for socialising, he didn't enjoy restaurants or anything too posh, yet he actually danced with my mother to Nat King Cole in the living room there. My father's health declined rapidly and my parents had to pull out of the pub. They had been in Tiptree a long time and were given a two bedroom bungalow in Tiptree, which is where they really wanted to be, surrounded by their friends and so they moved out of the cottage into the bungalow.

One night, I came home from being on the door and there was a message on my answerphone. It was from Anita. After five months, she had realized that she regretted ending our relationship and she wanted me to see her, which I agreed to. That was another bad error. She told me she had wanted to move in with me but as her mum, friends and family lived in Harwich and her daughter went to school there, she really wanted to remain in that area. Being as silly as I was, I put the cottage up for sale. I was back with her and moved into her place in Dovercourt. Yet, at the back of my mind, a familiar but unwelcome misgiving made itself known to me.

We viewed a detached house that was being newly built in Wix, just outside Dovercourt. I made lifelong friends of the chap who was building it, Sam Brazier and his wife Lisa. This was the first house he built on that development, Willow Tree Cottage, and we agreed on a price. Poor Sam had been turned over by his solicitor and there were all sorts of problems with rights of way, it was all going boss-eyed for him. He apologized to me for all the delays and promised me that he would do extra work, such as building a big garage on the side for no extra charge and landscaping the garden. He was a man of his word but it was all very long winded. Now I would recognize the whispers from spirit that delays and disruption often represent, but back then I wasn't quite so tuned in.

My cottage sold very quickly and fortunately I made money on it. An American chap wanted to buy it and I wanted to move into the new house, Sam was doing the best he could to finish the project, throughout all of this my father's illness worsened, it all felt a bit of a mess really. In the end, Sam completed the house, I had banked the money from the sale of the cottage and temporarily lodged with Andy Reid, staying on and off with Anita. Just as the new house was being finished, my father took a real turn for the worse. Sam had done everything he said he would and Anita and I were geared up to move into the house in January.

Anita rarely met my parents as I didn't socialise with them a great deal and she hadn't seen them during my father's illness. Just before Christmas, I took her to their pub when it was still theirs, although by that time they had the bungalow. They were going to do one last Christmas stint in the pub. Sam had given me a jeep for being so late with the house and I had given it to Anita but that night I was driving. At the end of our visit we both said goodbye to my parents. Anita went out to the jeep and as she did so, my father called me to him. He laid on the settee and looked terrible. He summoned all of his energy to speak to me.

"I want you to make me a promise," he forced the words out.

I didn't quite know what to expect next, my father was never one to share his thoughts with me.

"I don't know what it is Dad, I can't make you a promise if I don't know what the promise is about." I answered intrigued.

"I need a promise from you," he was resolute.

"Tell me what the promise is," I felt confused by his words.

He beckoned me closer. "Please, please, don't end up with her," he pleaded. "Whatever you do, don't marry her, she'll ruin you."

Stunned I tried to make sense of his outburst. Throughout all of my relationships, my father had never said anything like that to me. He would make comments about how nice looking the girls were, but nothing like the comment he just had. I told him I couldn't make such a promise.

"Even if you don't do anything else for me, please don't end up with her," he was adamant.

It's strange to think that my dad had the gift of prophesy. Yet, just a short while later, with my father fading away and the paint on the walls of the house barely dry, Anita called it a day on our relationship. Once again, she had completely changed her mind and told me goodbye. I was able to keep the promise that my father had begged of me.

I think this was the worst period of my life, everything went wrong at once. I still worked the doors, as well as the Furber Collection, and between the two I earned decent money. My father was at death's door, he was losing weight fast, Anita had said goodbye and now I had a house in Wix, in the middle of nowhere, in a place where I didn't know anyone. I felt stuck there in the middle of no-man's land. Anita had said that nothing had been going on outside of our relationship. The bus that she often caught to go to Colchester stopped right outside my cottage, I often felt a twinge when I saw it. She had done her usual, called it a day and never contacted me again. I never did get to the bottom of her and never will do.

Soon after, the Furber Collection started to have problems. A massive order had been made for one of the big department stores, they promised to take it at a certain time but then delayed it by three months. Ian Lindsey needed them to sell the order but the department store refused because it had been designed especially for them and they threatened to sue the company if he sold the goods elsewhere. In short, the company went under and I was suddenly out of a job. Luckily, I still had the door work at The Windmill. They say bad things come in threes. My main job was gone, the woman I was supposed to be with had left, and my father was dying. I felt washed up and stuck on a spin cycle of misery.

Chapter 21
One Door Closes, Another Door Opens

It was winter and I was back working the doors for a living, feeling really down in myself and unhappy with my lot, People would come up to me and tell me they had just seen Anita at whatever club, dancing with some bloke, needless to say I wasn't in the best frame of mind. Even as I stood in the cold doorway, my mind spun as I tried to make sense of recent events. There were lots of things I wanted to say to my father, I had been running him backwards and forwards to the hospital and taking my mother to visit him, but I couldn't get the words out. Instead I just went through my days, living from one hour to the next, apprehensive about what was around the corner.

Instead of taking time out to take stock of my life, assess my situation and come to terms with what had happened, I started seeing someone else. Deanna was my brother's then wife's best friend, the two women worked for the NHS. She was bubbly, intelligent and compassionate, all qualities needed for her job as a specialist nurse in heart care. In the past, she had worked in the rescue helicopters and had been in the sharp end of nursing care. Eventually she became a matron at a hospital, beating all the other applicants hands down.

Deanna was a lovely girl and was naturally very caring towards my father. Although she was probably one of the nicest people I had ever met, I was still smarting over Anita and Deanna knew it. Understandably, she never wanted to be second best, so it never went anywhere. When she managed to get the job at a BUPA hospital she moved out of the area. If the experience with Anita hadn't happened, then perhaps things would have turned out differently. Although it fizzled out, she played a bit of a role in my life. The experience was yet again trying to teach me that not giving time to process the end of a relationship can impact others negatively, as well as myself, although at the time I still hadn't learned that lesson.

I was back to square one, another relationship had dissipated into nothingness and I was still working the doors. Luckily, The Windmill was a buzzing place and to a certain extent it took my mind off life outside. Even so, an inner tension began to uncoil within me. The club had been sold by Bob Wheatley, who had lost a lot of money and gained a lot of problems, and it was subsequently bought by Jack King. Luckily I retained my job on the doors, and Dennis was reinstated. He had been sacked by Bob but was now back and the atmosphere in the club was vibrant.

There was usually a group of doormen at the entrance, but on one particular night I was working the door by myself. The club had a strict 'no jeans' rule but this lad came along wearing jeans. I told him he wasn't coming in wearing jeans and he told me to get Dennis. It was nothing to do with Dennis, it was my decision who would get in and I made that clear.

"You're just a doorman," he sneered. "Don't tell me what to do, just get Dennis."

"Look mate, I've knocked a dozen people back tonight and made them go home and change," I told him, "If I let you in they're all going to be on my ear, so do yourself a favour and change."

He didn't take the hint, instead he started asking how much my trousers cost, bragging that he was wearing Armani jeans and on and on he went. Not budging, I told him he wasn't coming in. I was on the steps, he was on the floor, both of us staring each other out. In a flash of movement, he whipped his mobile phone out and started to ring Dennis in an effort to overrule me. My anger exploded out of nowhere. Kicking the phone out of his hand, I grabbed hold of him and gave him a beating. The other doormen came running and pulled me off him, I don't know what would have gone off if they hadn't intervened. Other doormen took him into the club to patch him up. I had given him a terrible hiding and it was only Dennis stepping in that saved me from being nicked. To this day, it's something that I'm not proud of.

The Kings, Copford, with Sean Harris (RIP), my long term friend Roy Stewart, Joe and myself.

Dennis pulled me to one side. "Ronnie, you've been my head doorman for years, you're a fantastic doorman and you've got a great way with people," he told me. "But mate you're a loose cannon and I just can't have you here. I'll pay your wages for a month or so, you can have full money but I can't have you on the door."

It felt like another knife in my back. My father was dying, I had lost my sales job, yet another relationship had gone wrong and now I couldn't do the door work that I loved. They say one door closes, another one opens. In my case a whole row of doors had banged tightly shut. I couldn't blame anyone else for what had happened, in my heart of hearts I knew that this time the problem was me. But still, that old saying proved to be true and no matter how many doors had closed, one was about to open up. That was all it took.

By chance, I went out for a drink and stopped off at a pub called The Saling Oak. There behind the bar stood Bob Wheatley and as we chatted he revealed that he had plans to turn the place into a nightclub. He knew a lot of comedians such as Jimmy Jones, Frank Carson and Mike Reid, he had employed them all many times and intended to have cabarets there. In need of a good doorman, he asked me to take the job. Needless to say, I took Bob up on his offer and started working for him. Luckily it was very busy, which was timely, because around this time, my father passed away with cancer and there was the funeral to deal with. It was sad but emotionally I dealt with it pretty well, perhaps partly because I could throw myself into work. We also made the decision to employ other doormen at The Saling Oak because it was incredibly busy. One of them, Lenny Wilson, was the man who would later introduce me to the love of my life. Life was a whirl, work was busy and kept me on my toes. Still, in my mind I asked myself, Is this it? Is this going to be the sum total of my life? Even before I had thought to ask the question, spirit had been trying to answer me, trying to catch my attention, but up until that point I hadn't been open to listening. That was about to change because spirit was about to roll up its sleeves.

Chapter 22
Enter The Dragon

When spirit want you to listen, they will begin by gently whispering in your ear. The more you ignore their message, the louder they become. Looking back, the first incident where Susan and I had been in bed and saw the ghost of a young man before he disappeared into the wall, for most people would be enough to spark their interest in the spirit world. But for some reason I didn't feel the need to question what had happened. I just went about my business and got on with my life. Yet quietly spirit began putting mediums within my vicinity when I started working at The Saling Oak.

I worked on the door on my own for several months, and then needed to get another doorman with me as it was so busy. I called on a chap I knew, Dave Woodyard, who was married to a woman, who I knew from years back as Lou Nastri, a medium and tarot reader. Ten years prior she had told me that I had the ability to be a medium, but me being me, I totally ignored it all.

Unbeknown to me, I was soon to meet the person who would be instrumental in putting me on the right path. As I was at a low ebb, a good friend of mine suggested I visit a medium to find out where my life was going. Out of curiosity, I went to visit a medium, Lyn, at her home in Witham. She gave me some interesting information and told me that I had an incredibly strong psychic ability. It was true that I often had feelings and knowledge about situations. Even so, I had no plans to pursue any psychic ability that I might have. But Lyn had other plans. One of the first things she did was to take a ring off her finger that said 'Mum' and she asked me to hold it whilst she made a cup of tea.

"Should any little visions or thoughts pop into your mind that aren't your own, tell me about them," she instructed.

When she left the room, I put the ring on the side table.

"Pick that ring up, don't go all macho on me," she shouted from the other room.

Somewhat surprised, I picked the ring up and held it and as I did so, visions and information poured into my head. I passed all that I had seen and felt onto Lyn. She was astounded because she knew exactly who the information had come from.

"Are you sure you've never done any of this before?" she asked.

"Honestly," I replied, "No, I haven't."

Immediately I was told by Lyn that I was to join her circle. During my reading with her, she told me all about the situations around me, including Anita and said that she didn't think the relationship was fully over yet, but in the long run it would never work out for me.

Early in my circle days, when I had been in circle for just two or three months, there was that one event that was never planned, it came completely out of the blue. It let me know one million per cent that there is a fantastic power out there that lives on, there is definitely a spirit world and it can influence us. That event was when Lyn's son James came through me to speak to her. As I said at the start of this book, that event changed both Lyn and myself completely.

It enabled Lyn to move on, she cleaned James's room out, threw stuff away and was a completely changed woman. She still says to this day that it was the amazing proof she needed. In time, Lyn thought about the possibility for me to do physical mediumship and she contacted the Society for Physical Mediums. They asked her to describe what had happened and wondered if my heart had raced. She told them the exact opposite had happened and that my heart had beat had slowed down to the point that I thought I was about to pass out, or even die, and then it beat again. The society advised her that was correct because the heart needed to slow right down for the next spirit to enter in.

Of all the thousands and thousands of readings I have done, of all the messages I have given since, of all the things I have seen and experienced, and there have been many, this was the ultimate proof for myself, for Lyn, and also for Pat, who had sat watching the whole experience, that this is a very special life that lives on.

My early days of sitting in circle were fantastic, I had a great time. The way it worked was that during the evening we would sit in circle and Lyn would take us in for meditation. After the meditation, Lyn would go around the group asking each of us what we had seen. No disrespect to anyone else sitting in circle, as they were very nice people, but some would take journeys in canoes with Red Indians, fly with eagles, visit caves with bears, dance around totem poles, mix with angels and do all sorts of things.

One night Lyn asked me what I had seen. "Purple," I mumbled.

"What do you mean purple?" she questioned.

"Just purple," I felt quite disappointed, "I never had any of these big epic visions of Red Indians or the like, I just saw purple."

It was quite the same for Bill Brockwell, who was slightly more elaborate than me about what he had seen. Strangely, we were the only two out of that particular circle who ended up working for spirit as professional mediums. Lyn took a special interest in me, she predicted that in no time at all I would work in front of a thousand people, that I would be on television, would write books eventually and lots of other things. It all seemed a mile off to me at the time but it spurred me to really work at the meditation and other exercises that Lyn taught within the development circle.

Luckily, I have always had an extremely vivid and strong imagination. Not so much with my meditation but I have always done what I call 'mind walks.' I would relax with my eyes closed and imagine different scenarios. My favourite was imagining I was in the country, getting out of my car, walking across the pavement, across some grass through a gate, sometimes near the sea. In each case, I would make myself really feel and I mean really feel everything, such as the stone under my feet changing to grass. In my mind I would decide whether it was dry or brittle, soft and damp underfoot, sunny or overcast. In each case, I would stick to that and literally make myself feel the heat from the sun's rays or whatever. If I imagined myself in a hot air balloon, I would feel the weave of the basket, the heat of the flame, and I would take it on a journey wherever I wanted to go, land it and then get back in the car, all the time feeling the different sensations. If I made a mistake, say when I started the 'mind walk' the balloon was red but towards the end it was blue, I would start the mind walk from the beginning again until I could do it correctly all the way through.

Often this would lead into a meditation because I would land somewhere different from where I took off and there would be spirit people waiting to greet me. So that strength of imagination was useful. I often use it now when I am giving messages to people, I'm able to really feel what that personality was like, feel their gestures, how they spaced their words out, their feelings. I can literally 'feel' people and that really helped with my mediumship. More than meditation, these mind walks really helped me develop my abilities and I still do them now. I have had some wonderful experiences.

One incident I remember vividly was when one night I was stretched out in bed but still wide awake. In my mind, it was as if I had a television screen in front of me. I was watching the 'mind movie' in my head, yet I was there, present in the movie. It had to be another life that I saw, the most unbelievable thing. I was standing in the shadows of viaducts with a cobbled road in front of me. Roman soldiers were marching by, four abreast, and it was the incredible detail that surprised me. I could see the dust their feet were kicking up, broken toenails, stained feet and ankles, every face was individual to me. They were marching by, snapping their heads towards me as they passed me, raising their arms to salute me. I knew I was an officer, a centurion or something, and also that I was very harsh and strong. The strange thing was I had received a reading some time before with a wonderful old medium, Helenia Brieley who told me that I had actually been a Roman soldier in a previous life. She saw me wearing deep red, which meant I was a centurion.

Another thing she told me, "You were a bastard then and you can be a bastard now."

During another mind walk, I remember being in a field. I wore rags and had two children with me and there was a wooden plough and horses. The children climbed onto the horses and rode them bare-backed, as I shouted instructions to them. Again, I was wide awake watching this unfold before my eyes, like watching a film. It doesn't happen often but when it does it's amazing. It's part of the training and I do believe that behind the scenes, spirit have worked on me, as I feel great emotion, sense things strongly and can pick things up easily. I've never found the discipline necessary to train as a medium hard. Discipline is something that has always come easily to me, which is perhaps why it was easy for me to stick to weight training, and also why I found the regime of borstal fairly easy to deal with.

Lyn was an encouraging teacher, she would go to work at a factory and ask friends to drop bits of jewellery into an envelope for me to practice psychometry. Then she asked me what information I received from the piece of jewellery, subsequently checking the accuracy of the information with the owner. Lyn would also take me to watch other mediums work, we would sit at the back and she would tell me to watch, listen and learn how not to do it.

"What that medium's saying, everyone in this room could take that," she would tut.

For instance, the medium would say they had an old gentleman with them, drinking Guinness and feeling a bit short of breath. Lots of people could relate to it.

"That's how I don't want you to do it," Lyn would repeat as the various mediums performed.

The circle was progressing and I started giving messages. Guests would attend the group and Lyn would invite people in for readings and I would do odds and ends there. One night she suggested that I go along with her to a psychic supper in a spiritualist church in Clacton. On the drive there I remember she had terrible nerves. Even now I can understand her apprehension, because even after twenty years, I still get nervous, although not as bad as the early days.

"What we need is a nice table full of gentle old ladies," she smiled.

At the spiritualist church, there were lots of mediums there and around thirteen tables. The idea with psychic suppers is that each table has a number on a piece of paper turned upside down.

"Go on, be lucky," Lyn pushed me towards the tables, "Pick a number."

Naturally we picked number thirteen. It was a table solely of old ladies, about eight in total. I followed Lyn towards the medium room, she went in and I stayed outside. I was in awe of all the well-known mediums in attendance. Georgina Bloomfield was there along with Adrian Pasotti and other popular mediums. Lyn popped her head round the door and signalled me to go in.

"I can't go in there Lyn," I said nervously.

"Yes you can, you're a medium, come in here," she insisted.

The other mediums introduced themselves to me and I introduced myself as a fledgling medium. At a psychic supper everyone has fish and chips and then afterwards the medium goes round the table that they have picked and, holding each individual's hand, gives messages. We sat down together at the end of the table, had our fish and chips and then everything was cleared ready for the readings to begin. I sat there waiting for Lyn to start because she was a fantastic medium and I wanted to hear her give messages.

"C'mon then, what's happening?" Lyn asked me expectantly.

"What do you mean what's happening?" I asked.

"C'mon, do your thing," she clipped, "It's not my night, it's your night."

Flummoxed, I quickly exclaimed, "Me? I can't do this!"

Well I had a look from Lyn that told me not to argue, I bloody well was going to do it.

"Start with this lady here, hold her hand and tell her what's coming through," she commanded.

Nobody said no to Lyn, I did as I was told but she had her timing right, she knew I could do it and she had faith in me. During the course of the evening I managed to give each a message, many had lost husbands and I can honestly say I gave good messages. They were all so lovely and appreciative, and I received a big round of applause. Lyn patted me on the back and smiled. When the evening ended and we returned to the car I called her a sod for dropping me in it.

Lin laughingly replied, "Well, it was always going to be your night."

Of course, I didn't realise what she had planned, but that was Lyn. She was always someone who gave enough praise but not enough to make anyone big-headed. What a wonderful teacher.

It is much easier to 'think' than it is to do mediumship. I might pick up 'A' from spirit or 'B' from spirit and then sometimes the logical answer would seem to be 'C' so my mind would go for 'C' and it would be wrong. Lyn always knew when a trainee threw a guess in and would go absolutely ballistic.

On many a time she shouted at me "Do you realise you're dealing with people's most inner thoughts, their pains and anguishes. How dare you throw a guess in." She sometimes steamed in even more, "If I see you guess again, I don't care how good you're going to be or what you are, I'll throw you out this bloody circle and ban you for weeks."

Hence why she was called the Dragon Lady.

There was another time at the same church in Clacton, Lyn was up on the platform to do the introduction for my first official public demonstration. Nerves flipped my stomach over and over again like an acrobatic bartender shaking cocktails. There was a lady in the right-hand aisle to whom I had been introduced to as a fledgling. I gave this particular lady a message from her husband, detailing how he had passed and I thought I was doing okay. He suddenly said to her to go on long walks. Before I could say that I felt she was unable to do these long walks, and that he meant reliving them in her mind as she had enjoyed walking, she swung her artificial leg out into the aisle,

"What with this?" she mocked.

Talk about not knowing what to say, I felt it wouldn't be well received if I said that he meant reliving them and that she would think I was making it up. Of course, I wouldn't have been making it up but she was quite harsh. Before Lyn could say anything, this lovely old gentleman, Ted, who turned out to be a healer, stood up.

"Dear Lady, have you any idea how much guts it takes for these young people to get up and give messages?" he asked her., "He's given you very good proof, it looks like he may have got one thing wrong but I don't think he had finished talking and I'm sure he was going to say that you would take these walks in your mind and it's exactly that."

At this point Lyn stepped in to diffuse the situation, took the message over, and that was the end of that. Not quite the start I would have hoped for but at least it was experience for me.

Not much later, I was at Pitsea Spiritualist Church, a very nice church, where I actually ended up giving a message to Ted. I hadn't recognised him but he came over and mentioned that he had met me at Clacton when he had been there on holiday. His wife came through for him. He was a wonderful healer and I became very good friends with him. Another old lady was there from Canvey Island. Often on Sundays, I would drive over, pick them both up and take them to Finchingfield or another pretty village for something to eat and then drive them back. I remained good friends with Ted for many years until he passed to the other side.

I wasn't in the development circle long. Like the fledgling chick being pushed out the nest, Lyn told me that I should get out there and start doing some private readings. The only thing we disagreed on was that I found it very hard when sitting in front of someone. I felt embarrassed that for some reason it took longer to tune in, nowadays it's instant, back then it took longer. Tarot cards were one of the tools I used to develop my abilities. Lyn wasn't overly happy that I used them as she felt that I should set my sights higher than being a tarot reader and concentrate on being a medium. I found as the cards were being shuffled by the clients and then spread out by myself, the clients would concentrate on looking at the cards rather than me, which felt easier, then I would introduce the spirit world into the reading. This was how I worked for the first year or so of readings.

It's surprising how the spirit world works. At the time it was a case of 'who's Ronnie Buckingham, he's no big deal,' but I was making good inroads with my abilities. I remember my very first solo spiritual church appearance as a non-fledging was at Canvey Island. They were a very kind crowd and my initial foray into working alone went really well. It was on that day that I had my last ever conversation with Anita, right out of the blue. I had been back living at Andy Reid's place, the house in Wix had sold and I had the money in the bank. Luckily I had made, rather than lost, money on it. Anita rang me quite unexpectedly and asked where I was and if I was okay. I explained I was a bit nervous as I was about to do my first church service that day.

"Oh you're back to your silly little hobby," she quipped condescendingly.

I explained it wasn't a mere hobby but she continued along the same vein. To this day I have no idea why she felt the need to try to belittle me like that. In the end, I thought I'd had enough of listening and ended the conversation. I went along to the church, the mediumship went well and the chairlady told the others that the church had better book me for the following year. She also told them that if anyone wanted a private reading with me they had better book it soon, otherwise they wouldn't be able to get in to see me in time, as she felt I was going somewhere, which was encouraging. I had left the circle and embarked on working myself and her words were heartening.

Eventually I bought a little maisonette in Hatfield Peverel, as I had a big deposit I managed to get a mortgage on it with no problem. I started doing readings from there and I was also working at the Saling Oak. Just as Lyn had predicted, I was developing a reputation as a good medium. Bob cottoned onto this and within a short time I worked the doors some nights, but on other nights I did clairvoyant nights there. Bob was interviewed by Radio Essex, he was a fascinating chap, who had lived an interesting life. When the radio interviewer came in, he noticed an event board that detailed a night of clairvoyance coming up.

"It's really popular now, this clairvoyance thing, it seems to have taken off big time," he said to Bob.

I stood on the doors, my bulk all suited up with my bow tie on and Bob pointed me out to him, "This is the medium."

The interviewer's jaw dropped as his eyes took in my no-nonsense demeanor. He obviously thought this was a good story as he invited me along to be interviewed too. Bob had a lot of stories to tell, but the interviewer gave us equal airplay. After the interview was broadcast, a lot of people contacted me to congratulate and encourage me for coming across so well on the radio, which was great. To this day, I still think spirit was behind that initial meeting because after that radio interview my mediumship work soared.

Chapter 23
When You See A Rubber Duck

A steady stream of clients came for readings at my new maisonette. Having made up my mind that I wanted to become a very good medium, it was important to get honest feedback from the people I read for, so I bought a big book. Every day it would be open ready, with just the date and time of the reading, for the client to note their thoughts, which they would do in another room to enable them to have total privacy and the chance to be truly honest.

"Please, please write in there and make a comment about what you truly felt about the reading," I would ask, "If you felt it was terrible garbage and didn't give you proof, or whatever you felt, please put that and I promise you I won't look until you've gone and I swear I won't take it personally."

It was important to me that I did the right thing, not for myself but for my clients. I still have that book to this day for anyone that would care to look through it, and I can honestly say there's not one bad comment in there at all, not one. I did that for over a year, just to make sure, and it's lovely to look back on now, some of the messages are so touching I could cry. There were some wonderful readings in that flat, I have such great memories. I became great at sussing dialling codes as I had answer-phone messages and had to dial back to speak to people from all over the country.

One particular time comes to mind and I tell this story because it just shows how spirit can display such wit at times, as they listen in on us. This incident is backed up by a note in the comment book, so I can easily prove this story. For every story in this book there is paperwork or a testimony to back it up. I read so many books where mediums just write about 'Mr. A' and 'Mr. B' and this and that happened, but can they prove it? Whoever reads my book, if there's any doubt, I can produce proof.

Getting back to the story, there was a message on the answer-phone from a young lady, who wanted to book a reading for her husband and wanted to come along as a couple. For once, I didn't recognize the dialling code but it turned out to be Eastbourne. When returning their call, I commented that they were quite some distance away. They were insistent on travelling all that way to see me because they had heard a recording of a reading I had done. I always record readings, in fact I insist on it, as then my proof is there in the recording. A one o'clock appointment was arranged, after what would be a long journey. There was a pub just up the road, about fifty yards along, called the Duke of Wellington and they parked in the car-park there. They were a bit nervous about how the reading would go and who would come through. As they passed the time waiting until the allotted time, they recalled stories of those who had passed. Bang on time, they knocked on the door and I invited them in, took them into the little kitchen and as they had travelled such a distance, I offered them a cup of tea, which they gladly accepted. Right out of the blue, I saw in my mind two twin boys running around the couple. I connected to the boys whilst I made the tea. They told me they had been perfect in every way but had been stillborn, and that the lady had a photograph of them together, wearing little bonnets, in her handbag. I returned to the reading room. The couple were really nervous.

"It's okay, I know why you're here," I assured them.

"You do?" they were surprised.

"Yes, you lost stillborn twins."

The couple were astounded. The two little boys came through with amazing stuff. I knew the man had fallen out with his dad big time but had reconnected with his dad after the loss of the twins. Moving on, I described the couple's house perfectly, which was very unusual because you had to go from the road and up some steps onto the pavement, as the house was set back.

"Your dad's painting your house as we speak and he's using the colour yellow," I told them, all of which they confirmed was correct.

The twins described to me how they had passed and also other information, which they gave me in great detail.

"Why on earth have you been laughing about cacti?" I questioned, "What's all that about?"

With gasps of surprise and peals of laughter they told me that when they had been sitting in the pub car-park, they had been talking about a visit they had made to Las Vegas. On the drive there, the husband was bursting for a pee, so they stopped the car on the outskirts of the desert. There he was, hiding behind a cactus relieving himself, when his wife crept out of the car, camera in hand and called his name. Of course he turned round, with his bits in his hand. Spotting the camera, he jumped back and one of the spikes on the cactus went right into his backside. The couple had been giggling about this memory whilst they waited for the allotted time for their reading. The twins had been with the couple as they recollected this funny event. It was such a beautiful message and proof for them.

I have loads of letters from clients and keep each and every one of them. My first ever letter of thanks, which I will always treasure, was after a particular reading in the maisonette in Hatfield Peverel, A lady had lost her husband and the reading had brought her such peace and happiness that she wrote to thank me and tell me what a great medium she thought I was. Knowing that I had given her comfort and happiness meant the world to me and I was very grateful she had taken the time to write to me.

Nowadays I have a long waiting list of over a year but obviously at that time I was relatively new, having not long left circle, I was beginning to build up a reputation and clients would return regularly to see me. The lady who had written the letter contacted me to make sure I had received it and asked for another reading. I gave her a date two or three weeks away. Even before she was due for her appointment, I sat up in bed one night reading the letter. There was no clue in the letter as to how her husband had passed, whether he had suffered with a stroke or cancer, if he was young or old, or whether they had children. For some reason I started to panic and question my abilities. She had come for one reading that had gone really well, but what if on the second reading it was not as good? Would I undo all the good of the first reading? What if I said this time that he died of cancer but he had died of a heart attack? What if I say she has three children when before I had said she only had two? What if I said he was a big man but it turns out he was only a little man? What do I do, what do I do? The letter had stated that the reading had been marvellous proof and yet I was in bed, wide awake, worrying and not knowing what to do. Softly, a wave of peace washed over me and I could feel spirit. I didn't hear them shouting in my ear, just a voice, so full of calm and gentleness, asking me a question.

"Why are you worried? it asked, "Why? You'll pick it all up."

I had even been thinking that I would tell her that I had already given proof of how he had passed and other information, so it was best to move on from that with other information. I was worried in case I said the wrong thing. Yet, even with all the worry I felt, I couldn't cheat. I've never been able to fake mediumship in any way, shape or form. At the second reading, I went through it all again, how he had passed, in order to link with him again and then went on to tell her other information, such as his body would have to be moved because of vandalism around the grave. That information hadn't come out in the first reading but she confirmed it was absolutely correct. After the reading she sent a further wonderful letter of thanks. Following that reading, I've never worried about reading anyone twice.

This is very important and what I want all my readers to understand is this. You've read about my previous life, my prison convictions, my door work, my affairs, my marriage break-up and all that I was. So why me? I couldn't for the life of me understand why I had been given this gift. Readings were starting to pour in and the comments book that I have kept will prove that. Everyone finished their reading feeling blown away. One woman put in the book that she felt that I must have lived in her house for several years without her knowing, so factual was the information I gave her. There were many messages like that.

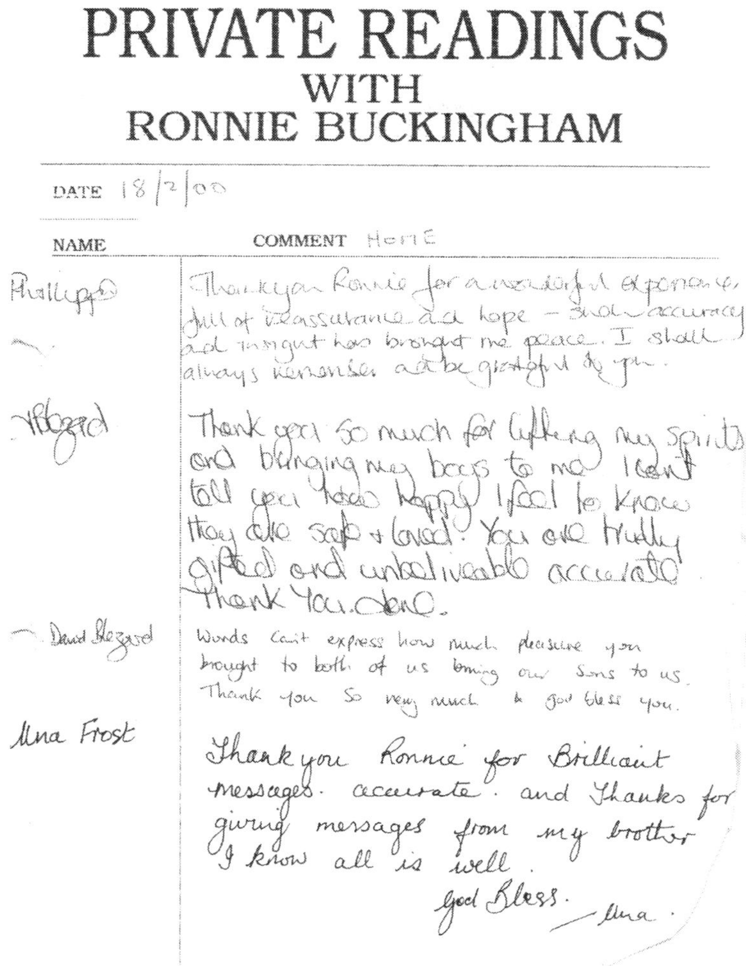
PRIVATE READINGS
WITH
RONNIE BUCKINGHAM

DATE 18/2/00

NAME	COMMENT Home
Phillipps	Thank you Ronnie for a wonderful experience, full of reassurance and hope – Your accuracy and thought has brought me peace. I shall always remember and be grateful to you.
Blezard	Thank you so much for lifting my spirits and bringing my boys to me. I can't tell you how happy I feel to know they are safe + loved. You are truly gifted and unbelievable accurate. Thank You. Jane.
David Blezard	Words can't express how much pleasure you brought to both of us bring our Sons to us. Thank you so very much & god bless you.
Una Frost	Thank you Ronnie for Brilliant messages. accurate. and Thanks for giving messages from my brother I know all is well. God Bless. – Una.

I couldn't work it out, why did I have this gift? Because in spite of it all, there was still the old Ronnie in there. There was a battle raging inside of me. Not between 'good and evil' because I was never evil, but between the old life and this new life. For instance, I felt that I couldn't really swear if I was a medium working for God and the higher realm of spirit, but swearing was part of my language, not in an extreme way but I did use the f-word regularly. It was how I was. To begin with, I still worked the doors and if someone played up or tried to put it on me they would get a right-hander or throttled. Bob Wheatley used to call me the Boston Strangler as a nickname because of my habit of grabbing people by the throat when they were out of order.

So, this new life, working with spirit, was quite difficult to cope with. In a lot of ways it caused me a lot of turmoil, as I questioned myself. Who am I? What am I? At the time I wasn't seeing anyone, I was spent as far as relationships went. To be honest, all I wanted to do was become a good medium, to be really good at something, on my own merits, for perhaps the first time in my life. That was my focus. I wanted to be the best at what I could be and I felt that mediumship was the way to do this. And yet, the battle between those conflicting parts of me, my old self and the person I was becoming, was just beginning.

My closest buddy, Andy Reid is an ex-paratrooper, the most down-to-earth, straight talking man I've ever met, not a crook at all, a wonderful carpenter and great friend. You'd have to know him to appreciate just how straight down the line he is, although he can be hilariously funny, the way he so blatantly speaks his mind. Whilst I was still living at the maisonette, Andy had gone through a bust-up with a girl he had been seeing. To take his mind off his troubles, we decided to go on holiday to Zante. I was working the doors, training hard and hence on the big side, seventeen stone of pure muscle and covered in tattoos. As Andy had his own gym, we used to train together there.

Off we went to Zante and met a couple of women there slightly older than us, nothing romantic in it, just people we were talking to and I gave one of them a message from spirit. The four of us decided to hire a car to go across to the other side of Zante to visit the beach where all the turtles are. The car was a tiny Fiat and after seeing the turtles, we drove along a cliff road. It was very mountainous in parts, and I wasn't used to driving on the wrong side of the road. We were enjoying the scenery, driving along with the windows open, happy as Larry, when without warning a big Peugeot taxi came screaming up behind us, lights flashing, making hand signals out of the window to indicate 'go faster, go faster.' I put my foot down but the car was very near to the edge, there were no rails and it was a sheer drop to the side. If our car went over we would be dead and the ladies in the back were really frightened. Andy warned me to ignore him and to slow down, so I slowed to a sensible pace. The driver behind hung back and then accelerated really fast behind us. I could see him in the mirror, he was stopping just short of hitting our car at the back end, continuing with his hand signals. At this point I became very wound up, Andy noticed and tried to calm me, telling me not to take any notice.

As we approached the town, I looked in the wing mirror and noticed the driver behind tried to pull out a couple of times but there were cars coming the other way. As we continued along, he positioned his car so that his front wing was in line with our back wing and he tried to overtake. A car was coming the other way, so he dropped back suddenly. All the while I kept my eye on him. There was a skip parked in the road and our door mirror hit the skip, the glass came out, shot over my shoulder and caught one of the ladies behind in the chest. She was unharmed but was really upset. At this point, I saw red.

"Just pull in and let the bastard go by," Andy tried to placate me, "Don't go getting angry with him."

As I pulled over unbelievably the driver pulled in behind me. Instantly I was primed for a fight. I slipped off the seatbelt, jumped out of the car and, within seconds, I had hold of him through his car window. My fingers gripped his throat tightly as I attempted to pull him out of the car. I was right in his face. Flailing desperately, he tried to close the windows to prevent me punching him. Shaking him like a rat, I called him everything under the sun. With that, some local men were out of their cars and they surrounded me. This made me totally lose the plot and I started on them like a man possessed.

Andy grabbed hold of me, "Get in the car, let's go or we'll get nicked here."

"No, fuck 'em, if they want it they'll get it," I was livid.

The taxi driver was holed up in his car, there was no way he was coming out. I called him a coward and a few other choice words, all the while Andy begged me to get back in our car. The two ladies couldn't believe it, I was an absolute lunatic. Eventually Andy stepped in and calmed me down. Everybody stood still as I returned to our car. I drove them back, after which we had a bite to eat and a drink. At around nine o'clock, I decided to head off to bed and soon after Andy came in. We were in single beds with around four feet of tiled floor between them. The lights were turned off and we both laid on our beds in silence.

All at once it came to me that if I had managed to get the taxi driver out of the car, I really would have given him a good hiding. If I had started punching him I wouldn't have stopped and might have done him some severe damage before turning on the other men. Like a bolt of lightning, it hit me that the space we had pulled into had been a taxi rank. The taxi driver hadn't stopped for a fight, he had simply pulled into the taxi rank. I hadn't thought to simply understand the Greek mentality and how his behaviour wouldn't be seen as out of the ordinary to other Greeks. I was mortified. As I laid on the bed, I inwardly began conversing with spirit.

"Look, I'm never going to be what you want me to be," I silently pleaded with tears rolling down my cheeks, "I can't do this, you've got to let me go."

I knew and spirit knew what I would've done to that man.

"How can I be what you want me to be? I can't," I repeated over and over. "You know and I know that I would've hurt him, alright he caused problems but look at me."

Shame ripped through me, I felt terrible and the tears continued to stream down my face. I wanted to sob but with Andy there I held on, continuing to speak to spirit, telling them I was just a doorman and could never be a medium. I begged spirit to just cut me loose. Suddenly there was a thunderous bump.

"What the fuck was that?" Andy sat bolt upright.

"I don't know," I had been shocked out of my tears.

He leaned over and flicked the light on. Right between our beds, almost as if someone had measured the exact distance, was a small, brand new, pencil eraser about two inches by one inch. The most down to earth man on the planet, Andy looked at the eraser, then looked at me.

"Where the fuck did that come from?" his eyes were as wide as saucers.

Truthfully there was nowhere it could have come from. The wardrobes were the other side of the room, the side tables were the other side of the bed, there was nothing at all between us, so there was nothing it could fall from. There was nobody else around apart from us two and besides, why would anyone take an eraser and throw it. Curious, I leaned over and picked up the eraser and an incredibly strong charge went through my body, like an electric shock. It's something I'll never forget. Now I'm not claiming it was Jesus or anything like that, but the most beautiful , calming voice spoke to me.

"It doesn't matter, rub it out, you start again," I listened intently as the words rang in my ears. "Just rub it out, start again, it really, really doesn't matter."

A sense of peace and wellbeing enveloped me, such as I had never felt before. In that moment I realized that as long as we're honest, we can do what we do. We can swear, we can like sex, okay it is wrong to beat people up of course, but basically we can simply be who we are. Spirit will always love and support us.

Strangely enough, since that fracas with the taxi driver, I've never been involved in another fight, not on the doors, not ever, and now it is some twenty years later. It was absolutely the last fight I ever had. I totally understood the meaning of the eraser because if I had only heard the voice I might have thought it was my subconscious. Have you ever had that experience where you have done something wrong, yet you always come up with an excuse for doing it? People have affairs but think to themselves 'Oh I bet he's done it to me and gone and slept with someone else, what's the harm in it?' or 'He pushed his luck as well so I'll give him a slap because he's asked for it.' People are always making excuses for themselves.

The eraser cut out the excuses. I put the eraser in the drawer and the next evening it was gone. Andy had never been one to believe in the spirit world, yet he didn't have an answer to explain what had happened. He couldn't get his head around it and was completely flummoxed. It dawned on him that there must be something going on but still he couldn't accept it. He knew I'd never lie to him because no matter what I've always told him the truth. If mediumship was just a con, a money making idea, I could've said to him 'It's all bollocks mate but I could earn a few quid at this,' and Andy would never have grassed me up. He might not have liked it because he's a very straight man, but he would never have let on. But he knew there was nothing in the vicinity of that space between the two beds that the eraser could possibly have fallen from. That incident was a turning point for me. It made me realise that I could be who I was and yet still be a good medium.

Chapter 24
Seeking Sanctuary

In my early days performing at spiritualist churches and still relatively unknown, I had a very fortuitous meeting. I was invited to Ann Walmsley's open day, even then she was an old lady and has since passed over, God bless her. She had her own sanctuary in White Horse Lane in Halstead, Essex, and had been on the circuit for a long time. Without a doubt, Ann was the most humourous, funny, Yorkshire born and bred lass, who although advanced in years when I met her, was such a character. A rather large lady with platinum blonde hair, she was both an appealing and straight talking individual. In mediumistic circles Ann was very well known. The open day was always the first Saturday in August at The Sanctuary, which was built on the side of Ann's house. It could hold around forty people and there would be meditation nights, clairvoyance nights, Sunday services and it was a proper little spiritualist church set in about a third of an acre of garden. In the summer there would be tarot readers, mediums and healers, and Ann would hold court in the middle of it, with demonstrations of mediumship and clairvoyance in the morning and evening by different people. Wearing short sleeves with my tattoos showing, I entered the garden. Ann was sitting in the corner under a shade, she never moved about a lot. Ann asked who I was and I told her I was a medium.

"Well, I've never heard of you," she huffed.

"I've only been doing it a little while," I replied, "But actually I wondered if I could work in your sanctuary as I'm looking for work."

After a quick glance up and down, she asked me how much experience I had. I told her I had performed one show, sat in circle and had done a few readings. Curious, Ann asked how long I had sat in circle and I answered five months.

"Where else did you sit in circle?" she quizzed me.

"I've only done the five months," I answered.

"Well, why did you leave circle?" Ann was intrigued.

I mentioned that Lyn had told me to go out on my own. Ann asked me for a card, which I didn't have, instead I wrote my number on a piece of paper. We continued with a few pleasantries and then I made my way home.

"What a big headed sod asking to perform here," Ann grumbled as soon as I was out of earshot. "He's only done five bloody months in circle."

In time, Ann and I became such wonderful friends, but bearing in mind that people sit in circle for five to ten years, I can understand why she thought that. A fortnight later I was sitting around at home without a great deal to do when I received a call. Apparently Ann had booked a medium from Yorkshire, Les Driver, to work at the sanctuary that Saturday, unfortunately he had broken down on the motorway. He phoned her to let her know there was no way he would reach her in time and that he was sorry to let her down. This put Ann in a bit of a pickle as she only had ninety minutes before the evening to find a replacement. As she knew everyone attending that evening, she didn't want to do the service herself. All the local mediums were either out or working, nobody was available at such short notice. Whilst going through the various numbers, Ann came across mine. Reluctantly she asked me if I was free, which I was.

"Do you really think you can work in my sanctuary?" she sounded doubtful.

"Yes, I believe I can," I replied, "I'm willing to have a go."

At that point she put me in my place. "No matter how big you are, if you come here and make me look stupid I'll have your guts for garters."

That's how she was, no beating around the bush. Small wonder I turned up feeling sick with nerves, it was early days for me. The evening started with Ann giving a short talk before introducing me to the crowd. Spirit came through for me and thankfully the evening went exceptionally well.

"My God, what a gift you've got!" Ann exclaimed. "You're the next Gordon Higginson, I've got to have you here again."

Our friendship and mutual respect was cemented and within a few weeks, she asked me to work at The Sanctuary again.

There is another medium and healer, Steve Barry, who at the time was starting his own psychic centre, called Cawston College, which was in Aylsham in Norfolk. He converted a huge old school with the help of his friends into a spiritual centre and hotel, where you could stay and take courses. It was a very old Victorian type place, incredibly beautiful and set in nearly a hundred and thirty acres. They were looking for someone to be the opening clairvoyant, the first person to work there. Now bear in mind I had only been working for spirit then for a matter of months, Ann had contacted Steve, unbeknown to me, and asked him to come down and be in the audience when I did her clairvoyant night.

Afterwards, Steve came up to me, "You're definitely something else, I've never seen anyone so surrounded by spirits."

He asked if I would be interested in being the first medium to work the new centre when it was ready, which was a few months off at that point. Feeling incredibly honoured by his request, I agreed. It turned out there were a few mediums vying for the chance to be the first to appear, it was a great privilege. A few months later I was there demonstrating mediumship in front of a crowd of sixty people in a Portakabin. My next appearance there in the main hall was in front of hundreds of people.

I performed on platform with a chap called Brian Wells, a very short man who was a brilliant psychic artist. We immediately gelled and worked well together. I remember there was a little girl who came through and I was able to give wonderful proof. She had stepped out from behind an ice cream van in London and had been killed. I was able to give the door number of the house the family lived in. All the while, Brian sketched a wonderful image of a girl. At the end of the demonstration, the family came up to see us, they had a photograph of the little girl with them. The sketch that Brian had drawn was absolutely the image of this girl, it blew me away as well as the family.

The Opening Day of Cawston waiting to go on with Brian Wells and Steve Barry

Ann would often visit Cawston to teach and I would accompany her to do demonstrations. Steve always billed it as how mediumship should be. The centre had a booklet into which people would write what they thought of the medium. One particular time I was working well and had a link with a lady and her great aunt came through, who she was very fond of.

"Oh you've got a pair of her Dutch clogs," I told her.

"No, I haven't," she countered.

Undeterred, I smiled to myself, as I knew where I was going with that but went on with other messages for her. I came back to the clogs.

"Ronnie, there are no clogs," she came back at me.

This went on and on and other messages came through but still I returned to the subject.

"Of course, there's the wooden clogs you've got," I continued.

It caused a ripple through the crowd when she replied yet again "I've not got any clogs."

"Your aunt is telling me that you're a collector of little miniature dolls," I thought I would let her know that what I was getting was true. "You've got dolls from all other the world."

She confirmed this was absolutely correct.

"This aunt is also telling me that she went on a trip to Holland," I smiled as I told her.

Suddenly it dawned on this woman exactly what I was going to say.

"Your aunt says she sent you back a little Dutch doll in national costume," I told her.

With a wry smile she confirmed this was true.

"And on the feet of that doll are….?" I raised my eyebrows quizzically.

"Yes, very good Ronnie, there's a pair of clogs," she rolled her eyes upwards as the crowd chuckled.

Steve's centre only lasted two or three years as it was such an expensive place to run but it opened a lot of doors for me. Many visitors from abroad, especially Swiss people, came to watch demonstrations, and this lead to invites to perform in Switzerland and other countries to work as a medium. The world was opening up for me in more ways than one.

As I said, Ann Walmsley and myself became great friends and had such a laugh together, she was a complete riot. Everyone loved Ann, she had the most wicked sense of humour, especially for an older lady. The first time we went to Worthing Spiritualist Church together, we couldn't find it and were driving around in circles looking for it. It was a lovely summer's evening and we saw a lady digging her front garden, I pulled over, wound the window down and called over to the lady, asking her if she knew the way to the spiritualist church. This lady was probably in her late forties or early fifties, she wore a vest and had big boobs, a very nice looking woman. As the woman walked towards the car, Ann started to laugh. The lady leaned into the window and literally positioned herself so that my chin was centre on to her boobs as she gave me the directions. There was no way that I could move my head otherwise I'd be banging my nose on them. I could feel Ann chuckling next to me. Anyway, the lady pointed us in the right direction, I carefully retrieved my head, and she walked back towards her garden, turning round to make eyes at me.

As we drove off Ann asked "Which way do we have to go?"

"I don't have a bloody clue!" I spluttered laughing like a hyena.

In the end we found somebody else to ask but Ann didn't stop laughing until we arrived at the spiritualist church. She repeated that story on many occasions. As I said, Ann was a great inspiration to me and pushed me forward all over the place, we shared some great experiences.

Very early on in my career, Ann told me she wanted us to go to Stansted Hall for an open day. Anyone that reads this book and remembers Ann will laugh about this. She was a big lady with a ferocious appetite. Off we went to Stansted Hall and the first thing Ann wanted was breakfast and I treated her to a full English breakfast and tea. She went to look at the day's events and decided what we would see. We sat through a clairvoyant demonstration and as we came out Ann asked if I fancied a cup of tea and a bun, which we had. Then we sat through another demonstration and had lunch. Coincidentally, whilst I was there Ann saw that Mary Duffy was there, a lovely medium, who I believe used to work with Doris Stokes.

"Right, don't let her see you with me," Ann instructed, "But have a reading with her."

As I knocked on the door the most beautiful voice told me to enter. I walked through the door to be met by this lovely old lady, a well respected medium.

Immediately, she looked up and said, "My God, come and sit down young man, what a gift you've got, the energy and love surrounding you is amazing."

She went on to tell me that I would work all over Europe. "You're a medium, you'll never be a fortune teller, you'll be asked to tell fortunes, that's par for the course," she declared, "But you're going to prove life after death and you're going to make so many people happy. You're going to mend hearts and minds That's all you're going to be, a clairvoyant, you won't go into trance and this and that, you'll be giving messages and readings and you'll be wonderful."

I was gobsmacked by her comments and didn't quite know what to say. Was she buttering me up or did she really mean it?

"My time is not long," she confided, "I just wish I could be here to see your progress, because you'll be something else."

In my work as a medium I have worked in many countries such as Switzerland, Denmark, Germany, Cyprus, Spain and Gibraltar, where I have a big following, thus she was right. Getting back to Ann, we went to see another demonstration and then it was tea time. What can I say? We had tea as well. After watching the final demonstration, we made our way back from Stansted, passing through Dunmow. As we went down the high street Ann asked me to pull over.

Concerned I asked, "What's the matter Ann?"

"They do the most beautiful fish and chips here," she chirped.

Needless to say, we stopped and had fish and chips. Well I had to eat it with her, I couldn't let her eat on her own. I couldn't stop laughing as I was blown away at how much she could eat, polishing off this huge portion of fish and chips, after all those other meals. There are so many happy memories of Ann that I treasure.

At Cawston College with Ann Walmsley

One time she received money via an insurance or investment payout and decided to have the windows changed in the house to which The Sanctuary was attached. She had several children, all lovely people, who told her not to do the windows but spend the money on a holiday instead. Ann thought about it and said to them that she had always wanted to do a cruise down the Seine and all through northern France.

"But there's not enough money to take all of you," she said, "I can't just take one or two of you, that's not fair."

All the children suggested that she take me with her and hence she asked me to go, I agreed and we had a wonderful time. We spent a week on the boat but obviously in separate cabins, and she had everyone on the boat in fits of giggles. Ann would come down the stairs via the stairlift giving everyone a queenly regal wave. Her jokes and sense of humour were beyond infectious. The trip was amazing, we stopped at lots of different places, such as Honfleur, and I fell in love with France. That trip was instrumental in my decision to move to France sometime later.

Ann passed over when she was well into her eighties. Her family asked myself and Steve Barry (Ann used to call us 'her boys' because she had trained both of us for mediumship) to be pall-bearers at her funeral. It was a lovely service, but also very funny with the words she left behind for us to hear. Her son John made the greatest speech ever about his mum, and of course her appetite came into that as well and her love of eggs. Bless her heart, she was cremated and, along with her sons, Steve and I carried the coffin. The song that the coffin went away to was one of my favourites, Matt Monroe's 'Softly As I Leave You.' There wasn't a single dry eye in the house. What a well loved, respected and sadly missed old soul.

Chapter 25
The Godfather

I still lived in the maisonette in Hatfield Peverel and worked the doors at the Saling Oak for Bob Wheatley. A friend from way back, who I had worked doors before with, Lenny Wilson, contacted me and we met up. I told him what had happened in my life and mentioned I was completely on my own and had not had a girlfriend for quite a while, which was unusual for me. To be honest, I was so wrapped up in my mediumship and enthralled by what I found I could do with this wonderful gift, that I wasn't really worried about seeing anyone, for perhaps the first time in my life.

Lenny told me about a lovely girl that he knew, who was widowed and had been on her own for five or six years, and that she had a little daughter of around five years old. He said that her husband had been a good friend of his and that he was a lovely chap, but since he died this girl just didn't go out. Wherever he and his wife went, Nicky would go along too, but basically she was on her own. Lenny said there was an event coming up soon and he wondered if I would tag along and be her date for the night. I really wasn't keen on the idea but agreed anyway. Evidently, Lenny had told Nicky about me. She came up to the Saling Oak with a crowd, including Lenny's wife Jan, some other friends and her parents. Yes, I thought she was an attractive girl, about eleven years younger than me, but not my sort really to be honest. We spoke and I found her to be a very intelligent, well turned out girl. Afterwards Lenny quietly asked me what I thought of Nicky and I told him I thought she was a nice girl.

"Ron, she's lovely," he said. "She's a fantastic cook and one of the nicest people I know."

He had known her for years because he and his wife were great friends with her parents. A Chinese meal was arranged for the group of friends and I agreed to go. Nicky and I clicked and we started seeing each other. Often she would arrive at the maisonette in a pair of overalls, ready to help me strip wallpaper, paint and suchlike. In turn, she would ask me over for a meal. She was a lovely girl but I'm not going to lie and say it was fireworks, love at first sight or a great attraction on my part because it wasn't, but there was something refreshing about this girl. I admired the fact that she had been on her own for five or so years and not been out with anyone. Amy, her daughter, was a sweet kid and Nicky was a very good mother to her. I started to go to her house and found out for myself about her marvellous cooking. I think things were tight for her, having been on her own. A very clever girl, with a quick mind, she used to work in the banks and dealing rooms in London. After a while we talked about moving in together. The idea suited me fine, I had someone that I knew I could trust completely, not like other girls I had met. Nicky wasn't a nightclub person, she was steady and loving. I sold the maisonette and moved into Vernon Way with Nicky.

Life was running along nicely. I turned the spare bedroom into a reading room and Nicky had a part-time job. I hadn't been looking for a great romance and I wasn't sure where this was going to go. It wasn't a convenience or anything like that, I really liked Nicky. She knew I had always wanted a dog and encouraged me to get one. Bandit was amazing, it was great having a dog again and being able to walk him every day on the nearby fields. He was something else that dog, the little sod.

One day, I had a one o'clock appointment booked in, which was a no show. There was no phone call to cancel or anything. I felt peed off and was wondering to myself why people couldn't just pick up the phone. Even now that sometimes happens, there's a tendency for people to not show up, no call, no excuse, nothing. Unexpectedly the phone rang and I could tell by the voice on the other end of the line that it was someone youngish and from London due to the Cockney accent. It was a young lady, Nicky Russell, who pleaded with me for a reading as soon as possible. Even at that time I had a waiting list of a few months, I was really busy. However, the pain and the energy that came down that phone line was enough for me to offer to read her straightaway.

"We're in London but can be with you in a couple of hours. Please see us," she implored.

"No, I'll read you now," I answered.

"What do you mean by that?" she questioned, "How can you do that?"

"How do I know that you've lost a son in a tragic accident?" I asked, "It involved a car and he's telling me he was run over."

Nicky was astounded as I continued, "I know that your mother is standing very near you and is holding the photograph of the little boy we're talking about, and I feel his name could be Jack."

His name was actually Jake. Nicky couldn't believe it but I could see it so vividly, it was a terrible thing to have happened.

"He's showing me that he was run over by boys in a stolen car," I continued, "I feel it was a silver estate, possibly a Volvo. He's showing me that one boy was black and two were white and they should never have gone down the turning they went into."

I could hear her saying to her mum, "Mum he's telling me all about Jake, he knows all about Jake, how can he know?"

Nicky asked if I could actually see Jake. I asked her did she mean what he had been dressed in, to which she said that was exactly what she meant.

"He was buried in a West Ham strip," I went on, "And he's telling me that the day he died he met the West Ham team and Frank Lampard."

It was true, he had in fact been to the West Ham ground on the day of his passing and had met Frank Lampard. Jake gave his mum such incredible detail. At the end of the reading, which was on a Friday, I arranged a time to see Nicky and her mum on the following Monday, I just had to fit them in. As I put the phone down, I started to cry and simply couldn't stop. The visions of this lovely little boy being trapped under the car were so upsetting. It turned out that the police had been chasing these lads in the stolen car. Jake had been to the West Ham club, met Frank Lampard and the team, and had a ball and some photographs that had been autographed. When he returned home he asked his mum if he could go round to his cousin. Nicky took him round so that he could show off his ball to the kids indoors. He pleaded to go outside to play but he had never been allowed to go outside there to play and she told him no. It was pointed out to her that it was a cul-de-sac and that no traffic went down there, so she relented and let him go with strict instructions he was to stay on the pavement. Jake was on that pavement when the car swung into the turning, up onto the pavement, crushing Jake. It was terrible, much as I tried to stem the tears, they continued. The pain was awful, I couldn't believe the emotions and the hurt I had felt coming through the telephone wire and the visions I had seen of this little boy's end.

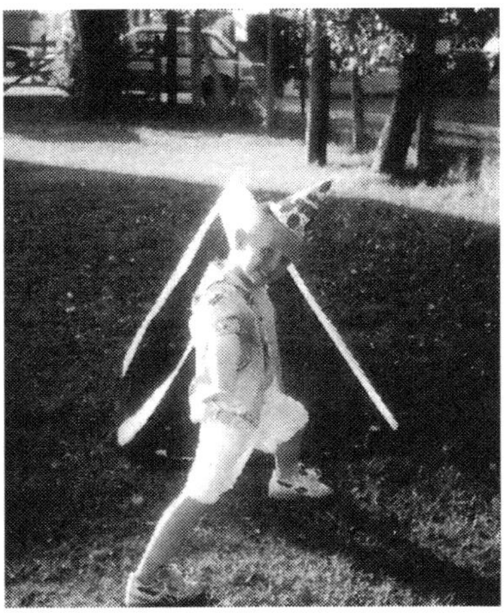

Jake Russell

It became so bad that on the Saturday I went to the emergency dentist in Colchester to get some antibiotics because my gums were raw, by Sunday I had settled down. Nicky and her mum Kath turned up on Monday. Now I have to point out that Kath would be considered the scourge of mediums. She had been known to stand up publicly in a hall in front of mediums and belt out that they were no more a medium than she was, that they were con artists and that they should get out and stay away, they were useless. That was how Kath was, but she came along with her daughter, already intrigued by what I had picked up over the phone. During the reading, I gave them names, conditions, where Nicky had her tattoo. all sorts of information came through, which blew them both away. Kath actually wrote a beautiful letter to the Psychic News, which I still have, saying that if ever there was a real link between the spirit world and life here, then I was it.

This lovely family then went on to name a star after me and register it with the Star Registry, which I believe is in Switzerland. They asked me to go down to see them nearer Christmas time and they presented the registration document to me, which I still have to this day. So, there is a star out there somewhere called 'Our dear friend Ronnie Buckingham.'

Nicky came to see me again and I told her that she was pregnant. She told me no, absolutely no way, God had taken her only child and he would never get the chance to hurt her again.

"Nicky, it's out of your hands, you're going to have another little boy,"

I told her, “He’ll be heavier than Jake by a pound or so, he’ll be darker and he’ll be born on the 31st January.”

She wasn’t having any of it but lo and behold, a while later she rang me to tell me I was right, she was pregnant and that the date I had given her was about right. As it turned out, I was wrong by four minutes. Little Callan Russell was born on 1st February. They asked me to be his godfather, which I readily agreed to and I’m very proud to be his godfather. This was a while back and Jake would be a young man now. Whenever I do shows in the London and Romford area, Nicky will get up and do an introduction for me and tell people how I saved their lives and brought this knowledge of God and an afterlife to them and that their son, Shaky Jake, is still there around them.

Chapter 26
Carry On Up The Hospital

Thanks to Ann Walmsley and a network of other people, I worked many churches in Suffolk, such as Sudbury with the lovely Clara Henderson, Ipswich, and also Norfolk working in Great Yarmouth, and other lovely churches in Kent, Essex, Cambridgeshire and London. I worked a lot of churches and was becoming more well-known and developing my reputation. The Kilroy television programme asked Woodford Spiritualist Church if they knew of a healer and the church put my name forward. I took some people with me, such as Terry Pottinger and Anne Harding. Terry is still alive and kicking, doing well and earlier this year actually put in fitted wardrobes for me. Terry had developed cancer that had subsequently disappeared under healing. Now in his seventies, he's in good health and living in Felixstowe. Anne had chronic emphysema, three experts had told her she would never be able to do this or that. Terry wasn't really given the chance to speak during the Kilroy show, Steve Barry was given the opportunity to say a little bit, but for some reason Kilroy focussed mainly on me.

Bless her, I had been giving Anne healing for three months for the emphysema. Previously she had been unable to walk upstairs and could barely put one foot in front of the other, she was out of breath all the time. It's some time since I gave Anne healing, maybe sixteen or seventeen years, but she's still with us and comes to see me from time to time. Anne told me of the story of the last healing I had given her, she felt wonderful, left my house on wings and arrived home. Later that evening, she began to feel extremely ill and was violently sick, breaking out in a severe sweat and thought she was dying. Taking a bucket with her, she went up to bed, in case she was sick again. On the bed, she began shaking and shivering. Hello, she thought, this is it, my time's up. She began to retch and actually filled the bottom of the bucket with about an inch of black tar, after which she fell into a very deep sleep and woke up feeling she could actually breathe easily for the first time in a long time. Anne came along with her medical documents and walked from the hospitality lounge of the television set along to the studio, which was several hundred yards. She never had to use her inhaler and actually had a lovely rosy glow on her skin and looked well.

Of course there were the knockers there, who questioned if it was simply a placebo effect and all that business. I pointed out that even if it was the placebo effect, if it cures people then healing does its job. Someone jumped up and said that emphysema is curable, to which Anne replied she had three letters from three different experts saying that it wasn't and that nothing could be done for her. She also told them I had never charged her for healing, or ever told her to stop using the inhalers or not go to the doctors. When it was my turn to speak again, I advised that spiritual healing can work with formal medicine as a back-up. The healing was a success and Anne is still here, yes she has to use the inhaler from time to time but it's a massive improvement on her condition before receiving healing.

In the early 2000s, a family from London contacted me. The mother, another Ann, was a tiny little lady with terminal cancer of the esophagus, one of the worst places to have it. Ann's dream was to do a cruise and her husband had booked one for the August. It was March when Ann visited me. The doctors had said that Ann wouldn't see May. Her family said they knew it was a big ask but could they bring her along for healing, of course I said yes. She came along, very skeptical, this tiny, incredibly brave lady. I tuned in first of all and gave her some messages from her loved ones on the other side, just to prove to her there was a spirit world and they made her no promises but I set to work. Ann really took to the healing. The months passed by and Ann managed to go on the cruise. She put on several pounds in weight before the cruise and had a wonderful time, she even danced with her husband on board.

In the meantime, I suffered a hernia in the stomach through weight training, I had split the lining of my stomach from the naval down at least seven inches, and had to wait until late August for an operation. Finally I went in for what was supposed to be a two day stay and from the off everything went wrong. To begin with the anesthetist couldn't get the epidural into my back. Apparently I was far too muscular and after four attempts, which were really painful, they decided to knock me out with something else and then insert the epidural afterwards. After the operation I woke up in terrible pain, the epidural had fallen out. The staff rushed around to administer some morphine to me. Nicky was there in the hospital with me and, as she sat by the bed, she noticed I had a catheter fitted and that there was no urine in the catheter, which there should have been after all this time. Quickly she alerted the nurses, who agreed that wasn't right. As they removed the catheter, blood began to pour out of me. A young doctor who had fitted the catheter had gone through my urethra and I began hemorrhaging. The blood was gushing out and I began to drift in and out of consciousness, whilst the nurses continually changed blood packs and tried to stop the bleeding. Even in my dazed state, I could sense the panic surrounding me. To top it all, I had been given the wrong type of blood, which sent me into shock.

A few days later, I had recovered somewhat, but was still very weak. Being continually woken up during the night for blood samples and for other procedures took its toll. An infection then began in my privates and everything swelled to a ridiculous size. I called the nurse over to let her know I was having problems and asked her to call for a doctor, but no doctor arrived. Again I asked for a doctor and again no doctor arrived. By the next day my testicles resembled a balloon and my privates were all out of shape. Despite all of this, my sense of humour was still there. When the doctor finally came I asked him if he could take away the pain but leave the swelling. The infection was so bad it really affected me and the medication prescribed for me made me feel very strange and delusional. I remember I couldn't just sleep on the bed, I had to keep my legs wide apart and ended up sitting for a couple of nights on a commode with my privates hanging down in the pan, it was that bad.

From there, things went from bad to worse and I couldn't pass urine at all. The medical staff decided they would have to give me a suprapubic catheter, which is a hollow flexible tube inserted into the bladder through a cut in the stomach, a few inches below the navel. My stomach was badly extended, I was again drifting in and out of consciousness, barely lucid and felt awful. It was a terrible experience and I thought to myself 'Why has spirit let me go through this? What have I done that is so wrong?' It wasn't anything I had done wrong, it was just that mediums, like everyone else, sometimes have to go through these things. Anyway, I remember coming to and the doctor telling me he would make a little incision and he wanted me to cough whilst he punched the catheter through the stomach area. I coughed and bang, the catheter was in. The urine shot out of this catheter like a hosepipe, over his shoulder and drowned his little assistant, who was covered in it. Shaking with laughter, even though I wasn't completely with it, I had seen it and it struck a funny chord. The doctor and nurses laughed too.

My stay in hospital was twelve days in total. Nicky was there morning, noon and night, she didn't leave my side. This made her special to me, she didn't stop fretting and worrying and I thought that was a lovely sign. The day I arrived home was actually the day of the 9-11 tragedy. Watching the television whilst those dreadful events unfolded, I thought at first it was a movie. Barely able to walk, I was in a wheelchair for quite a long time. During my stay in hospital, I lost so much weight and strength and knew I had been close to death. This was later confirmed to me when one of the nurses came for a reading some time later. She told me off the record that the staff at the hospital had panicked terribly because they thought they were going to lose me at one point. Everything that could go wrong went wrong. Yet here I am today.

For three months I did nothing about the experiences I had gone through in hospital, I simply spent the time recuperating. After that time, I wrote to the hospital asking for some compensation for the time I had off and the pain. I also put in the letter that I didn't want anyone to get into trouble, nobody had done it on purpose but it had been handled badly and I ended up being three months out of work and in that time would have probably earned a reasonable sum. Mr. Kennedy was the solicitor who contacted me to ask if I wanted representation. I declined because, as I told him, I was telling the truth, it wasn't my intention for anyone to get into trouble but that small amount was what I was claiming for. Test after test was asked for, I was sent from one hospital to another, and eventually the test results came back with all the notes. They confirmed I was telling the truth. During this time, I had to go back into hospital for another operation. Scar tissue had formed in the urethra, it had closed up and I was unable to pass urine and I had to have that cut out. In total, that procedure had to be repeated three times. Looking back, I could have claimed for probably two hundred thousand pounds. I received a phone call from Mr. Kennedy. He told me I was the most honest, decent man he had ever dealt with, I had not tried to scam them, or claim for big money. Then he advised me that he was putting a cheque in the post to me for thirty thousand pounds. Querying this, I told him I had only expected a much smaller amount but no, he confirmed a cheque for thirty thousand pounds was being sent to me. He also said that if it wasn't enough, and by his tone it appeared he didn't think it was, then it was highly likely I could expect a lot more. Even so, I told him I had only asked for a small amount of compensation and thirty thousand pounds was more than sufficient.

What really broke my heart was that from the time I was in hospital and for quite a while after, I didn't have the energy to give Ann healing and sadly she passed. She went downhill incredibly rapidly. I was really upset about it because if only I could have kept up with the healing for her because she had been improving, it might have helped. Nicky, wise as ever, explained to me that I wasn't God and that I had done the best I could and had helped to extend her life so that she had her dream of a cruise with her husband. Ann's family were wonderful and came down to see me, they shook my hand and gave me hugs and kisses, thanking me. They let me know that she had died in peace, knowing there was an afterlife and having lived her dream of going on a cruise.

I don't do healing anymore and that's because during the healing sessions, I never had the illnesses but would take on the symptoms. An older gentleman that I met, Albert Lamb, who has since passed over, but a wonderful man, very knowledgeable about spirit, told me that because I wanted to help people so much and cure people if possible, I was actually using my own life force when giving healing, rather than just letting spirit work through me. It made sense for me to stick to being a clairvoyant, which is what I am today.

Chapter 27
The Show Must Go On

Working for spirit as a medium isn't always easy, especially when I'm feeling under the weather. But as they say, the show must go on and often the power of spirit will intervene at such times. Many years ago I was booked in to drive a hundred miles to Yarmouth to serve the spiritualist church there. That morning I woke up feeling absolutely terrible, sweating profusely, I felt sick and had trouble keeping anything down. I was so ill but how could I cancel at the last second when so many people were hoping for a message? Feeling really rough I set off for Yarmouth but had to stop the car several times on the way to be ill but eventually made my way there, went in and had a glass of water. All of a sudden the symptoms disappeared. I went on stage and it was a wonderful service and great mediumship, with a fantastic ovation at the end with people coming to thank me. I felt wonderful. Half hour into the journey home, all of the sickness and symptoms came back. That's how spirit can step in and that's happened to me many times, especially when I've had colds.

Another time, I had been in hospital for another operation but things had not gone according to plan. The afternoon I came out of hospital I had an evening show booked at the Headgate Theatre in Colchester, which had sold out. What was I to do? I had to see the show through, there was no way I wanted to let everyone down. It would have caused the theatre great stress and disappoint those who had booked. Nevertheless, I was heavily strapped up, bandaged and in agony. The lady who organizes these shows for me had a word with the crowd beforehand. She let them know I had just come out of hospital that morning after a big operation and was in pain. A chair was put on the stage for me and I worked sitting down. Needless to say, the pain disappeared completely. The show was wonderful with messages coming one after the other and I had lovely feedback from the crowd. I remember someone put on Facebook that it was dedication to spiritualism to come out of hospital that day and go on stage, which was kind of them, but really it's the dedication of spirit, who work to bring healing to us, that saved the day.

Although mediums work with spirit, we're human too and feel pain and heartache just as much as anybody else. Yet spirit works with us to get us through the day in order to help others. One such example involved my dog Bandit, who I absolutely adored, and who entered my life when he was a puppy just a few weeks old. He was the cutest little Staffordshire Bull Terrier, a real character. Every morning, without fail, we would go for walks and we enjoyed our time together. There was a walk we used to take, with a river and a concrete section that went across it, level with the banks, to an island the other side. Now Bandit had a thing about ducks and birds, he would always chase them. In the summer, he would run across onto the island, chase them all off the island, and then come running back to me. One time, in the winter, he saw ducks flying overhead towards the island. Off he ran and I sensed what was going to happen and charged after him. He headed for the concrete section but now the water was flowing over it about two or three feet deep. Oblivious to it, his eyes were fixated on following the ducks heading for the island. Landing on the concrete, I watched him spin through the air, dropping at least eight feet into the white churning water below. My heart sank. I have a terrible fear of water but luckily my friend Nick was there, he reached the wall at the same time I did. We both looked for Bandit but couldn't see him, until all of a sudden his little nose and eyes broke the surface, before he was sucked under again. Straight away Nick and I tied the leads together, I jumped into the water and waded out until I was waist deep. Bandit came up for the second time but was too far away for me to reach him. His nose was flaring trying to get air and then he was gone. Knowing that one more time would be the last for him, I waded in further. Thank God, he popped up near me and I grabbed him by the scruff of his neck and literally threw him out and onto the bank. Soaking wet, I climbed out to find Bandit vomiting water and shaking, picking him up I carried him home. We were both ill for about two days after. To watch him go under the water like that was one of the worst moments. Yet when it came to doing the private readings that day, which had been booked months in advance, spirit enabled me to feel well enough to do them.

Another time, bless him, he had two cruciate ligaments replaced, not at the same time but one after the other and he was heavily strapped up. I moved the mattress downstairs and slept with him so that I could pick him up and carry him out to the garden and make sure he was okay. The bond between us was incredibly strong.

At a later time in his life, he was taken really poorly, I took him to the vets at Haverhill and he was in for just over a week. Unfortunately he was uninsured at the time as the insurance company wouldn't reinsure him again. But that wasn't important, even if I had to sell everything I owned, it didn't matter, I just had to help him. The vet wasn't sure what was wrong with Bandit, he was wasting away and there didn't seem much hope. Bandit looked so sad and my heart broke looking at him. The vet suggested that I should say goodbye to Bandit, but suddenly there was a phone call and it was a veterinary hospital in Newmarket . The vet had sent some samples off for testing at Newmarket but hadn't received a reply. Right on cue, the veterinary hospital phoned and asked if Bandit could be brought in immediately as they had an idea of what the problem was. With the help of one of the vets, who lead the way, I took him straight to Newmarket.

"Bandit hasn't eaten anything, we know how much he adores you, so see if you can get him to eat something," she said, "Please try because he hasn't eaten for days."

I put Bandit in the back of the Jeep and we raced to Newmarket, where they took Bandit from me. Half an hour later I was called in and they advised me that Bandit had E.Coli but it could be treated with certain medicines. Back we went to the vets at Haverhill for a new prescription. The other vet made her way back separately. Bandit looked so pitiful in the back. He was such a character, many people who came to me for private readings will remember him. I saw a bakers and stopped and I know you shouldn't give it to dogs but Bandit was a chocoholic. One time I had bought Easter eggs for my grandchildren, which he found and ate. Bella our other dog was on medication, which she would only take on a tiny bit of fudge and Bandit had to have a bit as well. Anyway, I zipped into the bakers and bought him two chocolate cakes, opened the back of the Jeep up and started stroking him. With great gusto he ate the two chocolate cakes. Back at the vets, I was asked if I managed to get him to eat anything and I told them I had.

When I told them about the two chocolate cakes the vet's reply was "Oh my God! You should never feed him them!" but it had done the trick.

Bandit was in there for a few more days and luckily picked up and lived for another fourteen months. Regrettably, he became ill again and I took him to the vets at Braintree. He was in for a few days, they managed to rally him around and then just a few months later he became desperately ill. Out in the garden in the freezing winter, he tried to bury himself in the snow. I picked him up, brought him in and cuddled him. Everything had been tried, I was feeding him by hand. Back to the vets he went for an injection, which they said he would either respond to or if not then it was the final option. He had the injection and I took him home. There was no improvement and he was a pitiful sight hardly able to walk. He was dreadfully unhappy.

In a last ditch attempt, I phoned the vets. They told me nothing further could be done for him and it would be best to put him out of his misery. I had him booked in for that evening at four o'clock but I had readings to do that day. People will wait a long time to see me and I didn't want to let them down. I kissed him and left him with Bella, and did the readings knowing that when I came back that afternoon, I would have to take him to the vets to be put to sleep.

I can honestly say that spirit took away all that pain and worry, and the readings went perfectly. When I arrived home I sat with Bandit and stroked him, put him in the back of the Jeep and took him to the vets. The vet came out and said not to bring him in, they would do it in the Jeep. I stroked him as he was put to sleep. The vets were lovely, they climbed in with him. Bandit was looking at me straight in the eyes all the time and then just drifted away. It was the kindest thing to do for him. I brought his body home and found a special spot for him, dug a hole, put towels inside the coffin for Bandit, along with his collar and lead, which he always would run and get every day for walks. As an afterthought, I put one of my slippers in there. He had always had a thing about my shoes and would take them into bed with him and I also put in a fudge bar, brand new in the packet. He was buried and I prayed over him, knowing one hundred per cent that he would live on. I knew it and yet the physical missing of him, that coming home in the evening and finding him waiting by the door for me with his tail wagging, it was so hard. People who love dogs will know exactly what I mean. I really missed him and I know my other dog Bella still misses him.

Life has to go on. The back gate leads onto fields and the next day, as I stepped out with Bella, there was a brand new fudge wrapper right outside the back gate, I picked it up and felt it was a sign that Bandit was okay. I still have the same Jeep that Bandit was put to sleep in, in a way it made the Jeep special for me and I can honestly say that car has never broken down. Often driving home from shows, I looked in the mirror half expecting to see his spirit sitting in the back but it had never happened. Obviously, I pass his grave every day and always speak to him and include him in my prayers and tell him how much I miss him.

Unusually I woke up in the early hours of the morning in March 2016 and just felt something was there. As I rolled over, there he was, sitting at the end of the bed with that look that he always gave me, he was only there for a few seconds.

"Oh Bandit, lovely to see you boy, God bless you," I whispered.

With that he disappeared. It was no illusion, I was wide awake and it was him, no mistaking it. That's how spirit can be, they can get you through the worst of times, the worst of illnesses, the worst conditions, in order that you can do the work they want you to do.

Chapter 28
When in Rome

At Witham spiritualist church I was working with spirit when a young man came through. His first name began with 's' but I knew it wasn't Steve or Simon, it was a different sort of name. A lady was there with her husband, who was a big, powerful looking man, in fact he looked a bit of a handful.

She put her hand up, "We lost our son in a car accident as you described and his name was Scott."

Carrying on I gave them more information, her husband just stared at me and showed no emotion.

"He's telling me that in the garage where he worked," I started to speak but before I could continue his father was up off his seat.

"He didn't work in a garage but in a tyre repair workshop and he fitted tyres." The tone of his voice was enough to inform the audience that he wasn't happy to even be in the building.

"Well, you're cutting straws, it's like a garage to me," I continued, "Scott's telling me there's a small red car, something like a small Vauxhall, he was doing it up with wide wheels and he had sprayed it up, to surprise you with how well he had done the car up."

The man looked at me and told me, "You're not speaking to my son because my son never had a red car and didn't do that sort of thing, I used to but not my boy," he was adamant, "You're wrong, you're not talking to my son."

To this I could only reply, "Well, I'm afraid I am."

By this time he was clearly getting upset. "Well, I'm telling you you're not. If my son had a car then I would've heard about it," he went on, "He never had a car there and wasn't doing cars up, I've had enough of this."

The message was cut short. His wife looked very apologetic. This man looked like someone not to argue with, so I wasn't going to push it. It was left at that and the show continued with messages for others in the audience. The couple left and didn't say a word to anyone. Evidently, on the way home, Linn, the lady in the audience, said to her husband, Malcolm, that she thought he had been a bit rude to me and he told her he thought it was all bloody nonsense.

"Well how do we know?" she asked him.

He was resolute that he would have known.

"Let's just pop in there and see," she argued.

There was only one way to find out. They went to the tyre company that Scott had worked at. Malcolm was dragged along there by his wife but thought it would be a waste of time. The couple spoke to the manager there.

"Well actually, there's a car under a tarpaulin," he told them, "It's out the back, it's one that Scott was working on."

It turned out to be exactly as I had described, the colour, make of car, everything. Malcolm was totally stunned. He questioned himself, how could someone tell him something about his son that even he didn't know? They contacted me and asked for a private reading. Malcolm came along in a different frame of mind, still a bit skeptical, but then Scott came through with such amazingly accurate information for them, including the three Staffordshire bull terriers they had. Then Malcolm's father came through, who had been a big, violent man. I think his name was John and he had been a boxer, he came through with information, including about his brothers and Malcolm agreed it was definitely his father.

"I've got a friend of yours coming through who's like a gangster," I said to Malcolm, "And either he was shot or I feel more that he accidently shot himself. Who is Mickey?" I asked him.

"Yes, that's him, that's my mate, he accidently shot himself," Malcolm confirmed, "I was at his funeral and used to work for him."

I continued talking to Mickey and relaying information to Malcolm. "Mickey was a big man, very smart and wore a white silk scarf" I described.

"That's him to a tee," he verified.

Then I said, "Mickey's going on about Italy but I don't feel he's Italian, but there's something to do with him and Italy, but he's not Italian." I couldn't work out what the message was about.

"Hold on, he's showing me the Coliseum," I could see it clearly in my mind, "It's something to do with him and Rome."

Apparently his name was Mickey Roman. Well, to say the reading completely changed their lives is an understatement and we became great friends. In fact we have appeared in magazine features together, as their story was in a couple of magazines. Malcolm is now a firm believer and that's the beauty of working with spirit, I meet some wonderful people, many of whom have, over the years, have become such good friends.

Chapter 29
Life After Life

For many years I worked for spiritualist churches but made the decision to stop working at them. For the simple reason that when I went back to a spiritualist church, there were the same faces there, week after week, year after year. It was like preaching to the already converted. I wanted to reach people who normally wouldn't go to a spiritualist church, to connect them with loved ones. I made the decision to start working in halls and restaurants, even though I figured I'd probably be preaching to the cynical.

One such place was a restaurant in Saffron Walden called Dish, a lovely place to work, I've had some phenomenal nights there. On one particular night, a lady was there and her daughter came through and told her how she had been in a car with her father, sitting in the back.

"The seat belt was on but it wasn't the right seat belt, please don't blame yourself," were the daughter's words for her mother.

She rightly gave me her name, Diana, and also mentioned a short name with a K, which was her sister Kim, and said that she had been eleven years old. Furthermore, she told me it was to do with someone driving a white Mercedes on the wrong side of the road, which hit her parent's car head on. I told the mother that her daughter's body went forward and that she knew she was passing. The mother said that no, she didn't and I insisted that was what had been confirmed by her daughter.

"Oh my God," her hand suddenly flew to her mouth, "You're right, she did."

Apparently, with the force of the impact, her daughter had been flung forward, went back but the seat belt she had on didn't save her because as she went back, it broke her neck.

As she was passing, very quickly, she looked at her mother and simply said "Goodbye Mum."

The whole restaurant was in tears, including me. The mother has been to see me several times at different shows and Diana often comes through. I do confess to the crowd that I've read this woman before but every time Diana comes through, she gives her mother or sister new information about their present circumstances. Diana obviously keeps abreast of what is going on.

One funny character that has come through a few times, but came through for the first time at Dish, was a short, dark haired, very good looking man. A little Cockney chap, an older man when he passed, he came through full of bounce. I described him to the crowd.

"And this man, he's singing at the top of his voice," I began to croon, 'Won't you come home, Bill Bailey, won't you come home."

Crying with laughter, a woman put her hand up. "That's my dad!" Bless her, she was so excited.

"Do you understand he's giving me the significance about this song?" I asked.

"Well, he would do," she gasped, "His name was Bill Bailey and he used to sing that song, saying it was his song because he was Bill Bailey!"

This chap came through a few times in there, always a bright and fun-loving character and he never failed to amuse when he came through with his little stories. His daughter, whose name I later found out to be Bernae Ellis, is a lovely girl, who often comes to my shows.

I've worked for so many different organizations, two of which were Jewish associations, Olim Wizo and Aquarius AVIV. The Olim Wizo one was the first I attended. It was in a lovely big hall, with a wonderful crowd, lots of fabulous food, it was around twenty pounds a seat, we're going back a few years now. The place was absolutely packed, mostly with women, most of whom were very noisy, chatty and hilariously funny. Entering the stage to a cacophony of noise I had to try to get their attention. A lot of them were there because the money was going to a good cause back in Israel, which they wanted to support whilst they enjoyed the sandwiches and a few drinks. Introducing myself to the crowd, I pointed out that I wasn't Jewish but I was saving up to be, immediately they chortled with laughter. Straightaway I asked spirit to get something through really quick to get the evening going. A gentleman came through and gave his name as Joe Green and said that he wanted to talk to a daughter figure and he hadn't been gone long.

"My father-in-law was Joe Green and he's only recently passed," one lady stated as her hand shot up.

Joe went on to tell me about hairdressing shops and gave other information. This really grabbed everyone's attention that I could give his first and last name. From there a couple of other messages came through. A leaflet was produced about the evening.

I said to the girls running it, "I bet the Rabbi won't be too happy about a medium being in your midst here."

"With the money you've raised here he won't complain!" they laughed. Let's just say the evening raised a lot of money.

One of the messages that came through was for a lady who had lost of son, which I told her had happened at quite a distance and it felt like the Winchester area. That statement caused her to gasp. I saw a little red car overturning and her son being thrown out of the car and there were other boys in the car. Also, there were MacDonald wrappers, boxes and food littered all over the road. I also felt that her son had been hit by a car as he rolled out of the red car. Further, there was a university link. It turned out her son was In Winchester University, the boys had pulled in to get a takeaway, came out onto a busy road, shot across the road, the car was clipped side on, which caused the car to go over. As it was summer, the windows of the car were open, hence the MacDonald's litter all over the road. It appears her son was hit by a large vehicle, a Mercedes I believe, that was travelling along at the time. The hall was stunned into silence, you could hear a pin drop.

Working with humour and laughter is important because I work with life after life, not life after death. Bearing in mind that the whole crowd was Jewish, a few messages in I couldn't believe what I could see. An Irishman was making his way down the aisle towards me, his spirit singing 'It's a long way to Tipperary' at the top of his voice, drink in hand, absolutely rotten drunk. Of course, I wondered to myself where he fitted into the proceedings, surely it couldn't be right. But, as Lyn had told me, time and time again, if you're given something by spirit, no matter how stupid or ridiculous it seems, trust in spirit and give it out. So, I did. There were gales of laughter from the audience.

A young woman put her hand up. "That's my father,' she told me.

"Well, he's Catholic Irish, not Jewish." I was curious about the connection.

"Yes, you're right but that was his song, he was a lovely man but often very drunk," she sighed, "I actually married a Jew and I converted and took the religion on, hence why I'm here. But yes, that was indeed my father."

The whole place fell about in amusement. There was another message where I told a lady that she had been burgled and her parents came through to tell her.

"You never set your alarm did you?" I told her, "You forgot to set the alarm."

Blushing, she admitted I was correct. Some numbers came into my mind and I realised her parents were trying to tell me the number of her safe. I gave her a few numbers, just two or three.

With a sharp intake of breath she exclaimed, "Yes, that's absolutely correct - no more, no more!"

I promise you it wasn't me. If that lady is reading this book and sees my criminal past, I do hope she appreciates it definitely wasn't me that burgled her!

At the end of the evening, I received a lovely compliment when an older, very suave and sophisticated gentleman in his seventies, came up to shake my hand. He asked me if I had ever heard of Joseph Benjamin. Yes, I certainly had, he was one of the all-time great mediums and I had read some amazing things about him and the messages he gave. A reporter once wrote about him and said Joseph Benjamin gave a mind-blowing spiritual evening of clairvoyance.

The reporter apparently asked him "If you spirit guides know so much, how much have I got in my pockets?"

Evidently, the reply was something like five pounds, eight shillings and nine pennies (this was in old money), consisting of a five pound note, so many two bobs, pennies, half-pennies and sixpences. The reporter checked his pocked and the exact same amount was in his pocket. I have to say, this would be way out of my league. Anyway, this older gentleman asked me did I know of Joseph Benjamin, which of course I did, he was a very famous Jewish medium and Cockney to boot.

"Well, I'm not going to lie to you and tell you that you're as good as him because you're not," he declared, "But you're the nearest thing I've ever seen and that, my boy, is a compliment."

As he went to walk away, he turned to me and queried "But hold on, how long have you been doing this?"

I calculated about ten or eleven years.

"Joseph Benjamin had been doing it all his life," he told me, "So, I think you can get there, God bless you." With that, off he went.

What a wonderful compliment to receive, not that I claim to be and probably will never be as good as the great Joseph Benjamin, but if I'm the nearest thing to him, then I'm pretty chuffed with that. I feel such gratitude to that wonderful gentleman because his words really helped me know I was on the right path.

Chapter 30
Tell It Like It Is

Part of being a medium is knowing how to 'switch off' from spirit to get on with daily life or to ensure a good night's sleep. Occasionally though spirit will come through no matter the time of day or night. One such example involved Nicky's childhood friend, Debbie Fletcher, who had married her childhood sweetheart, a chap called Kenny. Now I had met Kenny on two very brief occasions but knew nothing of him. Due to his work he had breathed in some sort of dust when he was working with MDF and he ended up with cancer in the top of the nose. He suffered for quite a long time and passed over as a young man. A couple of years after he had passed, I had a fitful night's sleep. In the morning, the remnants of my dreams swirled in my mind.

"You know I had a really strange dream last night," I told Nicky. "I dreamed about your mate Debbie's husband Kenny."

"That's really strange," she answered, "Because it's Debbie's birthday today."

I didn't think any further about it but Nicky thought it might be a sign that Kenny wanted me to have a word with Debbie, and she suggested I ring Debbie, which I did, to tell her of my dream about Kenny. Extremely skeptical, I could read straight away what she was thinking, that perhaps Nicky had put me up to it to make a birthday present for her.

"Honestly Deb, he's here and wants to speak to you," I sensed she wasn't at all sure about it. "Look, I'll prove to you that he's here. In the room you're standing in there's four photographs of Kenny in that room."

There was a pause for a few seconds. "Good try, there's three," she replied.

"No, there's four," I insisted, "There's also someone else in the room with you."

"Oh, you just probably heard my son in the background," she was clearly unimpressed.

"No, I didn't hear anyone but there are four photographs there," I stood my ground on this one.

Debbie turned to her son and asked him, "How many photographs are in the room?"

The answer came back, "Three mum."

"There you go Ron, there's three," came the emphatic reply.

"Deb, look behind the biggest photograph," I requested.

"Oh my God!" she called out to her son, "Quick look there are four!" her words rang out.

Debbie couldn't believe it and thanked me through her tears. Later, a text came through to me "You have made this the happiest birthday of my life, thank you so much."

Because of that, sometime later we arranged for a private reading for Debbie, I instructed her to ask a very specific question without letting anyone know what it would be and see what Kenny put through to me. What she wanted was for me to tell her that on their wedding morning that he had said to her "Good morning, what's it like to be Mrs. Fletcher."

I can't hear in sentences like that, it's not quite how I receive messages from spirit. Anyway, Debbie came for the reading.

"I don't know if this was what you wanted but Kenny is giving you a pack of Wrigley's spearmint and a packet of mints," I told her.

She started to cry and told me that they had been school kids together from a very young age and the first gift he ever gave her was exactly that. So even though she didn't get the specific message she wanted, Debbie knew for sure that was Kenny coming through.

I would like to give another example of the healing power of spirit and the messages given to us from the other side. A lady had booked a reading and when I answered the door in my tee-shirt, to my surprise she took one look at me, told me she had the wrong address and quickly began to skedaddle away back from whence she came. I called out after her to ask if she was looking for Ronnie Buckingham, because if she was then she had found him. Clearly flabbergasted as I wasn't her idea of a medium, Dolly came into the lounge, where Nicky was tidying up. As I invited her up into the reading room, I enquired as to whether she had experienced a reading before.

"Darling, I've spent fortunes on people like you," she declared, "And nobody has been able to get through what I really need to hear."

"I actually know why you're here," She didn't look convinced at my reply and so I continued. "In fact I can tell you right here on the stairs or we can go into the reading room."

There we were, perched halfway up the stairs, as she turned to me, "If you know why I'm here, you can tell me now."

"What in front of my partner?" I asked, to which she nodded yes.

"You're here about your son," I stated, "He hung himself in a flat and your husband is sitting up the road in a car blaming himself for this. Go and get him and we'll do the reading."

Her face had more colour changes than a kaleidoscope as she spun herself around and went out to fetch her husband. Five minutes later, she returned with her husband, who was in a very distressed state. Now this is where I want to point out to you that in many ways a medium has to be hard to be a good medium, because you have to give information across, warts and all. I told the couple that I had their son with me and that he had taken his own life by hanging.

"I'm sorry to say this but your son was one nasty bit of work," I told them straight.

"We know he could be a problem but we loved him," they answered in unison.

"Yes, I know you loved him but let me tell you something," I carried on, "He's telling me that he came round on the Friday night to borrow a hundred pounds off you."

The gentleman's eyes were downcast as he replied, "Yes, he did."

"You refused him and told him to fuck off out of it and that he'd had enough money from you," I said, "You were at the end of your tether."

Their eyes widened.

"He's also telling me that he had borrowed repeatedly amounts of money from you but never paid you back," as I said this, the gentleman's eyes again lowered.

"Do you honestly think that he took his own life because you wouldn't give him a hundred pounds?" I questioned them gently.

Calmly, I told them the truth about the situation. "Your son was a drug taker, a gambler, he beat his girlfriend up and he was a nasty piece of work."

"But we loved him," they spoke as one.

"I know you did," I reassured them, "But I've got to tell you what he's telling me. He's so sorry about his behaviour when he was here."

My eyes studied one face ravaged with emotion and then the other. It was so important that they listen to the next message.

"His death had nothing to do with your hundred pounds, nothing at all," my words were measured and slow. "It was all to do with his long-term girlfriend, who I believe had been made pregnant by a friend of his."

The air was thick with silence as I described what he was like and exactly what had gone on. As the reading was drawing to a close, the son thanked his father for the Japanese garden he had built for him. The gentleman's eyes lit up and he confirmed that he had arranged a piece of garden with a Buddha statue, stone area and plants, in memory of his son. They left me so happy.

A while after, I received a wonderful letter from Dolly detailing how her husband had been off work for ages and had suffered with terrible bouts of depression since their son passed. He often had suicidal thoughts himself and all because he believed that it was his fault that his son had taken his own life. She went on to say that thanks to the wonderful reading, her husband had brought his life back together again, was working and had regained a sense of hope and happiness in himself. My hands turned that letter over and over as I re-read each word. I can't begin to tell you how marvellous it felt to receive that letter.

Chapter 31
Full Disclosure

Spiritualist mediums meet a lot of people and need to be open minded yet discreet, because all sorts of information can come up. One such time I heard a car pull up onto my new block paved driveway. Looking out of the window I saw the most elegant lady, in her late forties or early fifties, get out of a Mercedes sports car, very obviously wealthy, with huge diamond rings. I answered the door and took her up to the reading room and made small talk for a short while to help her feel at ease.

Eventually she turned to me and announced, "To be honest, Mr. Buckingham, I really don't know why I'm here, I have a wonderful, privileged life. It's just that my business partner came to see you a while ago and he hasn't stopped raving about you and your wonderful gift." She continued, "I'm here out of curiosity really and I don't know what you've got to tell me."

"You've got a big problem," I looked her straight in the eyes.

Somewhat taken aback she questioned, "Have I? What would that be?"

"Your husband wants you to take part in a threesome," I said, "He wants to watch you sleep with a younger man."

Her face paled, she was stunned. For a moment there was a deathly silence, until she asked, "What did you say?"

"You know what I just said," I replied.

"Oh my God, how did you know that?" she cried.

"Well, your mother is telling me," I told her.

"What should I do?" she kept repeating, "What should I do?"

"Your mother is saying it's a slippery slope, it won't end there," I said, "But somehow your husband will have this, if not with you then somewhere else."

Anyway, for someone who didn't want to know a lot, this reading just went on and on but luckily it was my last reading of the day. After about an hour and a half, I told her that I really was exhausted and there was no more I could tell her. She thanked me for such a fantastic experience and for my advice. She was stunned that I had received the information I had from her mother and asked me how much the reading was.

"A normal reading is about forty minutes, you've been here about an hour and a half, but never mind a reading is forty pounds," I said.

This lady took out a Louis Vuitton purse, from which she retrieved a huge roll of fifty pound notes and handed me a fifty pound note.

"Hold on I'll get you the change," I said. And she took it, which made me think that was why she was rich. It did make me smile.

Another incident I remember involved a local osteopath, Mark Gurden, a very scientifically minded, clever man, who treated my back after I had injured it through doing squats at the gym. Unbeknown to me I had read for Mark's wife, an amazing reading. Mark was a complete skeptic, being a scientific man he didn't believe life existed after death, how could it? Until his wife went back to him and played him the tape. At the time, I hadn't met Mark, until I visited his clinic. I watched the routine, the people went up to the reception, paid their money and went in for treatment. When I was called, I went up and the receptionist said to me that she had a note not to take my money. Of course I questioned why but she had no idea. I was taken into a room and waited, in came through Mark Gurden, who went through his routine, tested me and carried out the treatment. At the end, I asked him if I paid him there or at the desk. He told me there was no payment needed. When I asked why he told me that his wife had come for a reading some time ago. I told him that I had charged his wife and therefore I would pay him.

"Oh no you won't", he stated matter-of-factly, "Because what you did for my wife, money couldn't buy. I listened to the tape and what you said and the detail in it was so exact I know there's no possible way you could've researched it or known about it. It was accurate to the point of being ridiculous."

Bless him, that was lovely to hear.

Chapter 32
Mystic Challenge

One day, I noticed an advert in The Psychic News about a programme called Mystic Challenge. At the time, it was run by Uri Geller and Paul Ross, the brother of Jonathan Ross. I had always wanted to meet Uri Geller as his abilities fascinated me. I rang the number and applied to be on the jury. The show had psychic versus psychic, or it could be a tarot reader, a medium, a rune reader, or perhaps someone who worked with astrology, palm readers and others. The jury members voted to decide who was the best psychic. The format of the show involved having a celebrity guest, not necessarily somebody very well known, it could be a stunt rider for instance, a politician, a singer, a soldier or an amputee, but a lot of the time there were famous faces . Once they had Cynthia Payne, otherwise known as Madame Cyn.

Two people with different psychic skills went head to head, they would bring the celebrity into the room, there was someone there who took quick notes, someone else from the jury, usually a newspaper reporter to ensure there was no cheating, who just watched the proceedings. The celebrity would be brought in totally covered with a hood over their head to make sure they couldn't be identified. Only the eyes could be seen and they remained silent throughout so that their voice couldn't be recognised. The psychics had about half an hour with that person in the room. Being a medium I was allowed to hold their hand, so of course I could tell if they were black, white or whatever, male or female, but apart from that there was no clue as to their identity. When a medium usually does a reading, it is normal to ask questions such as, "You father has passed over to spirit is that correct?" and individuals would confirm as the case may be. As the programme didn't want to deal with life after death, my main gift was taken away from me. The programme makers just wanted to know who the people were, what had happened to them in the past, what they did, and you had to give more information than the opponent.

In the meantime, they had a jury of ten people. The head juror would be the person connected with the newspaper world, such as Gary Bushell, or Sue Carroll. Anyway, the celebrity would talk with the audience about their early life, career, and life events, the information was put into categories, such as age, health and profession. Then the celebrity would be hidden behind a screen so that the psychic couldn't see them. Afterwards, the person who took the notes would ask the psychic to recap and leave what he felt were his best hits. For instance, the psychic would say "Well, I'm sure this person is a singer," or perhaps they would be certain the celebrity had been divorced and whittle it down to ninety seconds. Then the psychics would sit in a sound-proof booth with headphones on and there was another person in the box to ensure there was no cheating. The star would then speak with the audience, sit with Paul Ross, because with my luck Uri Geller had left the show, the psychics would be called out one at a time, and were given ninety seconds to give a profile. The jury would take notes and then decide who was the most accurate. Out of fifteen shows, I won twelve. When it came to reading the Marquis of Blandford he actually thought I had walked it. I had said something that Paul Ross didn't bring up, and on this occasion I didn't win, yet the Marquis of Blandford said there was information I had given that Paul Ross hadn't brought forth, such as a terrible shoulder injury he had. Paul Ross was a bit red faced and he decided to call it a draw.

It was fun and I won many shows on the spin. On the night before my first appearance there I actually dreamed that I would read a show-jumper or jockey and strangely enough my first reading was of the show-jumper Oliver Skeets. Although to be honest I didn't get that he was a show-jumper but I did get lots of other information, some of which I didn't actually say aloud on the programme, although afterwards I did mention to him what I had picked up. Some things are a more private matter.

I originally phoned up to be on the jury, not to go on the show. They asked if I had an interest in psychic stuff and I told the lady on the phone that I was a medium. She told me they were actually looking for contestants, as they had tested lots of contenders but most hadn't come up to scratch and actually some were a joke and she asked me to consider being tested. To begin with I told her I was quite busy but she asked me if I could read over the telephone. I confirmed that I could and she told me that she would pass the phone to someone that I had no information about, the phone would be passed to them but the person wouldn't say anything to me. I could take as long as I liked to start talking and the person would be listening, at the end they would decide if I was good enough for the show.

I tuned in and had a lovely mother figure coming through. I told the person I was reading they were female and I had her mother with me, that she had strong links to Birmingham and had trained as a hairdresser at one time but was now working for the television company, and on the reading went. Suddenly I could hear sobbing and crying at the end of the phone, then a woman's voice told me I was unbelievable and would definitely be on the show.

"I'm Nicky Cooper, the producer of the show, you're on the show," she told me, "Normally we'd see if your face fits the show but no, you're definitely on the show."

It was a Tuesday and she asked if I could do the show on Saturday, to which I agreed. It was a great show and I read some interesting characters. One reading that really touched me involved a motorcycling vicar, Rev. Lionel Fanshawe who had been a karate expert, a lovely man. As a priest, he had worked all over the world, helping children in various countries. After the show, Nicky Cooper told me then when I read Lionel he said to her that he looked into my eyes and saw my soul.

"That man's soul is beautiful,' he told her, which was very touching.

Being on the show was incredibly interesting and quite a grand affair. I would be picked up from my house by a limousine, taken to the studio and after the show would be brought back home again. This must have been at great expense as the cars were real quality, such as a big Audi A8 or a S Class Mercedes, always different drivers. One time, I came out of the studio and the driver this time was a small, stocky chap, who introduced himself as David. He had a beard and I could tell he had bad skin in the past. A very pleasant man, he asked if I wanted to sit in the front or the back. I told him it was a lovely evening for a drive through London and I would sit in the front with him, which seemed to please him.

After a short period of time, he turned to me and asked, "Are you famous Mr. Buckingham?"

This tickled me and I replied "Please, it's Ronnie and no, I'm not famous."

"Well, this business of me picking you up from Braintree and taking you back is not cheap you know," he informed me, "I can't imagine they'd have me picking someone up from the studio and running them back to Essex if they're not famous in some way."

He was obviously curious to know more about me.

"Well, I'm sort of well-known in what I do," I told him.

His curiosity got the better of him and he asked me what exactly I did.

"I'm a medium," I said.

At this he went absolutely berserk and totally lost the plot, letting me know in no uncertain terms how terrible mediums were and how they played on the emotions of vulnerable people, how we spoke in clipped sentences, and said obvious things, such as 'There's an old lady here with someone on the other side who drinks Guinness, and who knows a George or a Bert.' Basically, he thought mediums led others into false beliefs and were con artists. When he realised he was having a rant at a customer, he checked himself as he probably was concerned I would report him as being rude.

"I don't mean to offend you," he said quietly.

I told him I wasn't offended and could understand his views as there are some terrible mediums out there, I had seen some myself. I explained to him that as with drivers, there are good drivers and there are bad drivers in the world, just as there are good and bad mechanics, good and bad builders, there are good mediums and there are bad mediums, but I was one of the genuine mediums.

"There is a life after death," I began to explain to him but he told me that he simply didn't believe in any of it.

As you can imagine, the limousine was travelling at a slow pace as the traffic in London can be incredibly congested. As we were going along, the spirit of David's father came into the car and began talking to me. I felt his father was a horrible man and I was concerned about talking to David as he was very skeptical and heated about the subject of life after death. But it was so impressed upon me to give David a message from spirit.

"David, I've got your father here with me and he wants to speak with you," I was a tad apprehensive about the reaction I would receive.

"Mr. Buckingham, I'm fifty seven years of age, it doesn't take a genius to work out my father's probably dead," he was clearly not impressed. "You're not going to try that old chestnut with me are you?"

Quickly I reminded him there was no money being handed over to me by him and that I didn't need to give him a message, however his father was there.

"He's one very, very, very nasty man. I'm sorry but he is," I blurted.

"Well, you've got that bit right," David replied, "My father was one of the nastiest people God ever put breath into."

I carried on, "He's also telling me his name was Frederick, and that he died of a heart attack and lived in a bungalow by the coast."

At this David laughed, "Very clever, Mr. Buckingham, yes he was called Frederick, but then it was possibly the most popular name at the time."

I reminded him that other names were equally as popular, such as George, Albert, William and Charles. Still not convinced he countered that most people died of a heart attack or cancer, and most old people moved into a bungalow by the sea. I told him that his father was a nasty piece of work when he was alive, but David said that a lot of men in that era were equally nasty and Victorian in their attitude.

"No, your dad was worse than that," I said but then another image came into my mind, "I've got an image of Fred Astaire and your father is saying he looked very much like Fred Astaire."

This piqued David's interest "Well, I will give you that, people would stop him in the street thinking he was Fred Astaire." But still he was very offish and quiet with me.

"David, I've still got your father here, he wants to apologise to you, he's so sorry for the way he treated you." It was no good, I had to give the message.

David just nodded but I carried on, "Now I can't understand this fully but there's something to do with David Lloyd George and Clement Attlee and I've got to mention them to you."

He sat bolt upright in the driver's seat, now I had his full attention. It turned out his name was David Lloyd Clement Barry. His father named him after the two greatest prime ministers that this country ever had. David went on to tell me that he hated the name Clement so much he had it removed from his birth certificate, it wasn't on his driving license or anything else, so how could I have known that? I gave him more information about his father and that he was a bank manager, which David disagreed with, but then I realised his father meant that he used to dress like a bank manager but he was a furniture salesman. That was exactly right and apparently he always wore a bowler hat, pinstripe suit and looked the business. All of a sudden, a beautiful feeling entered the car, a totally different feeling and I wasn't sure if I was picking up the name Betty or Beattie.

"David, your mother has also just got into the car," I told him. "Was her name Betty?" to which he said no. "Then her name was Beattie, Beatrice." I said.

The penny dropped. "David, you had to pick me up tonight," I told him, "Because there are things I have to tell you."

By now he was totally intrigued, I had gone way beyond anyone's guesswork. I told David that his mother had given birth to a deformed baby boy and so wicked was David's father that his mother was made to bury that child with no cross, no flowers, and was never to mention him. He wasn't perfect, he was stillborn and that was it, end of, as far as his father was concerned.

"You feel you're an only son, an only child," I said to David.

"I am," he informed me.

"No, you're not, your mother gave birth to a deformed baby boy before you," I insisted.

David was adamant that he was an only child.

That was until I said, "David, I can even tell you the name she gave this little boy, Raymond."

His eyes widened with total disbelief. Evidently his mother had lived to be an old woman, had dementia and had been living in an old people's home, where he would visit her with his wife.

"Raymond, Raymond, it that you Raymond?" she would cry out when he visited.

"It's me David, who's Raymond mother?" He never had an answer to that question from her.

I explained to him that all those years of suppression of having to bury a child she had carried had erupted, because his wicked father had never allowed her to grieve or cry over him. She was never allowed to put flowers on a grave for him and it came back in her senile state to haunt her. Finally, we made it back to Braintree and David was a wreck, he asked if he could come in for a drink because he didn't feel able to drive home. Nicky made him a drink and he sat for an hour with us. He just couldn't get his head around it, but eventually calmed down and made his way home.

The next week when I was due to go to the show, the staff had asked for a driver and straight away David volunteered to pick me up. He told me that when he had arrived home that night, he woke his wife up and they found a piece of paper and a pen and they wrote down seven things that they thought I could have possibly guessed, such as his father being nasty, the name Frederick, being a small man, the illness that took him, living by the coast, that sort of thing. But, there were thirty plus bits of information that I had given him that nobody would have known. He was now utterly convinced that I was right and there was a spirit world but he was puzzled about the brother he had never known about.

As we drove along I explained about the spirit world and gave him other information that came through and I said to David that I was thinking of writing a book. Afterwards, he wrote a letter to me, which I still have and can be produced as proof of all this. David told me that his mother's brother was still alive and lived in the south-west of England. He went along with his wife to visit his uncle, who was a very religious man that went to church regularly and was a great believer in God, and would have nothing to do with mediums, believing they were the Devil's work, as many religious people do. Because of that, David couldn't come straight out with the fact that he had spoken with a medium. However, being a very shrewd man, he tested his uncle's memory as his uncle was in his nineties, although his uncle was as sharp as a tack. His memory was excellent and he remembered names, things from the past and was really on the ball. David slipped into the conversation that he had heard from somewhere that his mother had given birth to a stillborn baby.

His uncle shuffled on his feet somewhat before saying, "Oh, I think

Auntie is calling me into the kitchen," and off he went, not having answered David's question.

His uncle didn't return from the kitchen. Instead his aunt came in and said that his uncle was feeling a bit ill and had to retire to bed, and that his uncle wasn't to be disturbed. Deep down, David knew the answer. Sometime later, David received a letter from his uncle informing him that he was a close relative and he loved him but that he was feeling very weak and could he keep his communications to letter or telephone and not to visit again. Shortly after, the uncle died, but David believed his uncle was caught in a quandary really, as he had probably been sworn to secrecy and being a religious man he couldn't break that oath but neither could he tell a lie. The only thing to do was to avoid the question. Anyway, David took it all on board and truly believes, as I know to be the truth, that what I told him was absolutely true. I received such a lovely letter explaining how I had changed his outlook regarding the spirit world. For me it showed how spirit can come through, totally off the cuff, not planned. This man would never in a million years have gone to see a medium, so they sent him to the medium in another way. His father had come through in spirit, apologetic for what he had done, but a nasty piece of work in his time nonetheless.

On the Mystic Challenge show, one particular lady who I went up against, Claire Gabriel, was a tarot reader. We went head to head against each other and I won and we became great friends. She originated from Nottingham and had a huge following and had been on many radio shows in that area. Her daughter lived in Gibraltar and mediumship in that country had been really big. Some of the great mediums went there, Albert Best, Gordon Higginson, and perhaps even Doris Stokes, but they worked in public buildings. However, because it was a very Catholic population there, the government stopped giving permission for psychic or mediumship events to be held there in public buildings.

A lovely lady from Gibraltar, Lourdes, used to enjoy watching the mediums and longed to see them again. She had a business partner, Andrew, with whom she ran a shop. Andrew was a lovely man, very straight down the line, as was Lourdes. They had place at the time called Buccaneers, a wonderful vernacular property. Part of it went underground, like an old cave, which held around a hundred people. Originally it was used as an ammunition store in the Napoleonic times. It had a stage area and was a lovely setting. As Claire thought I was an extremely good medium, she suggested to Lourdes that she talk to me about visiting Gibraltar. At the same time, my partner Nicky and her parents were going out to Spain, it seemed the ideal time to go to Gibraltar to meet Lourdes and then catch up with Nicky and her family in Spain.

To demonstrate how straight up and down Lourdes is, evidently before my arrival, she had quite a big name in London do a clairvoyant night at Buccaneers and she told me he was atrocious. In fact she refunded everyone who went to see him, called him to one side and told him she would give him a chance and say that he had other shows booked for other people. Basically told him she thought he was a fraud and useless and that he had embarrassed her. Clearly she was a woman who pulled no punches. She wouldn't tell me who the medium was, only that he was quite a big name. Anyway, we met up and she was very straight to the point and asked if I could do mediumship, which I told her I could. To prove the validity of my claim, she asked me to give her a private reading, but I told her I wasn't playing that game. I was good at what I did and she either wanted me to do it or not. Relenting, she agreed to give me a go.

The shows went well and I ended up with a massive following in Gibraltar and went back there several times. It was brilliant to meet so many wonderful people. Even the staff at the airport had heard of me and I read a lot of the customs people, including the head of customs, who had lost his wife at the time. Hopefully I'll go back to work there. Andrew and Lourdes were very kind to me, I used to stay in Lourdes's flat, which was about ten floors up on the rock, so had stunning views over the sea and the Strait of Gibraltar. Sometimes we would sit and watch the submarines come up. It's a remarkable place.

One strange incident that happened in Gibraltar was when I did a reading for a lady, whose son came through. I felt he had died of a bullet in the head, her head hung low as she recounted that he had taken his own life.

"No, he didn't," I whispered, "He was murdered."

He was showing me someone jumping from an apartment window, it was about thirty feet up. I described to her what I saw. How there was a large slope of grass that went up, from the window, as long as you propelled yourself out, it was probably only a jump of about ten feet in height, which most people would be able to handle. Anyway, some other information came through and unbeknown to me the lady took the tape to the CID. Lourdes came in to see me whilst I was doing readings in the Buccaneers.

"I have a gentleman from the CID here to see you," she introduced Richard, the CID officer to me.

He asked if I would speak with him and could he record his time with me. It turned out that a lot of what I had said nobody knew, the police had never revealed it, they had kept it from being public information. It had been reported to them by a witness that someone had been seen climbing out of a window and jumping, along with other information. I told him that he wouldn't catch the murderer. It was to do with drug smuggling and foreigners on the island, that the lad's murder had been made to look like a suicide, as he had turned some people over. Richard told me I had phenomenal gifts and that nobody could have guessed the things I had revealed to him. He gave me his card and told me to contact him if I ever had any problems in Gibraltar.

They were the kindest of people in Gibraltar and I never had any problems there at all. I would go to Jimmy's Restaurant, which served the best tapas ever but it was embarrassing because I could never pay, as the owner wouldn't let me. There were people with clothes shops there and I remember passing one shop and a young man came out, who I had given a message from his father. The people in Gibraltar are very family orientated, and he beckoned me into the shop.

"Right, anything you want, just help yourself," and turning to his staff he said, "Don't charge this man anything."

I told him I couldn't do that but he insisted. Not wanting to offend him, I told him I would find something for Nicky and picked up a small item to appease him. It was incredibly touching to feel that my mediumship was giving such comfort that people felt they wanted to give something back to me. It was truly humbling.

There was a funny occurrence out there was when I gave a lady a message from her brother, who had hung himself. The message was absolutely spot on with names and other information. During the show's interval period, the lady and her daughter went outside and unfortunately the lady suffered a heart attack. Luckily she didn't pass to the other side but was rushed to hospital. The local newspapers jumped on the story. Needless to say, the headline was 'Medium gives lady heart attack." Fortunately she survived, however her daughters went to the newspapers furious about the story and when the lady recovered she gave them quite a blast too. The newspapers had to rescind the story and comment that it was nothing to do with me.

The lady thought that as her brother had died by his own hand that she would never hear from him again. She was thrilled to hear from him and it was she who insisted the newspaper retract their story that I was in any way to blame.

With Claire Gabriel, who is quite well connected, I did some work in Marbella, Spain, for Spectrum Radio, which is an English speaking radio programme out there. If anyone wanted their fortune told or advice, they would ask to speak to Claire, but if they had suffered a bereavement, they would ask to speak to me. A young lady called the radio station and wanted to speak to me. Straight away I picked up that she had lost her sister and described her sister to her, gave a name and said that I saw her sister passing with other people in a red convertible sports car. That was exactly what had happened. There were many tears and gasps of astonishment from the people working in the radio station. That evening we had a big show in a hotel and the young lady's family turned up to say thank you for the message, which was lovely.

Mystic Challenge led onto quite a few things in its way. Another occasion involved a friend of Ros, a Danish chap called Thomas, who was staging some mediumistic shows in Denmark. Mediumship was a fairly new concept in Denmark. Thomas contacted the Arthur Finlay centre in Stansted, which made sense as it is a big spiritual centre, in order to find spiritualist mediums. Ros insisted Thomas was to ask me and he agreed to meet me in London. In order to test me, he asked for a private reading and was blown away by what I revealed to him, I was hired and ended up going to Denmark. At the airport I was met by a chauffeured car, which I was allowed to use to go anywhere I wanted. The first performance was in a theatre in Copenhagen, followed by a town called Middelfart and then Silkeborg. The shows went down really well, although the television crew were actually frightened to come and speak to me as it unnerved them. Some wonderful messages were given and afterwards the crew told me that I had convinced them that there really was an afterlife.

I've been very privileged to be able to read for some wonderful people in my time, including celebrities. One in particular was Kate O'Mara and I have some lovely photographs of us together, including one she signed for me. What a stunning woman, I didn't meet her until she was in her seventies when she came for a reading. She was over the moon as her mum and dad came through. Sometime later, her son Dickon took his own life. Kate was beyond distraught and phoned me. Dickon came through with some wonderful messages for her, but I knew Kate would never get over it, she adored her son, she really did.

We remained great friends and I was sad to hear she had passed. When she had been in a hospital for actors and actresses, we had spoken. Although she had double pneumonia amongst other things, I believe it was a broken heart that took her. A sad loss because she was a wonderfully warm, lovely lady and it was a pleasure to call her my friend.

Another charming lady I met, who in the past had received some bad press, was Tara Palmer-Tomkinson. We met in the green room of the Big Brother set. I can read tarot cards, photographs, handwriting, anything like that, but this time I was there to read doodles. Tara drew a doodle wonderfully, she's a very talented woman, evidently a very good pianist. Quickly she drew a picture of a model woman with a hat on and high leg boots.

I gave Tara the reading and she was very open, straight to the point and never tried to lie about anything.

During the reading, I turned to her and said, "You know what, I keep seeing you in a forest, I've no idea why but you're doing something there and it's so beneficial to you." It all seemed odd to me.

"You don't win anything there, you might come up runner-up or something, but it's going to change your career and put you in the limelight again."

Tara was really pleased with the reading and asked for a private reading at my house, which was really sweet of her and it was booked for about four months. Even though she was a celebrity, I wasn't going to try to fit her in before anyone else, every reading is equally important to me. Anyway, a couple of months later I had a call from her agent, Willy, who told me that Tara was going to have to cancel her appointment as she was going to be on a programme called 'I'm A Celebrity Get Me Out Of Here.' So, it was a jungle and not a forest that I saw. Of course, she didn't win it but she went on to do lots of other things, such as the Walker's Crisps adverts. Willy actually said to me that I had obviously been right with my reading. After the reading in the studio, Tara wrote on the doodle, which I still have, 'To darling Ronnie, the man who knows more about me than I do.'

Chapter 33
It's A Small World

I would like to speak about the power of spirit and a wonderful, dear friend, a wonderful Turkish Cypriot, Yonja Ali, her husband Hussain and their children. Yonja is a superb medium, a lovely looking girl with a fantastic bubbly personality. I helped her develop her mediumship and she is doing readings herself now, and doing very well I might add. She invited me to work in Cyprus, as many people she knew were interested in the spirit world, and arranged some shows and private readings for me to do. Off we all went, with her lovely kids, to the Turkish side of Cyprus and I stayed with her parents, who were the loveliest people and I was made very welcome.

As we were pulling up to the house, Yonja warned me that there was a spirit of a little girl, four or five years old, in this house. She cautioned me that the little girl was right bundle of trouble, always causing mischief. The house was typical of the area, ornate with tiled floors, it was wonderful, and I was invited to stay in a lovely large room with its own en-suite. The first thing that struck me about the room was the huge bed. It was a 1960s style bed, if you can imagine this big padded headboard with a radio mounted into it, big cabinets fitted either side of it. It was enormous. It had a solid wood frame, probably about an inch wide, along both sides and along the bottom, and the mattress was positioned inside that on springs, which would come out. It must have weighed a ton and was sitting on a shag pile carpet.

On the second night, I decided to do a series of press-ups, because no matter where I am, I always find time for my keep fit regime. For years I have worn a crucifix and chain, which is very precious to me, which I rarely take off, but it was in the way of my press-ups and I ended up stabbing myself with it. I took it off and put it on the cabinet by the side of the bed. After three or four sets of press-ups and other exercises, I quickly showered, dried off and jumped into bed. As it had been a particular busy day, I fell asleep quickly. In the morning, I jumped into the shower, dried off and went to put on my crucifix and chain but couldn't find it. I looked for it on the cabinet and then searched high and low for it, even in the laundry basket and suitcases. It was nowhere to be found. In my mind, I retraced my movements the previous night, certain that my memory would reveal its whereabouts. Yet I was positive I had carefully placed it on the bedside cabinet. I popped downstairs and mentioned it to Yonja, who thought it was odd but volunteered to help me look for it, along with her parents and her kids. We went through the room with a fine toothcomb but couldn't find it anywhere. Nobody had been in the room except for me.

"I bet it's her, I bet it's that little spirit!" exclaimed Yonja.

The final day of my visit arrived and it was still missing. I felt gutted.

I turned to spirit, "C'mon, let's find this bloody cross and chain."

With just two hours to go before the drive back to the airport, we all decided to have one more look for it going through the room with a fine toothcomb. We even lifted the middle of the bed, the spring part that supports the mattress, right out. All that was left was the wooden frame. Still we couldn't locate it. Frustrated, we came up with the idea of lifting the wooden frame, which was so heavy that it was firmly embedded into the carpet. Hussain and I are both big and strong, but we only just managed to lift the bed frame up between us, the sheer weight of the frame meant that it was no easy talk. As we lifted it up, there glinting in the light, under the wooden frame, was the crucifix and chain. It was unbelievable because it took two strong men to lift the bed up, it was that heavy. One person couldn't have lifted that bed on their own, with one hand holding the bed and the other to lay the crucifix and chain in that position. There was no way.

But what was truly staggering was that when we examined the crucifix, there wasn't one single mark on it, it wasn't dented, nothing. Yet the solid wood frame of the bed really was heavy. Confounded we decided to replicate what had happened, to try and work out how it could possibly have occurred. Whilst Hussain and I lifted the bed up and lowered it slowly, Yonja tried to lay the chain and she couldn't do it. As we put the bed down, either some of the chain would stick out or some of the crucifix would poke out. She straightened it and time and time again we tried but we couldn't match what we had found. Yet it had been totally and absolutely hidden. If you had offered me a thousand pounds to lift the bed frame up on my own and put the crucifix as it was found, there was no way I could have done it. The only explanation was that it had been put there psychically. We were all witness to it and knew it was impossible for one person to do it. I also knew that nobody else had been in that room.

Another strange coincidence involved one night when I was booked at The Savoy Hotel in Korinia. Yonja knew one of the owners, a Turkish chap who lived in North London, where Yonja and her family had also lived. He invited me to do a show there and a reporter from the local press showed up. I think I was the first medium to do public shows there. The place was packed out and everyone had their meal out on the roof garden. Unfortunately one particular lady started to choke on her food, really badly. Quick as a flash, a man jumped out of his seat to perform the Heimlich manoeuvre on her. A huge lump of meat flew out of her mouth. The poor lady was blue in the face and the man had saved her life, without a doubt. When everything had calmed down, she took sips of water but was still clearly shaken by the event. I went over to her and asked if she was okay and whether she felt up to seeing the show, which she was.

"I'm the medium working tonight, have you been to see a medium before?" I asked.

She told me that she hadn't but her sister in France had.

"I listened to a tape the medium made for her and it was unbelievable," she enthused, "My sister told me he's by far the best medium she had ever seen and she's really into it. So I've got an idea of what you're going to do."

"Oh what a coincidence," I told her, "Because I used to live in France."

I asked her what part of France her sister lived in because mediumship is quite rare in France. It turned out to be Vermoutier.

"Her name isn't Elaine is it?" I asked.

"Why yes it is!" she exclaimed.

"Battersea John's other half?" I was incredulous.

Would you credit it, I was the medium she had heard on the tape. What are the chances of that? Inside the hotel the show commenced and I can honestly say there were some fantastic messages and proof that came through for the audience. There was a great write up about the evening by the local press, which ended up on the internet. The journalist had said it was a fascinating event, not to be missed. Along with some of her friends, she had received a message from spirit. She reported that there was no way on earth that I could've known the things I came out with and not to miss the opportunity to see me in action. Bless her, it was a lovely write-up.

CHAPTER 34
FAMOUS FACES

There was a time when I did a lot of television, such as Mystic Challenge, Kilroy, Big Breakfast, Inside Out and Rise TV, also I was psychic advisor to Big Brother when it first came out. On the Big Brother show I predicted that Kate Lawler would win. Nicky questioned why I wanted to go on what she thought were silly shows, reading pictures, paintings and all sorts of stuff. She felt it wasn't really me and thought I should concentrate on the real stuff. I figured she was right and began to turn down television work. We were watching Sky TV and found that I was on three different channels at the same time, doing three different shows. I had also done the television work in Denmark, although that was different as it was what Nicky described as the real thing.

It would have been great to do something like the Colin Fry show but it never transpired. But in essence mediumship for me is the real thing, it really is. I'm very aware that too many mediums sell their souls when they become famous. All this going into false trance business at the drop of a hat, or talking in a baby voice when children come through, it's all nonsense. What a load of twaddle, it's just showmanship. Such shows make all mediums look ridiculous and give mediumship a bad name but unfortunately, it's rife out there. If I received a pound for every time I read in some magazine that a so-called medium was having a séance and lo and behold Elvis Presley turned up and started performing Hound Dog or whatever, honestly I would be a billionaire! Frankly, it makes me cringe because it's just so stupid.

Mediumship should be kept real. It's important to me to work with humour, a bit of light-heartedness is a great thing. Spirits absolutely love humour. If you think about life, we spend so much time feeling sad, especially during bereavement, when there's much crying and upset and understandably so. When spirits do come through, they don't want you to be sad, they want you to know they're alive, well and happy in their new life. So, let's have a laugh about it, let the readings be accurate, let the messages be given with sincerity, but let us have some humour there as well. The spirit world isn't morbid and dark. We're not talking about life after death or death after life. It's life after life.

It's amusing that people have such a thing about celebrities coming through, the people that come through to me can always be researched. There was one time when I was doing some readings up in Yarmouth Spiritualist Church. I was reading one particular chap, who was an older, gay man. There was a lot of oohing and aahing and 'Ooeerr Missus' going on behind him.

"I'm sure you've got Frankie Howard standing next to you," I stated.

"Oh I would have," he smiled, "We were lovers for years."

Another time, I was working in a restaurant in Dunmow called Square One, and had been working there for virtually every month for about eleven years. One night, Mike Reid, the comedian, came through. It turned out his wife was in the audience, which I didn't know, and he gave some wonderful messages to her. One of the strangest readings, again in Square One, was an evening when the restaurant was packed out, and there was a long table with about a dozen young women. The spirit of a man came through. I turned to the audience.

"I've got this man coming through, I feel he was really, hard. A real tough man," I said, "He's massive, much bigger than me and I'm a big man."

In my mind I could see him with boxing gloves on and then taking the boxing gloves off and fighting bare knuckle. I could also see him being on television. There was other information I picked up about him, such as he was a Londoner, a big, aggressive man who passed with a brain tumour.

"I'm sure this is Lenny McLean," I stated.

Lenny McLean was a bare knuckle fighter, very famous, who featured in the film Lock, Stock and Two Smoking Barrels and played the part of a heavy, Barry the Baptist, just before he passed over with a brain tumour.

A young woman immediately jumped up from the audience, waving her hands as she shouted out, "That's my dad!"

Now, what are the chances of that? In all of the years that I've worked there, the only time that man came through was when his daughter was there. The table hadn't been booked in her name, I think she was married anyway, so her name was no longer McLean. I told her things that nobody could have read about in any books. She was amazed and came up after the show to hug me.

Another time, I was doing a private reading for an older, Cockney lady. Sitting down, I held her hand to tune in.

"Oh this is strange because your parents are here," I told her, "They both lived to a very old age, well into their eighties, which was unusual at that time."

The woman nodded her head and agreed I was right. I went on to describe all her brothers and sisters accurately.

"Hold on, I've got your brother coming through here," I felt a strong connection.

At this, her eyes lit up as she was eager to hear from him and I told her I would see what I could do. She gave absolutely nothing away, which is what I prefer.

"Your brother's a big lad and only young when he passed, just in his thirties."

She confirmed this was correct, and then I continued.

"But I don't feel as though I've got an adults mind, it feels a little bit childish." Again, this was correct.

"He's talking about his end being violent, in fact I feel he was murdered," I told her.

Again, this was correct.

"He's showing me this is something to do with the Kray twins," I went on, "I'm not saying they did it but the Kray twins were involved."

This, she informed me, was one hundred percent correct. At this point, she was breathing quite fast and waiting on my every word.

"Your brother's telling me he was shot," as those words came out of my mouth, the penny dropped.

In my mind, I saw him with an axe. I told her that her brother was Frankie Mitchell, known as the Mad Axeman.

"My God, you've actually named him, I can't believe this." she exclaimed, "I've been waiting for him to come through for forty years!"

She was astounded and then asked what had happened to his body. I answered her question, along with who had killed him and other information he gave me. The lady was so thankful and it was lovely to help her finally connect with her brother after all those years.

Chapter 35
Reigning Cats And Dogs

At home my relationship with Nicky began to stall. This had nothing to do with Nicky and everything to do with my insecurities, which stemmed from my past and the lack of love I felt as a child. In stark contrast to the sense of being insignificant to my parents, Nicky was incredibly close to her family and loved to be surrounded by them. It was natural for them to reach out to be together whenever possible, Nicky would go shopping with her mum, we would have Sunday dinners there, every Mother's Day, Father's Day, family birthdays, Easter celebrations. Whatever the occasion, they loved to celebrate it together. One time, when Nicky and I lived in Vernon Way, Braintree, although her parents only lived around the corner, they came to our house on the Christmas Eve and didn't return to their house until New Year's Day.

A sense of being almost suffocated by their sense of togetherness threatened to engulf me. Increasingly it felt to me as if I was in a cage, albeit gilded, in which I felt cramped. I longed for space away from everyone. It stirred up feelings within me that I couldn't process, simply because I didn't understand what was going on within me. Deep down I simply didn't feel part of their group but this wasn't down to them. They were incredibly nice to me, such good people, they really did their best to make me feel part of the family. But because I had never been close to my family, their world seemed so foreign to me. I had no reason to feel resistance to them, but progressively I subconsciously sought to exile myself from the family group.

Not having any reference points in common with my own upbringing, the way they were together just seemed 'wrong' to me. I began to slightly resent Nicky being so close to them and felt she was always putting them first, I felt like an afterthought. Nicky is the most generous person I know but she would spend money that she didn't even have. Christmas she would just load up with everything, nobody wanted for anything, yet she hated anyone else putting their hand in their pocket. She never wanted people to bring drinks or anything else and would always tell them we would do it. That's just how she is and how she has always been.

At the time Nicky didn't have much of a job, she was just doing a few part-time jobs and the doctor's surgery. I wasn't earning great money then and the money that I had from the sale of the flat had gone into renovating Vernon Way, having block paving put out the front, fitted wardrobes in the bedrooms, redecorating, landscaping the garden and fencing, and paying up some of Nicky's bills, which was fair enough as I was living there. Basically we weren't flush for money then and the readings were only cheap about twenty or thirty pounds per reading.

If I'm honest, I began to begrudge the way she lavished her time and money on others. Now of course I see that was simply a reflection of the hurt child within me that longed for parents who would demonstrate their love for me. Birthdays and Christmas were times when the sharp sting of resentment would well up. That at least was an easier emotion to cope with, rather than dealing with the past hurt and sadness that was at the root of my dissatisfaction.

Instead of facing the sense of vulnerability that being around her family brought up in me, I chose to run away from what I thought was the problem. In my mind I justified this decision by pointing the finger at my relationship with Nicky, which was becoming increasingly difficult. I convinced her to move with me to France. I think the relationship would have gone boss-eyed then if we hadn't.

We looked at several cottages and Nicky knew I wanted another cottage but we didn't have the money to buy the one we wanted. When I had visited France with Ann Walmsley, I fell in love with the openness of the country. Looking back, I had been working the nightclubs surrounded by a crowd of people and then coming home to be surrounded by Nicky's family. France represented freedom and a chance to put a large gap between myself and the sense of being hemmed in by others. It had all become too much for me. Nicky wanted to prove to me that she would put me first and that I came before her family. So the gesture to move away from them was her way of saying 'This is how much I love you.'

Eventually we found a lovely cottage in Normandy. It was an old timber framed cottage with about an acre of land and tennis courts, situated in the most beautiful remote valley. When we set eyes on the place, we just looked at each other and burst out laughing because it was a real 'chocolate box' place and better still, it was in our price range. We fell in love with the cottage. It needed quite a bit of renovation but we worked out that we could buy it, renovate it and still have a bit of money left over. The money I had received as a result of my time in hospital would help towards our dream home.

We took off for France, Nicky, Amy and myself with Bandit, our dog and Mr. Wheels the cat. When we got to the French side, the snow was incredibly deep and even the lorries had to stay off the roads. I remember stopping in some woods to let Bandit out for a run, together with the cat, on the way to our new home. Both of them were charging around in the snow. Bandit was such a livewire frolicking in the snow and when we called him back, he climbed into the car. We had a slight panic wondering where the cat was, but we called him and he came flying back into the car too. Arriving late, our first job was to get the big open fire going to warm ourselves up. The next day my brother Lee, along with Nicky's dad Les and her brother Brian, were on their way over with all of our furniture and possessions, but due to the snow were late.

When the lads arrived, Nicky's dad found an unwanted internal flush faced door, and he asked if he could have it, which we answered yes. The next thing we knew, Nicky's dad, who was in his sixties, disappeared outside with the others and we could hear copious laughing. We went outside to discover him standing on the door, using it as a snowboard down the slope and falling arse over head in the process. It was such a funny sight.

Nicky and I spent our time non-stop working on the house but enjoyed it and managed to make some great friends there. Just up the road from us there was an older couple, who were the greatest fun ever. They owned a massive mill house with a huge wheel that rotated around, which they were renovating. The local area had very few English people, it was mostly French and our nearest neighbours were farmers, Christian and Isobel. Because of our dog Bandit being a Staffordshire bull terrier and it being a rural area with cattle and horses around, Christian kindly fenced off all our land.

As our cottage was deep in the countryside, we were lucky to see any cars drive past, usually the most we could hope for was a couple of tractors. Sadly, just after a couple of months Mr. Wheels, our cat, was run over. It was so sad because in all the time we had lived in Braintree, apart from being clipped by a car and having a hip operation, in three years there had been no major events. Yet within a couple of months of being in France, in the middle of nowhere on a little road, that happened. We were driving Amy to school one morning and there was his little body. To say we were devastated is an understatement. Just like everyone else, mediums mourn the loss of a pet, and he was a lovely cat. When we lived in Vernon Way because I was at home all day, he loved me and used to come into the reading room, jump up on the table, sit there looking at me and then get his paw and play with my books and pens, swiping them onto the floor. He would then look at me as if to say 'So what are you going to do about that then?' After I had picked them up, he would do it again. We were really sad to lose him.

Nicky and I were sitting in our lounge one day and felt the energy of Mr. Wheels coming down the stairs. Both of us could see his spirit and then suddenly he disappeared, so that was lovely proof that he was still around us. On the day he was killed, we looked up and two planes had travelled through the sky and the vapour trails put a perfect cross right above our house. We buried him in the garden, bless his heart.

Living in such a rural area meant that we had to cohabit with the local mice, hence we decided we needed a cat to keep them out of the house. In France they don't have the big RSPCA centres as we do. Luckily we found a place in Lourgeres, a private establishment that took in stray animals. Often the French working dogs would be put in there when they could no longer work on the farms, rather than have them put down. There were lots of old labradors, spaniels and pointers. Anyway, off we went to have a look. Nicky came up with the idea of perhaps having two cats and we explained to the lady that owned the animal sanctuary what we wanted. She took us into a caged area that was tiny, just eight feet square at the very most and there were quite a few cats in there. There were shelves that clipped onto the wire at different levels on which the cats sat. I really liked the ladies that ran the sanctuary because they were totally self-funded, relying on donations only and they really did try their best with what little resources they had.

Two black cats caught our eye until suddenly this little grey cat with a misty eye jumped from its perch and landed on Nicky's shoulder and started licking her face. The lady picked up the cat and put it back on a shelf, telling us it was a bad cat that they had re-homed twice but each time it had been returned to the sanctuary. Again the cat jumped down onto Nicky's shoulder and started licking her face again and nuzzling into her. The lady picked the cat up and yet again returned it to the shelf. Well, this was a determined cat, because it then jumped onto my shoulder and started licking my face, before jumping back onto Nicky. According to the lady, this cat didn't like people and it was vicious, yet here it was wanting to cuddle up to us. Nicky and I both decided this was the cat for us and we told the lady we would take it. Well, it was so wild that I'm not sure it would have lasted much longer at the sanctuary. The lady begged us not to take the cat, as she was convinced we would just return it in a short while as it was such a bad cat. Nicky was adamant we would have it. The woman wouldn't take any money for the cat, so sure was she that the cat would be back.

Whilst the paperwork was being sorted out, I went into the office and I could hear a dog whining. I asked the lady what the noise was. She pulled the curtain back and there was one of the ugliest dogs I had ever seen looking through the bars at me. It had long ears, skinny legs, very odd muscular body, only young perhaps eight months old. The lady let the dog out and it came over to me, it was such a muscular, strange looking dog. Evidently it was half English bull terrier and half Doberman, not very big at all, the lady let it out and it trotted over to us. I mentioned it looked an unusual dog, she said it had to be put down because in France anything with bull terrier in it is classed as a dangerous dog, but she had fallen in love with it. It was a sweet dog, even though it wasn't the prettiest pooch in the world.

It was too late, my heart strings had been plucked and I revealed that I already had a bull terrier. Her mind began to whirl and she told me that perhaps an excuse could be made about the dog, she could make out that something had happened to it and asked if I would take it, otherwise it would be put down. Nicky put her hand to her head in a gesture of disbelief as I agreed to take it but I decided the dog would be good company for Bandit, who seemed a bit bored with his own company. We couldn't take the cat and the dog together, so I paid for the dog, and we returned home with the cat.

Curled up in his bed, Bandit looked up to see the cat coming through the door. Albert the cat walked straight up to Bandit and firmly swiped him with his paw. Luckily Bandit was very gentle with cats as he had been brought up with Mr. Wheels. Bandit looked astonished as Albert checked out our cottage. He padded around upstairs before coming down to snuggle into the settee for a cat nap. Albert had definitely decided this was Chez Moi. The French have a saying about a person being like a weathervane, and he was certainly a changeable cat. One minute he was all loving purrs, the next he was a martial artist with sharp claws, but we loved him and still have him all these years later.

The next day, we returned to pick up the dog, who we named Bella. What a nightmare. On our property we had a five bar gate that she jumped over with ease, so we put wire on the top of it. She jumped that too. This was no dog, it was an Olympian athlete. New gates seven feet high had to be ordered, which she couldn't vault over. Instead she decided to tunnel her way out.

We had a dog who was increasing in size daily and who couldn't be controlled. One word from us and she did what she wanted. Unfortunately, that was the least of our problems, because if there was one thing she hated, it was bikes. Now, as you may know, cycling is a popular hobby in France. Within a week of having her, she managed to escape, I ran out to find her. Just as I was about to catch up with her, a cyclist zoomed past on a racing bike. Unfortunately his speed was no match for hers and she had him off the bike. I was mortified and apologized profusely but luckily he wasn't harmed. What started as a nightmare turned into the most wonderful, sweetest dog in the world, who is still part of our family and has luckily ceased her racing pursuits. Pets help to make a house a home, and so it was with Albert and Bella, along with Bandit, as we all settled into life in what had become a new home for all of us.

Chapter 36
Healing Messages In Unlikely Places

I was living in France but travelling back to England to work, the readings and the shows kept going. I was serving the spiritualist churches and made some wonderful friends. Yet sometimes, even with all the work I was doing, spirit would prompt me in the most unlikely of places.

There was one time when I had travelled back to England and Nicky asked me to pop into the Freeport shopping centre in Braintree to buy some fragrance oils. As I picked up the various oils, I became very aware that the son of the lady serving in the shop was standing beside her. Now, you can imagine that when people come to see me at a show or for a private reading, they know what to expect. But out of the blue? Her son was imploring me to let his mum know that he was okay.

"Excuse me, but your son wants me to tell you that he's fine and happy on the other side of life," I started.

"I beg your pardon?" she was clearly startled.

"Your son, you lost a son in a road accident, something to do with a lorry," I said.

"Yes, he was hit by a lorry," she confirmed, "Have you read about this in a newspaper?"

I told her that I knew nothing about it, that I lived in France and had only returned to England that day. "Was his name James?" I questioned.

Of course, she was convinced that I must have read about it, but I assured her I wouldn't come into the shop to cause her distress. It was obvious that she was a bit put out and I could tell this was going nowhere. Mentally I told James that I couldn't do anything there in the shop, that his mother wasn't having any of it.

"Tell her this," James demanded.

I told the lady that I would take the oils and be out the shop.

"Before I go, he just wants me to tell you one thing," I said.

"What's that?" she didn't seem convinced at all.

"He's just saying you haven't got to pay for the tooth now Mum," I revealed.

Her face crumbled as she said "My God, you couldn't have known that. Nobody could've known that."

Of course I had no idea what it meant, I had just parroted exactly what James had told me. Evidently, he was due to get married and he had knocked his front tooth completely out. Not wanting their son to go up the aisle with a tooth missing, his parents offered to pay for a tooth implant, which is a very expensive procedure. Now, who would say that to a grieving mother, that she didn't have to pay for the tooth now? Apparently James had passed to the other side before the tooth was ever done.

There was another time when I was in Colchester buying new trainers. A very polite, young girl served me, who was probably only seventeen years old. As she was serving me, her granddad came through and she was somewhat bewildered when I informed her of this. I explained to her that I was a medium and talked to spirit.

"You were so close to your granddad, he hasn't been gone long," I revealed, "And he's saying he lived in Clacton."

The young girl confirmed this was all true.

"Will you please look after your nan Bet and make sure she's okay," I carried on, "He's telling me that he loves her and everything is okay."

Well, she went out into the back room and didn't return for ages but when she did so her face was wet with tears. The other staff gathered round me asking if I could tell them anything, but I explained that no, it was just a message for her that had come through. About a year later, a lovely lady came for a reading and told me that I had met her daughter, who had sold me a pair of trainers. The mother told me I had changed her daughter's life because she had arrived home from work transformed. Readings can happen off the cuff like that, which is great when spirit want to get a message across. But more than that, what I most appreciate about mediumship is that messages have such power to heal. Such is the beauty of mediumship.

An amazing story involved my brother Lee, who worked in the print industry for many years. A chap he knew, not terribly well but he was acquainted with, Brendan Boland, mentioned to Lee that he had heard about a wonderful medium called Ronnie Buckingham. Lee told him that I was his brother and Brendan asked if he could arrange a reading for him, which he did. Lee explained that he thought that Brendan may have lost someone close to him but that he didn't know any details.

Brendan arrived with his wife Martina. Their wonderful son, a young lad, came through immediately. He was only in his early teens and explained that he had been killed in a road accident and even gave the make, model and the colour of the car and even most of the registration number of the car that killed him, which was correct.

I described what I had been shown, that the events weren't as they had been described in court. Brendan revealed that he had always suspected that to be the case. He also confirmed the information I had been given, that Stephen had only had a few driving lessons and had never driven an automatic.

"I believe he was encouraged to take your car for a joy ride by this other lad," I told him.

The court case I understand found that Stephen had been driving. Stephen went on to show me what was in the coffin with him.

"He's got a snooker cue with him in the coffin and a condolence card from Ronnie O'Sullivan."

Again, Brendan confirmed this as true, apparently Stephen was a very good amateur snooker player, a real character, who would swear and carry on, a real lad. He has a brother, Niall and I mentioned to Brendan that he had a sister.

"Yes, I have, Eilish is her name," he verified.

"Who is Trevor to her?" I asked.

"That's her husband," he answered.

"Well, I'm being told you're seeing them very soon," I related.

"Funnily enough, I'm picking my sister and her husband up from Stansted Airport this afternoon," said Brendan, clearly surprised.

"I don't fully understand this but Stephen's talking about your sister wearing black with white socks," I said, curious myself with what it all meant, "And she's talking about Michael Jackson."

Both Brendan and Martina scratched their heads. They couldn't make heads nor tails of the message, but it was on the taped recording of the session for them to think about later. They left the reading thoroughly convinced and happy that their son had come through and was definitely still living on. A few hours later I received a call from Brendan. In his broad Irish accent he informed me that he had waited in the foyer at Stansted Airport, whilst his sister went through customs. She came through to the foyer, dressed in a black trouser suit, and as they met Brendan asked her if she was wearing white socks.

"Yes I was but I looked at myself in the mirror this morning," she told him, "And I thought to myself that I looked just like Michael Jackson, so I took them off."

When Brendan played her the tape, she was absolutely gobsmacked that Stephen could put that comical message across. I've stayed very good friends with Brendan and Martina and since that time have read for them on a few occasions. I have an empathy with young Stephen and one day I was mooching around at home and he came to me.

"Ring my dad Ron, please ring my dad, he's really in a bad way, he's crying and driving himself mad over me," he pleaded, "Just ring him up and tell him to stop fucking crying and tell him I'm alright."

Straight away I picked up the phone. After a few rings Brendan answered.

"Brendan, I've got your son Stephen here," I said, "He says will you stop your fucking crying and pull yourself together because he's absolutely fine."

It turned out that Brendan had been sitting on the stairs having what he referred to as a 'Stephen moment,' when the pain of losing his much loved son was simply overwhelming. He was sitting on the stairs with Stephen's photograph, breaking his heart, at the moment when I rang. Stephen was spot on again.

Quite a bit later, Brendan rang me up. "Ronnie, there's a question I need to ask you concerning my Stephen, could you throw any light on it for me?" he asked.

Immediately I said to Brendan, "You're going to dig him up," more information came to me, "You're moving his body to Ireland to be with your mum."

Brendan was taken aback that I had answered him in seconds.

"How did you know that?" he was incredulous.

"Well how do you think I know that?" I replied, "Stephen's telling me."

"You know, you've proved to me once again that my son must be alive," he said, "Because it takes a brave, brave man, to tell a grieving father that he's going to dig his son up."

"You think you're going to dig him up, but there's going to be a problem," I told him, "The Catholic church where he's buried will say yes but someone else will say no. You'll appeal and they'll say no. But on the third appeal, it will happen, and you'll get him there."

Silence echoed down the phone line as Brendan took in the message.

"Who's Anna?" I asked him.

"That's my mum," he said.

I calmly let him know that Stephen would rest with Anna and that he was happy with that idea. I also told him that he would have to get a big casket and that there would be some shenanigans at the airport around the time of Stephen's body being moved. Lo and behold, it was agreed by the church where he was buried about moving the body. However, it turned out that when a body is moved, you cannot put the body into a new coffin, because you have to put the coffin the body is buried in into a new casket. The only place they found that they could get a big enough casket was from the United States. Eventually Stephen was moved to Ireland. But at the time, when they were going over for the reburial, there was a mix-up and someone forgot to put the casket on the plane. So Brendan and Martina arrived in Ireland with their family but the casket was still back in England. Eventually this was sorted out and Stephen now rests with his grandmother. Even now Stephen will come through and I phone Brendan to tell him the message.

"Oh his brother Niall has just changed his car, has he got a Citroen," and everything this lad tells me is correct.

Brendan wrote a book about his experiences and in it he mentions me and how much the readings changed his life and what they have done for him and his family. They are words I treasure dearly.

Chapter 37
Healing Words

Another link to Essex involved a couple who later became special friends, Paul and Edwina Knowles. Although they live in Norfolk and had visited Cawston to see me do a show but had not received a message there, Paul's mother lived just up the road to me in Halstead, Essex, and had seen me a few times. As it was Paul's birthday, his mother paid for a reading for his birthday present. Paul and Edwina turned up at my house together. Edwina wanted to join Paul in the reading room and I told her no, as the reading was for Paul. If she was in the room too then it could be someone for her that comes through, rather than for Paul. She looked a bit disappointed but accepted my comment and sat back down.

As I followed Paul up the stairs, about half way I turned to Edwina. "Actually, you can come up Edwina, because I have your son here and he wants to talk to the two of you."

The reading that followed was extraordinary, what a wonderful little soul he was. William explained how he had passed of cancer at a young age. I was able to describe him perfectly to them. He gave amazing detail of the room he was in when he passed, what was there, such as the colour of the settee, the view as he looked through the french doors, even the basketball net on the side wall. I could see in my mind's eye what looked like a compass but it was a sundial. The details went on and on, such as describing their dog, he then gave thanks and love onto Stephen Turoff and wanted him to know he was absolutely fine.

The couple were amazed. They had received readings before but hadn't been impressed, but they told me that the reading I gave them turned their life around. I hear a lot of people, especially skeptics, say that when someone is suffering a bereavement they will believe anything that is told to them and that they will clasp onto any straw. In my experience, one in a hundred might do that, but most people, especially those who have lost children, want absolute proof.

I've found that I have an affinity with the spirits of young children. All of my best readings have been with children and that reading with William coming through to his parents was one such reading. Being a school teacher and an intelligent lady, Edwina questioned whether I could have found something out about them or looked up information. The couple didn't see how I could have any details about them but still they wondered, because how else could I give them such exact details? Yet they wanted to believe William was still around. I think Stephen Turoff, through his healing, extended William's life by at least two years. Evidently, when they took him for the last healing, Stephen pulled the couple to one side and let them know that sadly there was no more he could do and this wonderful little boy passed over to the other side.

A while after the reading, Edwina contacted me to tell me she had a lot of people in Norfolk interested in spiritualism, and would I consider going there. At the time I wasn't as busy as I am now, so arrangements were made for a few weeks later and off I went to their lovely home. Of course, Edwina knew that I didn't have a clue who was going to come through the door as they were her friends. She interrogated everyone who came out, asking them how the reading went and who came through. I can say hand on heart, and the couple will back me up on this, everyone raved about how amazing the readings were.

I remember one particular family had lost a son. The mother was German and she came for the reading. Her husband, was quite religious and a bell-ringer in the local church. Edwina brought the couple to see me in Braintree for the reading. I picked up how the lady's son Thomas had passed and other details. At the reading I asked what she thought of the reading. Although she said the reading was good, she didn't sound too impressed. She felt there was something about Thomas that if he had been really there he would have come out with. I asked her to come back into the reading room. We sat down and immediately Thomas came through with a big smile of his face. He told me he was a genius at playing the piano and the violin, able to play at a very high standard at concerts. That was the exact information that she wanted.

Sometime later I was back at Paul and Edwina's home, where I used to stay overnight. They were very lovely, hospitable people and would invite friends round. This particular evening they invited the German lady back and her husband came along. He was very skeptical. We all sat in the conservatory with various friends of the couple, and I gave messages. Thomas came through and I told his father things about his family and also Thomas, which he was clearly surprised to hear.

"Thomas tells me that you bought him a Steinway piano, even though you knew he only had months to live," I told him, which he agreed with.

Thomas also predicted another child for the mother, which was totally unexpected but that later turned out to be true.

"Have you looked on the lid of that piano?" I asked the couple, which they said they had not. "Well there's a burn mark on it, someone had put a cigarette on it," I informed them.

Later, when they had checked the lid they found the burn mark, it was absolutely true.

Another story involved Debbie Nelson, another friend of with Paul and Edwina. I first met Debbie when I did a show at a big hall in Norwich, a very posh place. Sitting right at the front, she was such a character with a huge grin on her lovely face, a real happy-go-lucky type of person. I ended up giving her a private reading, as her mother had passed, and then later on when her father had passed.

It's so important as a medium to develop your general knowledge and increase your vocabulary. It was something that let me down on this particular occasion because before he died, Debbie's father had agreed a secret password that only the two of them would know. The password was fuchsia. Now, I'm no Alan Titchmarsh, I know the difference between a rose, a daffodil and a pansy but that's about my limit. Debbie came for the reading and her dad came through with wonderful stuff for her. At the end of the reading, as I always do, I asked if she had any questions. She told me that her and her father had a password and that if he was really coming through to speak to her he would say that one word, and then she would definitely know it was him.

Hearing spirit is very difficult, most of my mediumship is done through feelings and symbols and it's not always possible to hear something exactly. Sometimes names can be difficult, for instance, Jenny or Jeannie or Irene or Eileen, Margaret or Margary, Mary and Marie, they can all sound very similar to me. So, Debbie's father tried to give me the password in the way that I would find easiest and showed me a vision. I felt frustrated because I knew it was the name of a flower and I told her she had a gutter and it comes down the pipe, maybe of an outside building and it ran into a water butt. Debbie agreed that it did. I could also see that at the base of the water butt were some flowers in a pot, a pinky red colour, which came up and bent over. It was the best I could do because I didn't know what they were called. Debbie burst out laughing and told me she would settle for that. If only I had known what the plant was, like a rose or daffodil, it would have been so much easier. That made me think that it was important for me to try to learn more about flowers and to improve my word power. It really can come in very handy when dealing with the spirit world.

Through my time in Cawston, I met the Buergi family, a Swiss family. I was invited out to Switzerland, originally not with this particular family but a girl who used to help with translation at Cawston, called Gabby, who invited me to Switzerland to do readings and workshops. One of the readings was for Ellen Buergi and her son Daniel. Incredibly clever people, I think Daniel speaks six languages fluently and has a grasp of a couple of others. He was very impressed with his reading and so his family asked me to go out again to Switzerland, stay with them and do readings. They actually lived just over the border on the outskirts of Germany. I had some amazing times there.

On one occasion, we were in Zurich, in a building that had four flights of stairs up to the office where the readings were carried out. A gentleman booked in called Sepp, as we waited we were advised that he would be late as he was heavily crippled. He was on two crutches as he had been hit by a lorry whilst he was riding his motorbike and had been smashed up badly. We looked over the stairwell to see him being helped up by other members of the family. Bless him, sweat poured off him as he made his way step by step towards the office. Eventually he made his way into the room and sat next to his wife. I picked up the details of the accident and what was going on with him personally. After the reading, Sepp had tears rolling down his cheeks, he felt so pleased that his parents came through and gave him wonderful proof. Although his English wasn't brilliant, Ellen kindly interpreted for us both and although she was originally from Holland, she spoke English and Germany fluently. As I mentioned earlier, I used to do a lot of healing but my problem was that I began taking on the pain and the symptoms of the conditions that people had. But now spirit prompted me to give Sepp healing and although he didn't understand what that healing was, I spent twenty minutes with him, after which the others helped him back down the stairs.

After my week in Zurich, I received a message from Sepp's wife asking if they could see me again. The couple wanted me to see the wonderful improvement in Sepp that had occurred since his visit to see me. They travelled to Eikberg to see me at the house there, I was situated on the middle floor, where he came for more healing. He managed the stairs surprisingly well and had another healing session. The difference in this man was unbelievable. Since that time, I have been back to Switzerland three or four times. Sepp had been on the two crutches and in a terrible way for some years. By my second visit to Switzerland he was walking and really showing off to me using just one walking cane. He would walk up the entire length of the room, turn around and walked back smiling triumphantly. Since that time he has made constant improvement, so much so he nicknamed me 'The Angel.' What a lovely man and I was so proud of what he achieved.

Healing doesn't always work and there was a tragic occurrence within the Buergi family. Ellen's sister, Nicolette, has a daughter Celine, unbeknown to them was that Long QT syndrome ran in the family and Celine had the condition. This is where the heart beat and the heart will stop and not beat again for a long time. Celine was the most stunning looking young girl and barely sixteen years old when she had a terrible heart attack. Medical staff took a long time bringing her back to us and regrettably she came back severely disabled, with no speech and confined to a wheelchair because her hands and legs were twisted. This was heartbreaking for the family. I travelled out to see her to give her healing, hoping that in some way I could help her to get better. Celine had terrible tantrums and tempers, which were understandable, as this once vibrant, stunning looking girl, who had lots of friends, was now in a wheelchair and completely dependent on her parents.

Ellen's parents were Gert, who is still with us, and Nicol, who sadly passed to the other side. Nicol was a pilot from the 1920s and worked for the Dutch airline KLM. He was a very special man, straight down the line and very strict and he wasn't having any of this mediumship business, he was very abrupt about it all.

Following my return to England, I received a phone call from Ellen to tell me they were at the hospital and Celine was dying. I was gutted to hear the news and couldn't take it in, I wanted to know what had happened. Apparently her body was boiling up and the hospital staff were trying everything to stop it, but if her temperature went a few degrees higher, the prognosis was not good. All of the family were with her because they were certain she was about to pass to the other side. I told Ellen that I would send her healing. Again, this can all be proved. Going into the bedroom and shutting the door behind me, I laid on my bed and said my prayers. In my mind I could visualize Celine. Using the power of imagination, I surrounded this stricken young girl with blocks of ice and I prayed with all my heart for this beautiful young soul. Some fifteen minutes later the phone rang again. There was sobbing at the end of the line.

"Ronnie, her temperature has dropped," Ellen cried, "It just dropped like a stone. She's gone right back to normal and nobody can get over it, not even the hospital staff, they can't explain it."

Ellen had said to Nicol that I would try some healing to cool her down but her words were met with tuts of disbelief but that one event completely changed Nicol. Whenever I went to Switzerland, I stayed in their lovely apartment in Zurich. I gave Nicol and Gert a reading. For once, Nichol was impressed, which coming from such a skeptic as he was, I took as quite a compliment. In front of all of his family, Nicol put his arm around me with such warmth.

"Friends you and I, friends until death," he said.

The family were speechless because they couldn't believe what Nicol had said. Funnily enough, I gave Nicol healing as he had some problems with his head and I diagnosed what was wrong with him, which was later confirmed by the hospital. The Buergi family swear to this day that I added three years to his life. We became great friends and I still speak to them on a regular basis.

CHAPTER 38
HELPING HANDS

As my mediumship work continued to expand, my relationship with Nicky began to contract. In retrospect, I think when I wasn't working abroad, we were with each other all day and probably both needed an outlet. I returned to England more regularly to work as we ran out of money renovating the property. When Nicky's family visited they spent two weeks at a time, as they made it their holiday destination. To be honest, I'm not totally sure why I felt it was a problem as we are now fantastic friends, but at the time it was too much for me. It always felt too over-powering for me. Her mum was, and still is, very opinionated and we would clash regularly, as I can be quite abrupt too. In the end, her family carefully timed their journeys to end when I would return to France. Often as I was at the port of Dover, I would see them returning back to England. I suppose I became a bit resentful. There I was coming back to England, working like mad, taking money back to pay bills and I just didn't feel I was getting anywhere with it all.

We made fantastic friends, enjoyed great parties and picked up a bit of the language. Although there were some fun times, my relationship with Nicky became strained. A lot of this I think was because whilst I was off travelling to work in England, Switzerland, Gibraltar and elsewhere, Nicky was on her own in France. Amy was fluent in French, as she was the only

English child in her school she had to be, but Nicky and I had only a basic grasp of French. Nicky felt alienated, compounded by the fact that the few English people we knew regularly returned to their properties in England. She felt totally alone. After four years, Nicky wanted to sell the cottage in France and return to England. It wasn't what I wanted at all. I felt at home in France, the tranquility and way of life suited me, it was so different from the daily rush back in England.

Things came to a head when Nicky was offered a full-time position at the doctor's surgery where she used to work. She decided to take it. We had been having some huge rows and everything was going from bad to worse, as we were around each other twenty four hours a day, without much distraction. Money was tight, as we had spent too much money on the cottage, and that became another battleground. If I'm honest, we had been a bit silly with it. To cut a long story short, her family came to pick her up, she took Albert with her and moved back to England. What was I to do, stuck in France with the two dogs? There was no way on God's earth that I would ever part with my dogs, neither Bandit nor Bella. That wasn't going to happen. However, my French wasn't fluent enough for me to be able to work in France. Besides mediumship wasn't big out there, the idea of talking to spirits bewildered people.

One such example involved our English friends, Elaine and a chap we named Battersea John, who loved a drink. They lived over in Vimoutiers and Nicky and I occasionally visited them, which was great as it was easier to chat in English. One night all four of us were in a bar. There was a barmaid behind the bar and I saw the spirit of a young man standing next to her, who told me that he was her brother. I asked John, whether he knew the barmaid and he said he knew of her as it was his local bar, but he didn't know her well.

"She lost her brother in a car accident," I told him.

"Did she?" His eyebrows shot up. "How do you know that?"

"He's got his hair in a pony tail with a bow in it and he's wearing a silver ring on his finger that he's saying is significant," I answered, "And I think his name was Francois."

John's eyes widened even more. "Are you sure about this?" he asked.

"I'm positive," I answered.

John deliberated about whether to tell her or not. Finally, he walked over to the barmaid and started conversing in French with her. She looked over John's shoulder at me and her face paled.

"Fucking hell mate, you're spot on," he gasped, "She lost her brother Francois, he had a pony tail with a ribbon in it."

He offered to translate and I gave her more information, which was absolutely right and it fascinated her. However, there was no way I could see that I could make a living doing readings out there in France.

Nicky moved in with her mum and took over the spare bedroom, but there was no room for me or for the two dogs. Her mum had two cats of her own and what with Albert, who terrorised the other cats, it was enough. Although they had very little room, the family are very close and made room for Nicky and Albert. My brothers couldn't accommodate me as they had dogs too. What was I to do?

As luck would have it, there was a lady that I had done a reading for, who was a friend of my brother's then partner Linn. She had a bungalow in Sible Hedingham that was being renovated but work had stopped on it because of planning matters. It had half a roof, the rest was a tarpaulin. There was a bedroom, one reception room, a bathroom and a kitchen, although parts of the kitchen was just canvas. It was a little short of a building site really, full of dust. However, as they say, beggars can't be choosers. A week later I put the dogs into the jeep, closed up the French cottage, put it up for sale and then made my way back to England. I moved into the bungalow paying a small rent, grateful for the opportunity to find somewhere for me and my dogs.

Luckily enough, I had wonderful friends, including Carol and Bob Martin, with their son Elliott, who had a beautiful house in Yeldham, which was just up the road, and they allowed me to do readings there. I struggled because all of our money was tied up in France, every penny we had. The cottage was up for sale but of course the garden had to be maintained, and the cottage itself needed maintenance. Worse still, it just wasn't selling. In the end It took two years to sell and Nicky and I travelled back to France to cut the grass and tidy it up, or else we would have to pay others to do it for us. Basically it was an absolute money pit.

Nicky is a very bright, clever and conscientious lady and luckily had a couple of promotions and eventually became the assistant practice manager at the doctor's surgery. I continued with the readings and work started to come in, such as a few shows, so I managed to make ends meet. After about three months, the planning issues on the bungalow I rented were resolved and further renovation works were due to start, so I had to move out. The problem was that it was difficult to find somewhere to rent. As soon as I mentioned I had the two dogs, nobody was willing to rent me a house. I figured my only option was to buy somewhere, the only problem being I needed a deposit but my money was tied up in France. Many hours were spent with my head in my hands trying to work out what to do. There was also the question of the couple of debts on credit cards I had to pay off before I could get a mortgage. Carol and Bob came to the rescue straight away and lent me some money to pay up my debts. They were a godsend and I worked hard to pay them back as quickly as I could.

I looked at a nice house in Great Yeldham with a thought of buying it. In the meantime, Nicky was looking for a house as well but she didn't want to move out to Yeldham, she wanted to be in Braintree, where I didn't want to be. Our house in France had still not sold. I needed somewhere and felt frustrated that I couldn't get everything sorted out. One evening I was on the phone talking to the Buergi family and Ellen asked me what the problem was. I told her I was experiencing problems finding somewhere to rent because of the dogs and that I had to look for somewhere to buy instead, but was being delayed regarding a deposit, due to the house in France not being sold. She asked me how much I needed and I told her it was a silly amount of money. Immediately she asked me for my bank details and she popped the money into my account straight away. Ellen and Heine, who was still with us then, God bless him, were so good to me. I had explained to Ellen that I had no idea when the house in France would sell, it had been on the market for ages and we had not had a single viewing. Nicky and I had already dropped the price but it remained unsold. The couple were insistent that I borrow the money and not worry about when it would be paid. It was such a blessed relief and so incredibly kind of them both.

With the deposit money in the bank, I managed to secure a mortgage and bought a lovely terraced house that had just been renovated. It was lovely to move in there with Bandit and Bella. I asked Nicky if she wanted to move in too but she declined as it was too far from work and she wanted to stay with her mum. We ended up seeing each other just on Fridays and Saturdays, Nicky would stay and then went back to her parents. It was quite hard work. So there I was with the two dogs, doing readings.

Before all of this happened, a serendipitous event happened on a golfing day out with my brother Lee. When we arrived at the tenth hole there was an old gentleman sitting down on his own. I invited him to join us as it was no fun for him going around on his own, and he was delighted to accept. Bill Dawson was an older, small framed man, and a decent golfer. We teed off and enjoyed the round of golf together. He asked what two big strapping men like Lee and myself were doing playing golf in the middle of the day, and asked us if we worked. Lee was still in the job I had managed to get him in the print industry with The Sun, he was there for around nineteen years in all, and he told Bill he worked nights and was free during the day. Of course Bill then asked me what I did for work. I told him I was self-employed and he asked what I did, and I answered that I was a medium.

Unbeknown to me, Bill had often sat in circle with Albert Lamb and had studied mediumship and spiritualism for a long while. It was summer and I was walking around in a short sleeved shirt, heavily tattooed and what with my Cockney accent, I'm sure he was surprised at my choice of career. He didn't say a great deal. We all went onto the next tee, Bill put his ball down to get his driver out.

"Right, so where is this ball going to go then?" he quipped.

"I told you I'm a medium, not a fortune teller," I laughed.

That meant something to Bill and to cut a long story short, he asked me if I would give him a reading. Well, I managed to get his family through and he couldn't believe it. He then asked if I would give his wife Margaret a reading, which I did. We became friends and then Margaret, who knew I was under a lot of pressure, offered to come forward and actually take over my bookings. Having my diary arranged by her took a lot of pressure off me. The reason it can be difficult is that basically even though there is a long waiting list, people beg to jump the queue. Of course, if I say no that isn't possible, then I'm called a hard-hearted so and so, and if I say yes then I am a soft touch and end up doing more than I can do. Bill and Margaret came into my life in a big way and to this day Margaret still handles all of my bookings. We call her the rottweiler because nobody gets past Margaret. Even if they tell her that they are great friends with me, or absolutely need a reading urgently, they are given a date and that is that.

Back in Great Yeldham, I worked really hard to get some money together. The house in France took a further two years to sell. When it did finally sell, I paid back the Buergi family and bought a decent car, after which I only had a little bit over. Of course Nicky had her share, but we lost an awful lot of money on the house in France. We still saw each other and Nicky continued to look for a house for herself. Surprisingly the house right next door to her mum came up for sale. Although Nicky had looked at other houses, I knew she would buy the house next door to her mum. It was semi-detached and needed quite a bit of work but it had a good sized garden. She definitely wanted it but it wouldn't have been what I had wanted. I suggested we buy a place together but she was adamant that she needed to be on her own. We were only seeing each other at the weekend and sometimes she couldn't see me at all because she had social events to go to. What with that and buying the house next to her mum, it seemed the only course of action was to end the relationship.

It was four months before we saw each other. By chance, I drove into a garden centre at exactly the same time as Nicky, we parked right next to each other and I ended up following her into the garden centre. We had a chat and decided to give our relationship another go. But it was the same old thing, she was adamant she was going to buy the house next to her parents, which eventually she did. Some friends of ours offered to help her with the building work but it turned out to be an absolute disaster. She ended up losing loads of money and I ended up putting some of my money into the house so that it could be renovated. I didn't want to move into that house and stayed in Great Yeldham. The situation was crazy. We had been together eleven years and yet we were basically just dating, it was stupid.

I still did the occasional reading at Carol's house and also at Margaret's place, the shows started to take off and my financial situation was improving and I even started saving a bit. I was with Nicky until her house was completely renovated, the extension had been added and it looked nice. But then things went from bad to worse between us. In the end I told her it was ridiculous and we called it a day. The only time that she was in touch with me was when Albert was in a fight and actually lost an eye. She knew how much I loved him and still do. Nicky wanted to let me know that he was in a bad way. Bandit went through a couple of illnesses and I would then email or text her to let her know, but we didn't actually speak to each other. Other than the odd text or email, radio silence prevailed.

Chapter 39
The Turnaround

Nicky and I went our own ways, although I think perhaps I went more my own way than she did hers. One night, I thought to myself that it was strange that there was this woman, who had been in my life for twelve years, longer than any other woman, yet I had no idea how she was doing or what was happening in her life. It felt really odd. We had been apart for a whole year and I suddenly felt the urge to contact her via email. I told her that it felt bizarre that I had been with her for all those years, yet didn't know if she was happy, sad, with someone or not, and that it all felt so weird, but that I wished her well and told her to take good care of herself. Nicky sent back the loveliest email back to me, telling me that she thought I should come round to see her and find out for myself how she was, and that she really missed me. She also told me to get a babysitter for the dogs or bring them, because I would definitely be staying the night. I went round to see her, she opened the door and that was it. In that moment I realized how much I loved her and had missed her. Nicky felt exactly the same. That was in 2013.

Earlier in our relationship I had mentioned to her about getting married. Nicky had been married twice, firstly marrying very young but her husband had played around, and then she remarried but unfortunately was widowed when her husband had passed at just twenty nine years old.

After that she remained alone for years. Whenever I brought up the subject, Nicky maintained that it wasn't necessary for us. That hurt me because she had married two other people, but despite her protestations that I was the love of her life and that she loved me more than she had loved anyone else, she wanted to keep things as they were.

On the night we got back together, I asked her to marry me and this time she said yes with no hesitation. We rushed the wedding through and were married within a matter of months on 18th November 2013. Since then, I've never looked back. I can honestly say, hand on heart, I've never ever been happier. They say absence makes the heart grow fonder and in our case that was certainly true. We had both missed each other so much during our time apart. Setting up home in the house next door to her mum, with all our pets back together, was total bliss. Nicky's parents adored Bella and Albert, although Albert could still be spiteful and Nicky's mum had a few reservations about him. There are now two big gardens for Bella, who goes from our house through the open gate into theirs. My relationship with Nicky's parents has been transformed, I get on so well with them. When we go out they look after Bella, often Nicky's dad will pop round and cut the grass for us, and we're all great friends.

Now I understand that my previous resistance to her family was simply me fighting with something that wasn't familiar to me. I didn't understand their love for each other, or the sense of togetherness they all felt. It felt so foreign to me. Luckily they gave their blessing to our wedding, any arguments from the past were forgotten. They have completely changed me for the better.

With my darling wife Nicky.

I hate karaoke but Nicky's brother, Robert, is an entertainer who sings and plays guitar and even has his own recording studio. There was a party at his house not long ago and of course he had all the karaoke equipment in the basement. This time, instead of giving messages, I crooned. Can you imagine a medium singing Monster Mash? It was hilarious but fortunately didn't go viral on the internet. Luckily for the world, I've decided to keep my usual day job!

So, in a bit of a turnaround, I'm totally happy living next door to Nicky's family. It's such a blessing to be part of such a wonderful family and I truly wouldn't want to live anywhere else. They really are great company and in the end, it was just that I needed to relax into it and discover how great family life can be. Sometimes, we just have to get over ourselves don't we?

Chapter 40
Feeling Blessed

My life has been full of sad moments, mistakes and, if I'm honest, one or two regrets along the way. But I can honestly say, hand on heart, that life for me is the happiest it has ever been. Nicky and I were married in a wonderful ceremony surrounded by friends and family. I'm totally in love and my life is at peace now. I still see my mum and I have no axe to grind with her, life is what life is. As I said, my dog Bandit passed over at nearly fourteen years old, bless his heart, and he is buried at the bottom of the garden and I have a little chat with him daily. Nicky and I still have Bella and Albert, the cat we brought back from France, both are old now but happy. Here I am, at sixty two years of age, with my beautiful wife, in a little home next door to my mother-in-law, which is ideal for us. I'm up every morning to walk Bella, I attend the gym virtually every day to train and keep healthy, and I play the odd round of golf.

Nowadays I never work weekends, I have a long waiting list for private readings and I also have about forty seven different venues that I work at, many of them restaurants, clubs and bars. Even after twenty years of working in the local area, I still sell out everywhere I go. Everything has turned out really well but I don't want to do as much because I become more tired now but I love what I do. I especially love the joy and happiness it brings to people. No way do I lay claim that every reading I've ever done has been fantastic, but there have only been very few that I would class as not being so good, although there has always been something there. As in this life, people communicate at different levels and it's the same with spirits. It seems I've always had an affinity with children, as they seem to come through stronger and better than anyone else. I could list a whole host of stories and produce hundreds of testimonials from people and I'm incredibly lucky to have such a strong following, as well as many lovely friends.

I've done my best to atone for the wrongs that I've done in the past. I was never a wicked man and never went out of my way to hurt anyone or be spiteful, I just stole for a living, that's what I did. In doing this spiritual work, I hope that I've paid back for some of the crimes I've committed.

Do I regret some of the things that I've done? Yes, I do, one hundred percent. But is it necessary to live with regret all the time? No, it's not. We can only try and be the best that we can be. I've dedicated myself to mediumship and I'll always owe a massive debt to Lyn, who spotted the gift in me, which went on to transform who I am.

I have the most wonderful family and Nicky's family are amazing too. Life for me now is fulfilling. Do I want to live for a long time? Yes, I do. Will I continue working for as long as I can? Yes, I will, even if I won the lottery tomorrow, it wouldn't stop me doing readings. Okay, I might have longer, more extravagant holidays, or maybe drive a nicer car, but I would keep on helping to connect people with their loved ones.

I've always loved all animals and people who see my shows know that I always have on hand an RSPCA box with a little man and dog on top. It goes with me everywhere and I probably fill it up around every six weeks and it holds on average about three hundred pounds. In addition the Danaher centre in Wethersfield, which is an RSPCA centre, has some lovely people doing wonderful work, and I've enjoyed doing shows for them. They kindly invite me as a guest of honour at their open day, where an auction for a private reading with me raises money for the centre. When I hand the money over to Big John, the manager, it's always a brilliant feeling.

I believe everything happens for a reason, we all have a path to follow and that life is a learning curve. Certainly I've learned a great deal in this life. I'm blessed to have great loyal followers, who I thank from the bottom of my heart for being there for me. Each day I thank the spirit world overall for the wonderful gift they have given me, the chance to work for them and the chance now to be proud of myself and be the best that I can possibly be.

Chapter 41
Another Day At The Office

As you will recall, at the beginning of this book I mentioned that being a spiritual medium is sometimes a funny old game. But then sometimes it isn't.

About four months into sitting circle with Lyn, she received a phone call from a chap, who was desperate. He explained to Lyn that he didn't really understand what mediumship was all about, he didn't know about ghosts and spirits, and frankly he hadn't believed in any of it. That was until it became clear to him that there was definitely something wrong with his home.

In her usual brisk fashion Lyn turned to me and announced, "C'mon Ronnie, we're going to go round and sort this place out."

From the outside there was no clue this place was any different to the others in the village. As we pulled up, the chap came to meet us, invited us in, and explained that he had built the bungalow himself. He introduced us to his wife, a very well spoken lady and we chatted amiably for a while. As soon as he could, her husband pulled us to one side and, as he recounted to us what had been happening, his face paled.

"She's just not the woman I married," he explained. "She's angry, she swears and is nasty to the kids, she won't cook, clean or even wash. It's not like her, she's always been perfect but now it's like she has a different personality.

With despair etched in his face he whispered, "I can't put up with it much longer, she's terrible."

He showed us around their home and finally took us into the big double bedroom, which had a range of fitted wardrobes. As he opened the wardrobe doors, the temperature in the room suddenly dropped, as cold air slithered up and enveloped us. In the wardrobe, amongst some stored clothes, was a camcorder in a green casing. The casing was covered in mould. The hairs on the back of my neck stood up as a feeling of unease crept over me. Lyn also sensed that there was something sinister in the bungalow.

His wife was seated in their beautiful, big lounge and we made our way back there to talk to her. Lyn and I sat side by side on a settee, approximately twenty feet across from her. She chatted away pleasantly to us, whilst her husband said very little. Out of the blue, a feeling of alarm snaked up from the pit of my stomach. I was on full alert, but why? Pure instinct warned me something was afoot. Out of the corner of my eye I saw something come into the room and slither over towards the chap's wife. Immediately I sensed the spirit of an elderly man, who was limping. He positioned himself behind her and, as he did so, the image of him in my mind suddenly disappeared.

I nudged Lyn and whispered, "There's something seriously wrong here."

"I know," she breathed, her lips barely moving. Lyn sat there motionless.

"You pair of bastards, get out of my fucking house!" the woman screeched as she jumped up and launched herself at us, "Who the fuck do you think you are coming here."

The obscenities continued to pour in a vile stream from her mouth.

Without batting an eyelid, Lyn said evenly, "This is their house, it's not your house. You're not this woman. Get out!"

With that the woman went ballistic and then literally limped, at high speed, over towards Lyn with her fist raised, spitting obscenities. Jumping up to protect Lyn, I grabbed the woman's raised arm and what amounted to a wrestling match followed with Lyn and myself battling her. Watching the whole scene open mouthed was her husband, who didn't have a clue what to do. Lyn and I managed to wrestle her into the bedroom and, enlisting the help of her husband, we fought to pin her to the bed but she was as strong as an ox. All three of us tried to grab her arms and legs, which flayed around and eventually we managed to contain her. During this Lyn became to speak and pray to the spirit world, reciting the Lord's Prayer and the 23rd Psalm. The obscenities continued to gush forth from the woman. Undeterred, Lyn commanded the spirit to be gone and to leave this woman be. As she did so, a beautiful energy began to fill the room. Lyn and I immediately sensed it was this man's wife.

"Call him across," we pleaded to her spirit, "Please call him across."

Lyn then continually repeated her demand to the spirit of the man contained within the woman's body. "Go towards the light, go towards the light."

She continued to direct his spirit towards the light for around twenty minutes, all the time the three of us were straining to keep the woman pinned to the bed. As strong as I am, I broke out in a sweat with the effort, we all did, but Lyn remained resolute and wouldn't give in.

Out of the blue, a bright white burst of light, almost like a huge sparkler, appeared at the top of the room between the wall and the ceiling. The light suddenly exploded into a massive flash and, at that exact moment, the woman's body became limp, as if she had fainted.

"He's gone, he's left her," Lyn was relieved and exhausted, "His wife came for him."

Just a few minutes later, the woman sat up as if nothing had happened, back to her lovely usual self. We led her into the lounge and as you do in such circumstances, all of us had a cup of tea. My brain whirred trying to make sense of what had just happened. I looked to Lyn for answers, who appeared unperturbed by the event. After a little while, Lyn and I went back into the bedroom and looked in the wardrobes. The mould was still there and yet somehow it was fading right before our eyes. Warmth filled the house as the temperature had risen to reflect the sunny day outside. There was a completely different feel about the place, it was now a loving, warm and friendly space.

Lyn and I investigated the history of the place to try to make sense of why the man had felt compelled to possess the woman. It turned out that the man did indeed have a limp, he and his wife had no children but both had lived to be a good age. His wife was the first to pass and the man was absolutely distraught. They had lived in a bungalow on a large plot of land, on which the man grew prize roses and he enjoyed spending time in his greenhouse raising various plants, as he was a fanatical gardener. When he had lost the love of his life, in his distress with no children to turn to and no real friends to help or advise him, he put the bungalow up for sale, which was subsequently bought by the builder. The elderly man moved into rented accommodation but immediately regretted his decision to sell and desperately wanted to have his bungalow back. It was where he and his wife had spent their life, everything that he held dear, all their special memories, were there.

The elderly man went to see the builder and told him that he wanted to buy the property back, and even offered more money than he had sold it for. However, the builder was unwilling to sell, it was a good buy and he had managed to obtain planning permission for a bigger bungalow. The man pleaded with the builder to reconsider his offer, but the answer was an emphatic no.

The builder proceeded to demolish the bungalow, and each shattered brick broke the old man's heart even more. His beloved home that had been shared with his wife, the greenhouse where he had spent so many happy hours and everything else was destroyed. In its place, the builder constructed a spacious bungalow with block paving and wonderful landscaping, it was a stunning place. Consumed with anger, grief and remorse, the old man made a decision. He gathered together the few items he needed and then hanged himself. The anger this man felt towards the builder for not selling his property back to him was immense and in retribution the man haunted the house and caused mayhem.

The builder didn't have any sense of the spirit world, he was a very down-to-earth type of man, not given to what he considered flights of fancy. On the other hand, his wife was immensely psychic and open. And so the man attached himself to her. He was able to make her life a misery by invading her with his angry personality. The relief the builder felt when the angry spirit of the man finally passed over was immense. But in a sense, although of course we helped him and his wife to live comfortably in their new home, it was less about helping them and more about helping the spirit of the old man because his soul was in torment.

About a month later, Lyn and I sat in circle, along with Bill Brockwell, Pat and a few others, and the old man and his wife came into the circle to pay us a visit. He thanked us profusely for helping him see the truth and for helping him across to join his beautiful wife.

I have to say, it was perhaps the most frightening, totally hair-raising experience of my life, but Lyn really was phenomenal throughout, completely level headed, she knew exactly what she was doing, what a great teacher. As they say, just another day in the office for a spiritualist medium.

Afterword

Dear Reader

I wanted to share some thoughts with you about my journey so far. Life hasn't always been easy for me but there have been some amazing experiences and I'd like to share a few pointers with you that I've picked up along the way.

The most important lesson I've learned is that without a doubt crime doesn't pay. It could be fun, I'm not going to lie about that, there was an adrenaline buzz with it. Perhaps I'd find a safe and when I managed to break it open I'd find thousands of pounds inside. What a massive thrill, especially given that one of my unspoken fears was being like my father, in debt and not able to provide for my family. But when I work it out, what with the time spent in prison, I could easily have earned that money legally. When I look back at the things I missed, the birthdays, the Christmas celebrations, seeing my kids grow up, the family times, the sex even, all that life happening on the outside while I was banged up inside, nothing is worth that price. I'm not a learned man, I left school early and became a laborer, a villain and suchlike, but now I've made something of myself. I live a life now where I don't worry about a knock on the door, being raided, being taken away, or having whatever I have being taken away from me. There's nothing more thrilling than being able to sleep soundly at night, knowing I'm doing my best to help others.

It's important to be true to yourself. The best way to discover that is to be true to those who are important to you, those who love and support you. To love and be loved by someone is paradoxically the best and, at the same time, one of the most difficult aspects of life. Relationships will test you to the limit, but in the end you'll realise they're simply a mirror of the relationship you have with yourself. I sought to find myself through others but eventually I stopped all of that crap, gained an understanding of myself and everything fell into place.

I've had many moments, in between the foolhardiness of youth, when I've doubted myself and wondered if I'm really cut out for a decent life. My biggest fear was always the fear of being a failure, of being a non-achiever, a run of the mill individual with no story to tell. Strangely, that fear worked to my advantage in some ways, as I avoided drugs and alcohol like the plague because I feared ending up a nobody in the gutter.

Yet we all have a God-given gift or talent somewhere, it may be communication, it may be something artistic, it could be all manner of things. The point is, there's something in everyone and you just have to search and find out what it is and dedicate yourself to it. Maybe you've done a lot of searching, most of it in the wrong places, but keep searching because it'll be okay in the end, I promise.

The most important lesson any of us will ever learn is the power of choice. I could've plodded along being a doorman until I was too old to do it anymore, and then found some other work to do. I could've gone that way but thankfully I didn't. Luckily I had the gifts of focus and discipline, which always came quite easily to me, but I think everyone needs a certain amount of focus and discipline in their lives, I really do. It's too easy to say 'Mañana, I'll do it tomorrow,' then it's the week after, then the month after, and things are put off. Focus and discipline can get you through anything because no matter what the task in front of you, you'll see it through.

Always have a goal and when you reach it, create another one. At the end of my life, like the great Gordon Higginson or Doris Stokes, I hope that lots of people will turn round and say "There was a fantastic medium, Ronnie Buckingham, who could give superb proof of the afterlife and he helped so many people." That's my present goal.

Never give up, never say never, never feel sorry for yourself. If you begin to feel sorry for yourself, turn that feeling into anger, and that anger into something else more positive and keep going forward. Always remember that no matter what, you have the ability to transform yourself and change your circumstances. It won't always be easy, but it'll be worth it. You just have to decide to do it.

Do I think a leopard can change its spots? Yes, I do. If there's something about yourself or your life that's not right for you, then change it. You have the ability to change anything and everything in a moment and if you need help, then remember that Spirit is always there, waiting to be asked.

With love,
Ronnie Buckingham

TESTIMONIALS

You gave me evidence of my parents only maybe a family member would know. At times in my life when I've felt I needed something but was not sure of what, I've opted to try and source a sign, or something, to help me know that what I'm doing is right for me. My parents are really the only people that could validate that, and with them not being here anymore, Ronnie you really fill that void for me in your evidence.

I'm not sure I will ever be able to thank you enough for the gift you are happy to share with me, but without a doubt, I endorse your professionalism and mediumship. Your gift to me has been priceless. Thank you so very much.

Kim Baker

I know you read for so many people, you probably won't remember me. You did a wonderful reading for me and my dad came through. You described his injury after a car accident, you knew my brother's name Ian (despite we sadly no longer talk). You kept asking me if I was pregnant and weeks later I actually was. My daughter is four now, nearly five. You also knew, and this part was mind blowing, that my husband had been painting our front door and you joked that my dad said he needed to do it again because it was rubbish! He did have to do it again, as he admitted it was a terrible paint job. You knew my husband and his dad both supported Tottenham.

You described my dad as handsome, yet he has grown a beard in the spirit world, plus you knew he had served in the Air Force.

Your reading brought me so much comfort, so thank you very much. You were amazingly accurate! You are very blessed with your gift.

Lorraine Spillane

My husband and I both came to the meetings in both February and July this year at Headgate in Colchester. At the first meeting people who had messages seemed to find that you were very accurate in details that you gave them. In the July meeting, you opened with a man that sounded as though he could have been my father. When I responded, you went on to give me a very accurate account of my life and my father and the rift that had been in my family. The accuracy with which you detailed the split was absolutely phenomenal. You knew about the sadness that had blighted my life and you told me my father wanted to apologize. He had been dead a number of years and because of the rift, he was the last person I would have expected to get a message from. Later in the evening, just before closing, you gave my husband and I a message from his first wife. Again with such a detailed accuracy.

We would both like to thank you so very much for the peace of mind that you gave to us both. Thank you.

Paula & Brian Beckwith

My first encounter with Ronnie was at my local gym. One evening, a few months after I lost my father, I bumped into Ronnie in the locker room. As it happens, it was just the two of us and he turned to me and said that he had been meaning to talk to me and that I had lost someone very close to me, my father. I was shocked to say the least but he continued. I was always very skeptical about mediums but as he continued and told me things only I knew about my dad, I started to realise the gift Ronnie possesses. The whole meeting was only a few minutes, but I knew I needed to go and visit him for a one to one.

Ronnie was very kind and delivered my father's message in a very sensitive way. I managed to get a one to one with him very quickly as he gave me first options on a cancellation. In our one to one he continued to astound me with more information only I would know. He also used terminology my father used, odd catch phrases that he used a lot.

I left both meetings feeling refreshed and enlightened. I felt like I had spoken to my dad again. When I got home I cried happy tears knowing he was somewhere at peace. I look forward to my next meeting as I know Ronnie will ease the suffering and allow me to connect again with my dad.

If you miss someone you have lost, or have unanswered questions. I implore you book in with Ronnie. He is worth every single penny. Thank you Ronnie for sharing your gift.

Stuart Goodchild

Ronnie, for a long time now I have found myself gravitating back to you for even the smallest of validation that my parents are around me and that they would be proud of me if they were here.

My very first visit to you was some years ago now. Seeking anything you would be able to embrace me with in terms of me, I'd lost me. And indeed still do. I've experienced life changing experiences, cancer scares, redundancy, divorce, financial hardship, abuse and loss, you would never have been able to know if it wasn't for your mediumship.

You gave me evidence of my parents only maybe a family member would know. At times in my life when I've felt I needed something but not sure of what, I've opted to try and source a sign or something to help me know that what I'm doing is right for me and my parents are really the only peeps that could validate that and them not being here anymore, Ronnie you really fill that void for me in your evidence.

I'm not sure I will ever be able to thank you enough for the gift you are happy to share with me/us, but I can without a doubt endorse your professionalism and mediumship. Your gift to me has been priceless. Thank you so very much.

Kim Baker

I had to write and tell you what a wonderful experience it was seeing you at Dickens Restaurant in Halstead last night. The comfort you must have given, especially to the ladies who had lost children, was immeasurable. I didn't get a message myself but it was lovely to see how happy you made other people. What an amazing gift you have, you are very lucky indeed. You constantly said how happy those on the other side were and this gave me great comfort.

Sarah Davidson

I had a reading with Ronnie on the 11th July 2009, it was myself and my sister-in-law Wendy. We came along together to see him. It was an amazing experience for us both and it has personally helped me so much to cope with the sudden death of my partner, Paul, we had been together for ten wonderful years.

Ronnie has a wonderful gift and I cannot find the words to tell him how grateful I am to him. If it wasn't for Ronnie I would not have been able to get through the past three months, it was such a great comfort to know that Paul is happy where he is now.

Although it still early days since Paul passed away, I feel because of all the things that Ronnie has told me, it has given me the strength to carry on with my life and I will be forever eternally grateful to him. I find it so hard being on my own now but knowing that Paul is in the spirit world and is close by me a lot of the time helps me so much. Ronnie told me that I might even find happiness again, with a new partner, who knows.

Thank you Ronnie - I owe you so much.

Carol Hopkins

I just wanted to thank you so very much for my fantastic visit with you yesterday. You said you were interested to know what my husband Pete's reaction was to the tape when he heard it and I can honestly tell you that you have turned a 'non-believer' into a truly amazed 'believer!' You gave us so many facts that it is impossible to argue with.

As you already know (and told us!) Pete's relationship with his dad didn't always run smoothly and sadly when his dad passed over, even though Pete drove like a bat out of hell, he wasn't able to get to him in time to tell him that he loved him or say goodbye. He has struggled with this badly for the last seven years. Shortly after that was when we lost Jim, who was not only our brother-in-law but one of our best friends. Since that time, our lives have changed in that we have been able to purchase a small motor repairs garage, something which Charlie himself always wanted to do and Peter has always regretted that his dad wasn't there to share in this with us. You said that Charlie knew that they loved each other very much and your parting line on the tape was 'but seriously, Charlie needs his son to know that he is proud of him.' That line means the world to Pete, we now know that although he isn't here physically to share it with us, he is here and he does know.

I can't explain this very well Ronnie, but today Peter is like a man that has had the heaviest load lifted from his shoulders, he even looks different. I honestly think that a spark has been re-lit in him and I don't know how I can ever thank you enough for that.

You are truly an amazing man with a wonderful gift. I have seen the difference in my mum since she visited with you and you were able to tell her that my two brothers were well on the other side, something she has been wanting to hear for forty six years. And I really don't need to tell you the difference you have made to my sister Sharron's life after her visits with you and the things you could share with her about Jim.

My whole family listened to your tape last night and there wasn't a dry eye in the house! Bt they weren't tears of sadness, not really. My children really needed to hear that their Grandad and Uncle Jimbo (!) was watching over them (and celebrating my son's birthday with him!) and my daughter was thrilled to know they had Molly her rabbit with them. It's the smaller things like this that you can tell that makes you cry and laugh and feel good again after felling so sad for so long. Sharron said that when she was waiting for me outside, she wanted to go in instead of me, but that after she had seen the faces of Pete, Scott and Amber as they listened to the tape she was glad it was me and not her because she could see how it affected them.

I'm probably not explaining this very well. Everyone I love most in life you have helped and I just have to say the biggest, biggest THANK YOU from the bottom of my heart. God bless.

Michelle Crossley

We lost my mum, Jean on the 28th August 2000. On Sunday 1st October 2000 my dad, Michael, on the spur of the moment, decided to go to Sudbury Spiritualist Church, the medium was Ronnie Buckingham. That day, Ronnie gave my dad and sister-in-law a lovely message from mum that dad still remembers to this day, but there were things in the message regarding a house move, etc., that were for me and as I was not present at the church I phoned Ronnie the following week to tie up some loose ends of his message.

When I spoke to Ronnie on the phone, he linked in with mum and began describing my new house, its location, where the rooms were, what the colour scheme was, the fact it had some alterations done to it prior to us buying, all of this I could accept as 100% accurate. However, there was just one thing that Ronnie was adamant about and that was a link to a boxer dog and a house move. Now this I could not link to at all, the only thing at the time I could think was the people we bought the house from were kick boxers. Ronnie was not really convinced this was the link and kept on that he was sure it was a boxer dog and linked to moving home. This I have never forgotten and always kept in my mind Ronnie's message about the house move and the boxer dog.

Six years later on in June 2006, my wife Amanda and myself decided it was time to move and had a look around a house and immediately fell in love with it. It was everything we had always wanted in a home, although it needed some work and alterations we went for it, we put in the full asking price, which was accepted and then arranged our mortgage. There were a few problems with the sale along the way but we got through them and the 23rd August 2006 was the day we exchanged and got the keys to our new home. Little did I know of the shock I was going to get when I picked the keys up! I went into town with Amanda to pick up the keys and when they gave me the keys, I noticed it had a fob on them and it was when I looked at what was on the fob that I nearly fell over in astonishment. The key fob was a picture of a boxer dog. I immediately remembered Ronnie's message - boxer dog and house move. 'This is it' I though, after all these years mum has guided us to our dream home and now the message Ronnie gave me has come true. I honestly couldn't believe what was happening, I was absolutely dumbstruck and very emotional.

It was a great pleasure to speak with Ronnie on the 7th January 2007 and tell him that finally his message he had given me six years earlier had finally happened. He didn't remember anything about the original message but when I told him the story he was very shocked, but it really does go to show the power and accuracy of Ronnie in the fact that he was definite all those years ago that it was a boxer dog linked to a house move. It really does go to show the power of spirit.

Robert Howard

I was part of your show last night at the Loughton Academy, actually I was the second person who you gave a reading to. I was the only man to get a reading and our table was quite close to where you were standing. First of all, I would like to thank you personally for the messages you gave me from my brother Andy. I'm sure you know how comforting it was. The messages you passed onto me were 100% accurate and the detail of information was incredible. As I left the show, I was able to assimilate more of the information that I was not too sure of, but after reflection, the information was once again 100%. I guess as it was very emotional for me, and trying to take in the vast amount of information was difficult at the time, but as I type this email, I'm remembering more relevant information.

Fivos Averkiou

I first met Ronnie six years ago when I attended one of his psychic reading sessions at Silver End. He clearly has a very special talent for connecting with people and with the spirit world. His session left a lasting impression on me and I was pleased to learn that Ronnie was a keen supporter of the Danaher Animal Home.

Shortly afterwards, I met Ronnie in my capacity as General Manager of the Danaher Animal Home, a self-financing charity that provides a temporary refuge for dogs, cats and other small animals awaiting a new permanent home. Ever since, Ronnie has come to the Animal Home almost every month with cash donations that he has raised at other psychic sessions, accepting little thanks but pleased to know that his donations go towards helping the animals that have been handed into our care.

The Danaher Animal Home is very privileged to have Ronnie as guest of honour at its annual Open Day, whatever the weather. At this event, Ronnie kindly auctions a psychic reading to the highest bidder, the proceeds of which all go to help our four-legged residents.

Ronnie has an abiding passion for animals and is hugely interested in animal welfare matters. He is cheerful, outgoing and gregarious and shares our ambitions to provide a better life for the ill-treated animals that we look after. We are very fortunate to have Ronnie supporting our cause and highly value the huge contribution he makes to our organisation. It is an honour for me to endorse this book. I hope it inspires people as much as he has inspired me.

John Kirkman, General Manager, Danaher Animal Home

About the Authors

Ronnie Buckingham - Medium Rare is the true story of Ronnie Buckingham, which charts his life from a childhood of want, to a life of crime, with many years spent behind bars, until finally finding his true life purpose as a healer of hearts through his work as a well-known and highly regarded spiritualist medium.

Since working with spirit, Ronnie has worked throughout Europe, appeared in numerous television shows and radio appearances, as well as countless magazine features, and he continues to give mediumship demonstrations to large audiences, astounding people with the accuracy of his messages from their friends and relatives on the other side. Giving undeniable proof that the spirit world can truly connect with us, his down-to-earth delivery, sense of humour and incredible compassion, has turned many a skeptic into a firm believer in the afterlife. With his plethora of tattoos and a Cockney accent, coupled with his extraordinary ability to deliver mind-blowing proof beyond all doubt from the spirit world, Ronnie Buckingham certainly is a spiritualist medium most rare.

Ronnie can be contacted via email ronaldbuckingham354@btinternet.com

Ruth Baker - Is a feature writer and ghostwriter with a special interest in EFT, holistic healing, psychic and spiritual matters.

Ruth can be contacted via email tappingbootcamp@gmail.com

19444332R00165

Printed in Great Britain
by Amazon